Interpreting in Asylum Procedures

TRANSLATION, INTERPRETING AND SOCIAL JUSTICE IN A GLOBALISED WORLD

Series Editors: **Philipp Angermeyer**, *York University, Canada* and **Katrijn Maryns**, *Ghent University, Belgium*

Translation, Interpreting and Social Justice in a Globalised World is an international series that welcomes authored monographs and edited collections that address translation and interpreting in settings of diversity, globalisation, migration and asylum. Books in the series will discuss how translation and interpreting practices (or their absence) may advance or hinder social justice. A key aim of the series is to encourage dialogue between scholars and professionals working in translation and interpreting studies and those working in other linguistic disciplines, such as sociolinguistics and linguistic anthropology. Books in the series will cover both translation and interpreting services provided by state and corporate entities, as well as informal, community-based translation and interpreting. We welcome proposals covering any combinations of languages (including Sign languages) and from a wide variety of geographical contexts. A guiding aim of the series is to empower those who may be disadvantaged by their lack of access to majority or official languages, and as such proposals which bridge the gap between theoretical and practical domains are particularly encouraged.

Topics which may be addressed by books in the series include (but are not limited to):

- Medical settings (including care settings and provision of public health information)
- Legal settings (law enforcement, court, prison, counselling)
- Educational settings (including community-based education)
- Asylum and migration procedures
- Access to democracy and citizenship
- Interactions with business and private-sector institutions
- The media and minority-language broadcasting and publishing
- Ethical and political considerations in translation
- Cultural translation
- Translation and language rights
- Translation and intercultural relations and conflict

Intended readership: academic and professional.

All books in this series are externally peer-reviewed.

Full details of all the books in this series and of all our other publications can be found on http://www.multilingual-matters.com, or by writing to Multilingual Matters, BLOCK, The Fairfax, Pithay Court, Bristol, BS1 3BN, UK.

TRANSLATION, INTERPRETING AND SOCIAL JUSTICE IN A GLOBALISED WORLD: 4

Interpreting in Asylum Procedures

Dialogist Interpretation

Hassan Mizori

MULTILINGUAL MATTERS
Bristol • Jackson

DOI https://doi.org/10.21832/MIZORI1311
Library of Congress Cataloging in Publication Data
A catalog record for this book is available from the Library of Congress.
Names: Mizori, Hassan, author
Title: Interpreting in Asylum Procedures: Dialogist Interpretation/ Hassan Mizori.
Description: Jackson: Multilingual Matters, 2025. | Series: Translation, Interpreting and Social Justice in a Globalised World: 4 | Includes bibliographical references and index. | Summary: "This book presents dialogist interpretation as an innovative method for examining interpreter-mediated encounters within asylum procedures, uncovering hidden layers of meaning by engaging with participants' internal dialogues. It offers practical recommendations and calls for asylum reforms to enhance fairness and communicative equity" – Provided by publisher.
Identifiers: LCCN 2025011732 (print) | LCCN 2025011733 (ebook) | ISBN 9781836681311 hardback | ISBN 9781836681328 pdf | ISBN 9781836681335 epub Subjects: LCSH: Asylum, Right of | Refugees – Legal status, laws, etc. | Translating and interpreting | Law reform
Classification: LCC K3268.3 .M59 2025 (print) | LCC K3268.3 (ebook) | DDC 342.08/3 – dc23/eng/20250317
LC record available at https://lccn.loc.gov/2025011732
LC ebook record available at https://lccn.loc.gov/2025011733

British Library Cataloguing in Publication Data
A catalogue entry for this book is available from the British Library.

ISBN-13: 978-1-83668-131-1 (hbk)

Multilingual Matters
UK: BLOCK, The Fairfax, Pithay Court, Bristol, BS1 3BN, UK.
USA: Ingram, Jackson, TN, USA.
Authorised Representative: Easy Access System Europe – Mustamäe tee 50, 10621 Tallinn, Estonia, gpsr.requests@easproject.com.

Website: https://www.multilingual-matters.com
Bluesky: @multi-ling-mat.bsky.social
X: Multi_Ling_Mat
Facebook: https://www.facebook.com/multilingualmatters
Blog: https://www.channelviewpublications.wordpress.com

The policy of Multilingual Matters/Channel View Publications is to use papers that are natural, renewable and recyclable products, made from wood grown in sustainable forests. In the manufacturing process of our books, and to further support our policy, preference is given to printers that have FSC and PEFC Chain of Custody certification. The FSC and/or PEFC logos will appear on those books where full certification has been granted to the printer concerned.

Typeset in Sabon and Frutiger by R. J. Footring Ltd, Derby, UK

To my family –
whose presence, conversations, and quiet reflections have formed an essential part of the dialogic space within which this book emerged.
In ways both spoken and unspoken, you have co-constructed the background against which these ideas took shape.
This work stands not only as an inquiry into interpreter-mediated communication but also as a testament to the enduring dialogue we share.

Contents

A Note to the Reader

This book is the product of a dedicated effort to create a comprehensive assessment of communication within asylum procedures, with an emphasis on interpreter-mediated encounters. This project stemmed from my firm belief, developed through both research and personal experiences as a practising interpreter, researcher and former asylum applicant, that certain layers of communication in asylum procedures are underexplored and poorly understood. I seek to convince concerned parties of the importance of these layers, and to propose a methodology aimed at making procedures more equitable and more sound in terms of underlying communicative theory, enhancing fairness. To this end, I call for a wider integration of a contemporary version of dialogism in the approaches to communication taken in asylum procedures in the Global North (i.e. the First World). Dialogism, a concept introduced by Mikhail Bakhtin, focuses on the significance of dialogue and the interaction among various voices, perspectives and cultures. It posits that meaning is fluid, continuously shaped and reshaped through the engagement of differing viewpoints. In this process, participants' voices are not inherently equal; moreover, they exist in a state of mutual reliance, with each voice impacting and being impacted by others. This entails a possibility in any given interaction that certain voices are supressed, elevated, exaggerated or distorted by the complex interplay of the sense-making process. This idea holds particular importance in the fields of language, literature and culture, offering a lens through which the intricate dynamics between diverse voices and perspectives can be examined.

It is my belief, based on the analysis presented in this book, that *dialogist interpretation* presents a concrete avenue through which advances can be made in understanding, efficacy and fairness in asylum procedures. By dialogist interpretation, I refer to a novel approach towards interpreter-mediated communication structured around engaging with and reflecting on the internal dialogues of participants when and where needed. Such a process may involve general reflection, or an examination down to the level of individual utterances if required. While advances in the study of interpreting and communication already account for the active role of interpreters as primary participants in communicative events (see Chapter 4), the approach presented in this book is innovative in terms of its practical application. In the context of an interaction, understood dialogically, one's internal dialogue encompasses the complex and overlapping cognitive and linguistic processes by which one hears, understands (or miscommunicates) and responds to what is communicated. Thus, an internal dialogue is the dialogue one has in one's mind when evaluating what has been said and re-evaluating one's own thinking – it is one's thinking, cognition. In light of this, dialogist interpretation aims to uncover the often unexpressed, critical layers of meaning that contribute to the overall sense-making process in interactions, such as those in asylum procedures. Dialogist interpretation seeks to enhance fairness and efficacy by ensuring that these internal perspectives are considered and integrated into the communicated outcomes. This approach is grounded in the broader field of dialogism, which focuses on the co-constructed nature of communication and the importance of multiple voices and perspectives in understanding interactions.

This effort, and this book, has at its core an empirical case study. In this study, I conduct a detailed analysis of the dialogue (an interpreter-mediated encounter) during a legal consultation in an asylum procedure in the Netherlands. At the heart of this book, then, lies an empirical case study drawn from real data – recordings made during a legal consultation between a lawyer and his client, a Syrian asylum seeker, in a lawyer's office in the Netherlands. This case study contributes to the field of interpretation studies through its methodological innovation and comprehensive approach. It combines in-depth textual analysis with reflective interviews at both the micro and macro levels. All primary participants are interviewed: the asylum seeker, the interpreter and, to some extent, the lawyer. By engaging directly with the interpreter, the study delves into their internal dialogue, attempting to trace the rationale behind translation choices. This provides valuable insights into the interpretive judgements made during the legal consultation. Similarly, a reflective interview with the asylum seeker offers a deeper understanding of whether he comprehends the lawyer through the translation and what he understands exactly. In all interviews, I have also sought to uncover how the parties theorise their roles and responsibilities, as well as those of the other parties, during the interpreter-mediated interaction. This holistic approach enriches our understanding of all participants' perceptions and interpretations, making this study a valuable resource for scholars in interpreting studies as well as practising interpreters.

In undertaking this detailed examination, I harness dialogism as my analytical lens to navigate through the complex layers of meaning and sense-making within the asylum dialogue. Dialogism, with its focus on the interaction among various voices, perspectives and cultures, allows me to uncover significant insights from the collected data, including the nuances and intricacies of communication that often remain unexplored in asylum procedures. The choice of the Netherlands as the venue for this study not only allows a probing into the specific communicative challenges within its asylum procedures but also sheds light on similar dynamics across the Global North. Further, having lived in the Netherlands for almost 17 years, first as an asylum applicant myself and later working as a professional interpreter, I am well acquainted with the Dutch asylum context. The findings derived from this rich empirical foundation provide scalable insights and suggest improvements applicable across varied jurisdictions and communicative settings not only in the Netherlands but across the Global North as a whole, where asylum processes (though varied) operate on broadly similar principles. These scalable changes, which range from small reforms to existing processes and procedures to more wide-reaching changes in institutional philosophy, are grounded in a call for the integration of the contemporary version of dialogism in the analysis and interpretation of asylum procedures worldwide. This approach underlines my belief in the potential to enhance communication in asylum procedures, to transcend the confines of local legal cultures and to offer a new paradigm for understanding and improving these critical processes across the Global North.

Over the course of the case study, I scrutinise the communicative dynamics at play, probe the accuracy of translations, assess the judgements made by the interpreter and question the degree of understanding the immigrant has of the proceedings. I argue that some potentially crucial sense-making information remains unexpressed, remaining concealed within the minds of the interlocutors and constricted by the design of the wider asylum procedure, and hence does not receive the attention it deserves. This unvoiced information is critical to the communication process that unfolds during the legal consultation. I posit that both the asylum procedure and the associated legal consultations often suffer from this lack of attention to this essential component of communication. Through discussion of the history of global asylum practices and the asylum system of the Netherlands, I suggest that this neglect partially originates from political motives and an absence of critical engagement with communication during the procedure. Furthermore, I propose that the political climates in the Global North contribute to these shortcomings, due largely to the institutionalisation of asylum procedures which, in the (understandable) pursuit of standardisation, have precipitated a lack of engagement with recent advances in the theory of communication. I assert that it is imperative for the civilised world to ensure that asylum seekers are treated equitably, with procedures that strictly adhere to domestic and international legal standards, ensuring objectivity and respect for their rights while mitigating the impact of a formulaic approach to diverse and individual cases. To achieve this, we must critically evaluate all aspects of asylum procedures and identify areas for improvement. My research, focusing on the communicative aspects of the asylum procedure, represents a modest contribution to these efforts.

Readership of the Book

Throughout this book and its case study, I explore a contemporary version of the theory of dialogism and its associated concepts, which are essential for understanding sense-making and meaning-making in a range of communicative settings, including asylum procedures. The book emphasises the inherently co-constructed nature of asylum narratives, calling for the incorporation of the crucial concept of internal dialogue into asylum procedures.

As such, the work provides empirically and theoretically grounded recommendations to guide various stakeholders, including immigration officials – particularly the staff of the Dutch Immigration and Naturalisation Service (INS) – lawyers, judiciary and assistance organisations, on how an understanding of dialogism and internal dialogue facilitates equitable decisions and effective support for asylum seekers. Lawyers and organisations gain strategies to advocate for clients, while the judiciary gains deeper insights into asylum narratives' complexities, ensuring justice reflects individual nuances. Incorporating internal dialogue into asylum procedures reveals a wealth of information that greatly enhances the quality of asylum narratives, informing decisions and enriching immigration dossiers. As will be seen in Chapters 2 and 4, prevailing procedure designs are poorly suited to capture such information, due largely to their underlying understanding of communication and the manner in which they are used to render verdicts in asylum applications.

This book will be of particular use to interpreters, highlighting the significant impact they have on communication. It shows how interpreters' choices can shape asylum seekers' narratives and highlights the need for accurate communication in avoiding misunderstandings and, in the studied context, subsequent unjust verdicts. It provides guidance on navigating challenges and ethical considerations, enhancing interpreters' professional development and effectiveness. Additionally, it illustrates how interpreters can elicit information from internal dialogues, enriching narratives and supporting clients effectively.

In terms of academic contributions, this book seeks to inform interpreting and translation scholars, contributing to both theoretical understanding and practical application. The empirical evidence produced by the case study offers new research avenues, helping scholars develop nuanced theories and understand real-world implications. Curriculum designers gain insights to equip interpreters for high-stakes settings, handling ethical dilemmas and communication nuances.

Structure of the Book

This book unfolds progressively, exploring the complexities of communication within asylum procedures, with a particular emphasis on interpreter-mediated encounters (IMEs). Each chapter contributes to the overarching aim of addressing systemic barriers, theoretical gaps and practical challenges while proposing actionable reforms grounded in dialogism.

Chapter 1 establishes the historical, legal and sociopolitical context of asylum systems, offering a comprehensive overview of their evolution. By situating the discussion within these frameworks, the chapter sets the stage for understanding how communication processes are shaped by broader institutional dynamics.

Chapter 2 builds directly on this foundation by demonstrating how political considerations influence procedural design, which, in turn, impacts the communicative dynamics essential for fair decision-making. This connection introduces the book's core argument: that the quality of communication within asylum procedures, particularly in IMEs, is often constrained by systemic design flaws.

Chapter 3 presents an empirical case study of an interpreter-mediated legal consultation in the Netherlands. It illustrates the loss of critical sense-making material in asylum procedures, providing concrete examples of where and how communication breaks down. These findings not only support but also extend the discussions from Chapters 1 and 2 by highlighting the practical implications of systemic challenges.

Chapter 4 provides the theoretical backbone of the book, integrating essential concepts from a contemporary version of dialogism to deepen our understanding of communication dynamics in IMEs. This chapter draws on, critiques and builds upon established models, such as Cecilia Wadensjö's *Interpreting as Interaction*, to frame the analysis of interpreter-mediated communication within the unique context of asylum consultations.

Chapter 5 discusses the findings from the empirical case study in detail, illustrating the significant impact of overlooked or lost sense-making material on procedural fairness. This chapter proposes methods to recover and incorporate these unexpressed communicative layers into asylum procedures. The distinction between Chapter 3 (empirical findings) and Chapter 5 (analytical dissection) ensures narrative coherence and methodological precision, avoiding the conflation of empirical challenges with their solutions.

Finally, **Chapter 6** synthesises the insights gained throughout the book, advocating for a dialogist approach to interpreting and communication in asylum procedures. It makes practical recommendations for improving transparency, efficacy and fairness, benefiting not only asylum applicants but also the integrity of the asylum system. By situating these recommendations within both academic and institutional contexts, the chapter highlights the potential for scalable reforms across different jurisdictions.

Acknowledgements

I would like to thank the participants of the study, whose involvement in the case study provided not only empirical material but also vital insights into the dialogic processes this book seeks to foreground. Their willingness to reflect on their experiences offered indispensable perspectives, without which this project could not have taken form.

I am indebted to the scholars and colleagues whose conversations, written works, and critical engagements enriched my thinking and encouraged the refinement of the ideas presented here. I am particularly grateful to those working at the intersections of interpreting studies, communication theory, and asylum law, who helped create intellectual spaces within which this inquiry could evolve.

Special thanks are due to the anonymous reviewers whose careful reading and critical feedback strengthened the manuscript and sharpened its arguments. I am also grateful to the colleagues who generously read parts or all of the manuscript in its earlier forms; their thoughtful comments and encouragement have contributed meaningfully to the final shape of this work.

I would like to acknowledge the support of the University of Leeds, where the initial research was undertaken and where many of the foundational ideas were first developed. My thanks also extend to the editorial team at Multilingual Matters for their guidance and professionalism throughout the publication process.

Finally, I am grateful to my family for their quiet support and understanding throughout the long process of bringing this book to completion. Their presence formed part of the dialogic space within which this work could emerge.

I acknowledge the broader dialogic conditions – academic, professional, and personal – within which this book has come to light. It is a product of many interactions, reflections, and silent collaborations, seen and unseen.

Use this QR code to access the Appendices for this book. They can also be found at https://vm7.ehaus2.co.uk/mmatters/page/iap/

1 Asylum – Historical Contexts and Contemporary Challenges

1.1 Introduction

In writing this book, I am driven by a dual sense of duty and scholarly curiosity to delve into the intricate and often overlooked nuances of communication within asylum procedures. My goal is to shed light on the subtle yet critical layers of meaning that unfold during these procedures, and highlight how their neglect can diminish the efficacy of the asylum process. In light of this, I advocate for a dialogist approach to interpretation in such procedures. This approach recognises and harnesses these nuances to enhance the integrity and fairness of the adjudication process, ensuring that asylum-seekers are treated in accordance with the principles outlined in the United Nations' 1951 Refugee Convention and its 1967 Protocol.

In the simplest sense, asylum-seeking refers to the process by which individuals who have cause to flee their homelands seek refuge in other countries (see Section 1.2.1 for detailed definitions). In its present state, asylum-seeking in the Global North, as both a practical phenomenon and within the public consciousness, is closely tied to the administrative and bureaucratic procedures by which such individuals attempt to achieve this – the asylum process. My experiences as a former asylum applicant and as a practising interpreter as well as my academic expertise in interpreting studies provide me with a unique perspective on the complex reality of contemporary asylum-seeking. This perspective is crucial for examining the nuanced interplay of legal, political and communicative elements during asylum procedures, particularly during the legal consultations which are integral to these procedures.

This chapter sets the stage for this endeavour by providing the essential historical backdrop needed to understand the complexities of communication within asylum procedures, which I will discuss in the coming chapters. This historical background is also foundational for contextualising the recommendations made in this book. By examining the evolution of asylum practices and the interplay of the legal and political factors that have shaped them, we can better appreciate the challenges and nuances that interpreters and other participants of the interpreter-mediated encounter face today. This historical context is crucial, as it informs both the theoretical and the practical approaches to dialogue interpreting explored throughout this book.

This chapter begins its examination of the historical context of asylum by tracing the evolution of post-war migration into contemporary asylum systems. It discusses the legal distinctions between refugees and asylum-seekers and highlights the legal framework that has developed to protect them. The chapter then examines the impact of changing public attitudes and policies on the asylum process, focusing on the potential effects political currents within societies have on the design of asylum procedures. This is followed by a detailed examination of the use and misuse of statistics in terms of public opinion.

1.2 History

Migration from one place to another has been part of the human experience 'since before recorded history' (Segal *et al.*, 2010: 17). Europe and other Western nations are no exceptions to this phenomenon. Indeed, Europe's history is 'inherently connected with migrations' (Lyons & Huegler, 2010: 439), especially emigration, which was the predominant form of migration in the cultural and economic history of Europe until the Second World War, whereafter (in addition to continued emigration) migrants, including asylum-seekers and refugees, have increasingly moved to Europe and other parts of the Western World (Weinar *et al.*, 2019: 38). Western Europe has in this period been a safe, democratic and developed part of the world, like the other traditional immigration (destination) countries: Australia, the United States and Canada (Glynn, 2021: 1–2). This said, and as this chapter will explore the point in detail (see Section 1.4), it is worth noting that the vast majority of refugees from the Global South (developing world) flee to neighbouring countries. The history of asylum-seeking is complex in both its social and legal dimensions, and for this reason it is pertinent to unpack the myriad terms commonly used when describing the phenomenon.

1.2.1 Definitions: Migration, immigration, emigration, refugee, asylum-seeker

For the sake of clarity and consistency, I define here the terminology I will be using in the book, especially given that terminology 'in the world of displacement, and migration, often seems very fluid in its popular, and even expert, use' (van Selm, 2019: 305). According to the *Oxford English Dictionary* (2023 edition), *migration* is a general term referring to the 'movement of a person or people from one country, locality, place of residence, etc., to settle in another', while *emigration* refers to an 'instance of leaving one's own country or region, either voluntarily or under compulsion, in order to settle permanently in another'. From the perspective of the receiving society, a person is an *immigrant* if she/he permanently relocates to a country that is not his/her home country.

Refugee and *asylum-seeker* refer to different things, even though the terms are often used interchangeably. Some people call any person in flight or seeking refuge a refugee, even if they have not yet gained official/ legal status (Kneebone, 2009) but in fact, formally, the term 'refugee' specifically refers to an asylum-seeker whose legal status has been determined (van Selm, 2019: 307). An asylum-seeker, according to international treaties, is someone whose request for sanctuary has yet to be processed (Chin & Cortes, 2015) and so is not as yet a refugee. It is international law that determines that refugee status comes with conditions. The United Nations' 1951 Convention Relating to the Status of Refugees deals with this in Article 1A(2) (Kneebone, 2009). The 1967 Protocol Relating to the Status of Refugees, an amendment to the 1951 Convention, does this as well. However, it is interesting that the United Nations High Commission for Refugees (UNHCR) calls every asylum-seeker a refugee, as long as they satisfy the legal definition set by the 1951 Convention (Kneebone, 2009). It does not 'wait' until a potential country of asylum (PCA) has assessed the asylum application in question. The UNHCR has a supervisory function in relation to the signatories of the Convention (Harvey, 2015: 43) and guards its implementation by said signatories.

It is also noteworthy that the term 'refugee' does not mean precisely the same thing in the different member states of the European Union (EU), even though attempts were made to unify its use in 1996. On this front, only general ideas have been laid down (van Selm, 2019). Regional and international forums have attempted to find a unified definition that PCAs can use. Unsurprisingly, however, as we will see in this chapter, this has been in vain.

Another term that requires consideration here is *forcibly displaced*. As defined by the UNHCR, the term refers to:

> those who are forced to move, within or across borders, due to armed conflict, persecution, terrorism, human rights violations and abuses, violence, the adverse effects of climate change, natural disasters, development projects or a combination of these factors. (UNHCR, 2018)

This definition thus includes not only asylum-seekers and refugees but also internally displaced persons (IDPs) as well as stateless persons (UNHCR, 2023b). IDPs are:

> persons or groups of persons who have been forced or obliged to flee or to leave their homes or places of habitual residence, in particular as a result of, or in order to avoid the effects of armed conflict, situations of generalized violence, violations of human rights or natural or human-made disasters, and who have not crossed an internationally recognized State border. (UNHCR, 2023b)

Many IDPs, either shortly after displacement or later, when the prospect of their returning home seems increasingly distant, may become asylum-seekers. As will be seen in Section 1.4, it is IDPs, not asylum-seekers or refugees, who represent the vast majority of the forcibly displaced. Of further note, although the UNHCR's own definition of IDPs includes those displaced by natural and human-made disasters, they are not included in the statistics provided by its own Refugee Data Finder database (UNCHR, 2023b).

Stateless persons refers to those who fall under the provision of the United Nations' 1954 Convention Relating to the Status of Stateless People, who are those 'not considered as a national by any State under the operation of its law' (UNHCR, 2023c). While not directly subjects of study in this book, an understanding of IDPs and stateless persons is essential to contextualising the statistical landscape. As Chapter 2 will investigate in depth, the figures presented on asylum-seekers and refugees are rarely neutral, and their selective use is a key mechanism by which agendas both for and against asylum are pushed.

On the subject of neutrality, it is posited in this work that the term *asylum-seeker*, particularly within the context of the Netherlands – the focal setting of the case study underlying this book – has increasingly acquired a range of negative connotations. In conjunction with widespread media representations in the Global North of those seeking international protection as free-riders and opportunists, or even outright liars (see Section 1.3), decades of controversy over asylum policy have given the term, at best, an unfortunate image. This said, the term remains in use legally and by the UNHCR itself. For this reason, the following approach is adopted in this book. In relation to the discussion of the historical phenomenon of asylum-seeking, and in discussion of the public debate surrounding it, the term *asylum-seeker* is used in the *neutral and factual* sense described above. In relation to the study presented in this book, the analysis of it and the recommendations that are made in relation to the findings, the term *asylum applicant* will be used to describe those who seek international protection but have not yet gained refugee status. My use of the term 'asylum applicant' reflects a desire to more fairly represent those described as such and emphasises the simple fact that they are indeed *applicants* – people applying to a national iteration of an internationally recognised process of identification and protection.

It does not follow that states and societies can spurn those who participate in legal processes of acquiring asylum while still seeking to wear the mantle of what we might call international decency – that is, status as nations that fulfil international commitments, hold humanitarian values and respect the rule of law. The negativity associated with the term 'asylum-seeker' is not inherent and therefore it is the position of this book that until such a time that discourse on asylum is more civil than antagonistic, more objective than polemic and pursues justice rather than political advantage, the term should be avoided by those seeking the betterment of asylum applicants and greater effectiveness of the processes and institutions with which applicants interact.

1.2.2 Migration to Europe

While the history of migration is as old as that of humankind, in the European case, contrary to much contemporary public discourse, 'immigration [from outside the continent] is a quite new phenomenon', which 'took off substantially in the decades after World War II' (Weinar *et al.*, 2019: 38). Indeed, over the post-war decades, Western Europe has become a desirable destination for migration. The economic growth in the Western World and consequent labour shortages from the mid-1950s onwards 'led to migrant worker recruitment in most Western European countries' (Lyons & Huegler, 2010: 439).

Different countries approached this recruitment differently. For example, Sweden, the UK and France offered long-term settlement schemes. In contrast, Germany, the Netherlands and Switzerland 'attempted to prevent settlement of temporary "guest workers" through systems of "rotating" recruitment' (Lyons & Huegler, 2010: 439). The latter countries recruited young male migrant workers mainly from Southern European states, North Africa and Turkey. France and the UK let in migrants from former colonies in Africa, the Caribbean and the Indian subcontinent to fill labour shortages (Segal *et al.*, 2006). Other developed nations, for example Canada and Australia, also offered residence opportunities because 'they needed labour for economic growth and people for demographic growth' (Castles & Loughna, 2003: 2).

In terms of those seeking protection in the first decades after the Second World War, the 'classical refugees of the Cold War' (Castles & Loughna, 2003: 40) had predominantly been dissidents from Eastern Bloc countries. These immigrants were relatively small in number and marginal in terms of their political and economic costs to the protection countries. Due to the political climate, their coming was not considered a problem as it was seen as a statement against the regimes of the countries they came from, and helped showcase the superiority of Western European morals over those of the Eastern Bloc (Neumayer, 2005; Trauner, 2016).

Over time, policies started to change. By 1970, around 11 million migrants were living in Western Europe, accounting for 5% of the total population (Castles, 2000). However, this number did not mean migrants were always accepted by their new societies as permanent residents. Policies changed drastically with the 1973 oil crisis and the economic downturn that followed, and in a number of European countries it was hoped that guest workers would return to their countries of origin (Hahamovitch, 2003). In the aftermath of the crisis, many states in western Europe decided they wanted to receive no new foreigners on their soil (Castles, 2000). These economic slowdowns meant politicians saw 'political mileage' in resisting the permanent settlement of migrants (Luedtke, 2019: 16). European political elites began to 'pander to xenophobic politics – in response to their declining legitimacy and electoral support – by proclaiming their nations to be "zero-immigration" vis-a-vis non-EU nationals' (Luedtke, 2019: 16).

This xenophobic climate did not convince migrants to return home, however, and European politicians failed to formulate a coherent strategy to deal in a constructive manner with them or with those who arrived subsequently (Luedtke, 2019). Further, despite the end of widespread further recruitment, many migrants chose to remain (particularly those from non-EU states such as Turkey or Yugoslavia). Many were joined by family members (Lyons & Huegler, 2010), as allowed under international law on family reunification. For example, Moroccan migrant communities remained in the Netherlands (Luedtke, 2019).

In the 1980s and 1990s, Europe witnessed a significant migration movement within its borders (and to a lesser extent from outside Europe) with the fall of the communist regimes of Eastern Europe and the USSR (Bhabha, 2004; Bhabha & Young, 1999; Keselman *et al.*, 2010; Rillof & Buysse, 2015). At the end of the Cold War, the Iron Curtain, which had separated and limited movement between the two competing spheres, ceased to exist. The end of restrictive emigration policies in the post-Soviet/post-communist space led many to seek better economic opportunities and living conditions in Western European states. Before the fall of the Eastern Bloc, many migrants from then communist countries sought to come to Western Europe as labourers instead of applying for asylum, even though their genuine reason for leaving their countries was political protection, because work permits were available at the time (Castles, 2000). The 1990s went on to witness bloody wars and large displacements of peoples in what had been Yugoslavia, leading to significant migration towards Northern and Western Europe (Hatton, 2004). In a pattern reminiscent of more recent 'refugee crises' such as that following the Arab Spring and the Syrian civil war, European countries were confronted with high volumes of asylum applications distributed unevenly across states (Kang, 2021).

Neither seeking safety through labour migration nor patterns of regional 'surges' in migration have been limited to migrants from Eastern Europe. Conflicts in Africa and Asia have led to intermittent increased refugee flows, from the 1960s onwards, with many of those fleeing managing to reach EU countries as labour migrants rather than refugees. When national recruitment schemes ceased, claiming asylum became the only available route to safety for many, including those with mixed motivations, that is, both escape from a repressive regime and economic migration (often following previous patterns), for example Turkish/Kurdish asylum applicants in Germany (Castles & Loughna, 2005).

1.2.3 The legal history of asylum and refugee status

As mentioned in Section 1.2.1, legally, there is a difference between an asylum-seeker and a refugee. In practice, however, it is 'often impossible to tell at the time of movement whether an asylum-seeker is actually a "refugee" in the sense of the 1951 United Nations Refugee Convention' (Castles & Loughna, 2003: 1). Among those who migrate are refugees who may not seek asylum. Some of those who do seek asylum and are genuine refugees may end up being labelled as economic migrants.

Europe has a long history of protecting refugees. During the first half of the 20th century, the international community made arrangements to protect refugees and displaced people through the League of Nations,[1] and in the second half of the century through its successor, the UN: 'the refugee problem [had become] the concern of the international community, which, for humanitarian reasons, began to assume responsibility for protecting and assisting refugees' (UNHCR, 2019: 13). In 1921, the League sought to resolve the problems posed by significant numbers of Russian refugees through the creation of the High Commission for Russian Refugees. This body coordinated relief efforts and considered the question of legal status, but its preferred methods of resolution were 'repatriation, colonisation and naturalisation' (White, 2017: 19). Nevertheless, these efforts represented the beginnings of a gradual movement in the international community to address the matter of those who sought refuge across international borders, and would eventually give rise to a number of legal developments. Those legal instruments and arrangements 'were driven by concerns about refugees' lack of formal legal status, need for material relief, and access to durable solutions' (McAdam & Wood, 2021: 194).

After the Second World War, when the numbers of refugees had dramatically increased to exceed even those produced during and after the First World War, it soon became apparent that no existing legal instruments were sufficient. The influential European powers felt there was an urgent need for such international instruments, to regulate and mitigate the human catastrophe created by the war. At this stage, refugee flows were conceptualised as part of the broader issue of 'surplus population', a term that also included out-of-work labourers, displaced populations and those affected by shifts of national borders following the war (Karatani, 2005). In this sense, the development of asylum policies was closely linked to the emergence of modern border regimes and involved the need to 'define the legal status of refugees' (UNHCR, 2019: 13) in order to promote, as far as possible, a uniform approach among all parties. The immensity of

---

1 The Arrangements of 5 July 1922, 31 May 1924, 12 May 1926, 30 June 1928 and 30 July 1935, the Conventions of 28 October 1933 and 10 February 1938, the Protocol of 14 September 1939 and the Agreement of 15 October 1946.

the overall problem could not be dealt with piecemeal. There was a call for an 'instrument containing a general definition of who was to be considered a refugee' (UNHCR, 2019). As alluded to above, this would come in the form of the Convention Relating to the Status of Refugees, signed in Geneva on 28 July 1951. During this period, refugee movements were framed as just one component of a larger 'surplus population' problem – a category encompassing unemployed workers, displaced group, and those compelled to resettle in the wake of newly redrawn national borders after the war (Karatani, 2005).

There has since been a continual search for updated solutions to the challenges of emerging refugee crises. The amended 1951 Convention has retained its influence some seven decades on. To confront the new challenges concerning refugees, the international community has been reinforcing its capabilities with new actions and new legal instruments. The Convention has been reinforced by the introduction of two seminal legal texts: the 2016 New York Declaration for Refugees and Migrants, and the Global Compact on Refugees, affirmed by the UN General Assembly in 2018 (McAdam & Wood, 2021). The New York Declaration 'fills what has been a perennial gap in the international protection system – that of truly sharing responsibility for refugees' (UNHCR, 2016). The Global Compact, as its Guiding Principles state, represents 'the political will and ambition of the international community as a whole for strengthened cooperation and solidarity with refugees and affected host countries' (UNHCR, 2023a).

The 1951 Convention entered into force in 1954 and initially applied only to post-war Europe (UNHCR, 2001). It became applicable around the globe when the 1967 Protocol was adopted (Lyons & Huegler, 2010). The Protocol removed the geographic and temporal limits of the 1951 Convention. Combined, they provide a 'universal code for the treatment of refugees uprooted from their countries as a result of persecution' (UNHCR, 2019: 9). The 1951 Convention and its 1967 Protocol are the 'only global legal instruments explicitly covering the most important aspects of a refugee's life' (UNHCR, 2011: 2). As of 2024, 44 UN member states were not party to the Convention, including India, Pakistan, Bangladesh, Indonesia, Thailand, Iraq and the majority of the Gulf states (Forced Migration Review, 2024).

It is important to remark that both the 1951 Convention and the 1967 Protocol, are considered one legal instrument, which means that a state that accedes to the former automatically accedes to the latter. The acceding parties to the amended Convention may, however, show reservations, although no reservations may be made regarding its 'fundamental provisions', namely: Article 1 (definition of the term 'refugee'); Article 3 (non-discrimination); Article 4 (freedom of religion); Article 16(1) (access to courts); Article 33 (non-refoulement); and Articles 36–46 (final clauses) (UNHCR, 2011). Notably, the 1951 Convention and the 1967 Protocol do not impose particular asylum procedures on signatory countries. That is, they leave it to acceding states to decide on these as long as the content of both instruments are respected.

Through Article 1, the Convention does not apply to all who seek protection. For example, it does not apply to people regarding whom there are serious suspicions that they have 'committed war crimes or crimes against humanity, serious non-political crimes, or are guilty of acts contrary to the purposes and principles of the United Nations' (UNHCR, 2011).

Joint regional frameworks have also been developed in an effort to co-ordinate the implementation of consistent asylum policy. For instance, the EU has established its Common European Asylum System (CEAS). The CEAS sets out common standards and procedures for dealing with asylum applications in EU countries. These standards are laid out in several key pieces of legislation (EU Commission, 2023), including:

(1) the Asylum Procedures Directive, which sets out common procedures for granting and withdrawing international protection;
(2) the Reception Conditions Directive, which ensures that asylum-seekers have access to certain basic things, such as housing, food and healthcare, while their applications are being processed;
(3) the Qualification Directive, which sets out the criteria to identify who is eligible for international protection;
(4) the Dublin III Regulation, which determines which EU member state is responsible for examining an asylum application;
(5) the Eurodac Regulation, which sets up a system for fingerprinting and registering asylum-seekers and irregular border-crossers over the age of 14;
(6) the Temporary Protection Directive, which provides temporary protection in the event of a mass influx of displaced persons.

The implementation of and adherence to these regulations vary by country.

The CEAS has been subject to criticism and there have been ongoing discussions on how to improve it, including sharing responsibility for asylum-seekers more equitably across EU countries (Kaufmann, 2021: 15). These discussions could lead to significant changes in EU asylum laws and regulations. These laws and regulations are meant to provide a minimum standard for the treatment of asylum-seekers and the processing of asylum claims. Individual EU countries may choose to provide additional protections or rights to asylum-seekers above and beyond what is required by EU law.

1.2.4 Response of the states

As may be inferred from the brief history of migration in Europe presented above, the response of the EU member states to the 'influx' of asylum-seekers has greatly changed since the 1970s (van Selm, 2019: 309). This change started with intergovernmental cooperation in the 1980s (Luedtke, 2019). In the 1990s, the EU decided to work towards standardising the policies of individual states, to develop more unified, EU-wide ones (Bendel, 2019). European countries also came up with their own national policies to mitigate or even bypass the obligations of the 1951 Convention. When the numbers 'peaked' in 1993, restrictive measures (border controls and deterrence) were increasingly introduced (Lyons & Huegler, 2010: 439). The CEAS started in the 1990s and it continues to evolve (see Section 1.2.3). In addition to restrictions, the member states have opted not to expand the definition of a refugee, even though the UN Convention's definition does not explicitly cover threats to one's integrity from other causes, such as 'people fleeing from war, political violence not specifically directed against them, natural disasters, famine, and the like' (Neumayer, 2005: 390). The motivation behind not expanding the definition stems from the consequences it would have in terms of asylum-seekers' rights. Some countries have even wanted to restrict access to the rights attached to the original definition of the 1951 Convention (Every and Augoustinos, 2008: 650), as it 'significantly curtails the power of national governments to control inward migration to their sovereign territories' (Baillot *et al.*, 2014: 107).

It therefore makes sense that asylum procedures in the EU, whether at a national level or Union-wide, have generally been characterised as restrictive (Every and Augoustinos, 2008). European governments have been aiming to deter potential asylum-seekers from making the journey to their borders (Affolter, 2021a), a sentiment perhaps most clearly expressed by the Conservative UK government between 2022 and 2024. Throughout this period, British politicians publicly stated they want to move asylum-seekers to Rwanda to deter others from coming to the UK via France, despite criticism from the UN Refugee Agency, current and former British politicians (including members of the Conservative party) and human rights organisations.

While perhaps the most dramatic example, the so-called Rwanda Plan is far from an aberration. Indeed, it has been noted that European governments have tended to enact legislation and policies from the 1980s onwards to restrict the 'number of asylum claims made on their territories' (Baillot *et al.*, 2014: 107). Such measures are not restricted to deterring asylum-seekers from travelling and filing applications or to stricter policies on those who are not granted asylum. Recently, for example, influential UK politicians, including the then Prime Minister Rishi Sunak, stated such aims publicly (Syal & Stacey, 2023). He and the then Home Secretary wanted to change legislation and adhere to a less broad definition of 'refugee' than that which was in use in the EU. In the EU itself, the policies adopted by the member states have involved measures such as 'stricter border controls, increasing use of detention, and limits on refugees' access to social and economic means of support (the so-called "pull factors" for migration)' (Baillot *et al.*, 2014: 107).

In terms of this impact of this political climate, and the associated institutional attitudes that follow, on the design and execution of asylum procedures, more often than not asylum-seekers are treated as guilty until they prove themselves innocent (Bohmer & Shuman, 2018: 80). It is not uncommon for asylum-seekers to be detained in centres immediately after they apply for asylum (e.g. in the Netherlands, when asylum-seekers typically enter via an airport). The taking of the fingerprints of every asylum-seeker is a characteristic 'technology of suspicion' deployed in the EU and other parts of the world, such as Australia and the United States.

Countries have been working towards standardising and mechanising asylum applications against the backdrop of a general desire to curb the numbers. The way narratives of escape are processed by asylum authorities is standardised, as Chapter 2 will discuss. As noted above, there have been attempts to externalise the asylum procedure (Bendel, 2019). For example, the EU at one time offered financial and political rewards to incentivise Turkey to prevent asylum-seekers from moving to mainland Europe. Priti Patel, when Home Secretary of the United Kingdom, long contemplated and attempted to receive asylum-seekers in countries or territories other than the UK mainland, in an effort called 'offshoring' (BBC, 2022). Another former UK Home Secretary, Suella Braverman, similarly considered offshoring migrants to the UK's distant island overseas territories (Forrest, 2023). While such efforts remain contentious and subject to legal review, they cannot be discounted as 'tough talk' in light of the associated payments made to Rwanda by the UK government (Bullen, 2022)

Dealing with asylum applications outside the borders of the destination country is not new and has been called the externalisation of the asylum procedure. Australia, for instance, has pursued such policies for some time. Sometimes applicants are expected by the countries in which they arrive to return to a safe third country, for example France with respect to those who arrive in the UK (Bendel, 2019: 294; Neumayer, 2005: 390), the logic being that France is safe and there is no need for asylum-seekers to travel on to the UK from there. Some asylum-seekers can risk being rejected at the port and being detained immediately on the ground that they are themselves from a 'safe' country (e.g. Jordan) and so do not deserve international protection.

Even those who do apply under national procedures have no certainty of gaining a permit to stay. Moreover, if they do manage to obtain one, it is often unclear whether residence will be permanent. In the case study dealt with in this book, the asylum applicant has just this problem. In Australia, to furnish another example, successive governments used Temporary Protection Visas as a way of discouraging arrivals by boat. These expire after a few years and do not allow people to sponsor family members. (These measures were, though, recently been abolished.) Some

EU member states have become less generous in granting 'political status' (i.e. international protection) and instead started giving more subsidiary, humanitarian permits, which are easier to withdraw (Fullerton, 2011). Those not granted refugee status are not provided with an international refugee travel document and can have their permits withdrawn whenever the national immigration services declare their home countries safe. Syrian refugees in Denmark, for example, started to lose their residence permits even before the Assad regime lost power in Syria. Many Syrians fled from Denmark to countries like Germany and the Netherlands.

In light of all this, it is evident that asylum is not a stand-alone phenomenon relating solely to protecting the vulnerable. Rather, it is 'implicated in other often competing agendas and discourses' (Bohmer & Shuman, 2007: 603). With asylum comes other policy issues politicians need to take into account, including 'border control, terrorism, border-crossing crime' among others in the wider 'internal security field' (Huysmans, 2006: 148). Thus, 'political asylum serves two sometimes contradictory ends: protection of the state and refuge for the applicant' (Bohmer & Shuman, 2007: 603). To complicate matters further, it is not the case that there is, on the one hand, the question of international protection and, on the other, security and security politics; 'sea patrolling, humanitarian assistance, border death, cooperation agreements and detention' are all policy areas which blend the politics of protection and the politics of security (Puggioni, 2017: 1). In the troubled period since the 1990s, the protection of the state has gained the upper hand for reasons dealt with below. Increasingly, asylum has become part of a 'larger system of surveillance, border regulation, and state sovereignty' (Bohmer & Shuman, 2007: 603). Therefore, the discourse surrounding asylum-seeking is no longer a matter of determining the legitimacy of asylum applications but, rather, a question of how to regulate, if not limit, the number of people who arrive in a given country and, in turn, the number who are granted protection. In this atmosphere of suspicion, the securitisation of asylum is well attested (Huysmans & Buonfino, 2008). Chapter 2 deals with this in detail.

1.3 Evolving Public Perceptions and Their Political Impact on Asylum Policies

This chapter has traced the evolution of Europe from a land of emigration to a destination for asylum-seekers and immigrants, and with this the evolution of international and regional legal frameworks. In this section, the focus is on the interplay among historical migration patterns, political forces and media narratives. By dissecting these elements, a foundation for a nuanced comprehension of modern asylum policies can be established. The historical insights are pivotal to current asylum debates, which are frequently shaped by misinformation and politicised agendas and underpin the recommendations advanced in later sections of the book. The discourse illuminates how political and media portrayals can skew public perception and influence policy frameworks concerning asylum-seekers, consequently impacting the communication dynamics during the asylum procedure. A thorough understanding of these narrative origins enables this book to advocate for a more equitable and effective management of asylum applications, as detailed in the ensuing chapters.

Moreover, this section not only sets the historical and discursive stage but also substantiates the book's advocacy for integrating dialogist interpretation into asylum procedures to bolster both fairness and effectiveness. Grasping the historical background to asylum debates enriches our understanding of the present challenges and distortions, and underscores the need for an informed and critical approach to asylum narratives and policymaking.

1.3.1 Debates on asylum, historical context and modern realities

The media's reporting of news in the UK and the Netherlands may suggest that both these countries, and in fact the EU as a whole, are overwhelmed by immigrants and asylum-seekers. These perceptions are misleading, as we will see in Section 1.4. Nevertheless, immigration is presented as if it has permanently changed the face of Europe, often negatively. Many politicians in recent decades have argued that multiculturalism has failed. Such voices are found not only at the political fringes but also in the mainstream, as the examples of Suella Braverman in the UK and Frits Bolkestein in the Netherlands in the 1990s. Both have been very influential. Braverman was a key member of the Conservative party for much of its 14-year tenure as the party of government, while Bolkestein influenced Dutch politics for decades,[1] and his party has been in coalition government in the Netherlands for a similar period. Similar claims are made by some Eastern European politicians in states that have more recently joined the EU, even though these countries are not major immigration destinations, at least from outside Europe.

In many countries of Europe, public discourse on immigration (especially asylum-seeking) has hardened since the 1980s and 1990s (Lucassen, 2019). Certain politicians have thrived on anti-immigration/asylum platforms. Examples include: Geert Wilders, whose Party for Freedom won

1 Bolkestein is a Dutch politician who served as leader of the People's Party for Freedom and Democracy (VVD) from 1990 to 1998 and as the European Commissioner for Internal Market from 1999 until 2004. Geert Wilders (mentioned below) is another prominent Dutch politician and adherent of nationalist-populist politics. He is known for leveraging national imagery and historical narratives to resonate with the electorate. His style, characterised by simplistic yet powerful imagery and an 'us versus them' rhetoric, often positions him against perceived domestic and trans-national adversaries, notably the EU and immigrant groups.

the 2023 Dutch general election by a large margin; Pim Fortuyn, who was a very influential Dutch politician before he was assassinated in 2002 and whose rhetoric impacted the Dutch for a long time; the above-mentioned Bolkestein; and Nigel Farage in the UK, who has influenced British politics for many years and who is also against the presence of asylum-seekers. This type of discourse receives much attention from the media, and some sections of the population have become quite sceptical about asylum and suspicious of asylum-seekers. Economic hardship and recession, it should be noted, do not appear to have played much of a role in fuelling such attitudes to immigration (Hatton, 2016). Rather, Euroscepticism and the growth of populist parties in the first two decades of the 21st century, in addition to the high-profile 'migrant crisis' following the start of the Syrian Civil War in 2011, have generated alarmist perceptions of migrants and migration across the EU (Kang, 2021; Lancaster, 2022).

Such views have persisted, if not continued to gather momentum, and have been utilised to mobilise political sentiment. In October 2022, for instance, the UK Home Secretary stated in Parliament that Albanian criminals have been 'invading' the UK (Topping, 2023). Even today, years on from the Syrian migrant crisis, these ideas of an 'invasion' are frequently drawn upon. It is against this backdrop that the debates surrounding asylum, discussed in the following sub-sections, must be considered. That such trends in asylum debates allude to closely related debates regarding multiculturalism, the desirability of economic migration, Euroscepticism and the expansion of the EU is an indication of the close ties between the matter of asylum and the wider trend of globalisation. This is because with globalisation also comes migration as economies become increasingly connected and barriers to free movement and trade are reduced. Many local communities have been affected by a foreign presence in their markets. This unease with immigration in general, and asylum-seekers in particular, has been felt across the board in the rich industrialised world – the Global North.

The fact that there is a tendency in EU member states to conflate the concepts of asylum, migration, economic migration and illegal migration has probably contributed to the feeling of insecurity and fear. As such, the perception that asylum protects the persecuted has changed in public discourse. It has turned into a 'discourse about protecting the receiving country from potentially dangerous migrants', and 'shifted into a discourse about international security and the fear of terrorism' (Bohmer & Shuman, 2018: 6). As Bohmer and Shuman (2018: 158–159) elaborate, 'today, in addition to the suspicion that economic migrants are trying to game the system by posing as asylum seekers, and despite evidence to the contrary, migrants are suspected of being potential terrorists'.

In trying to contextualise and analyse such narratives, data can be just as obfuscating as polemic and political rhetoric. Nevertheless, as Section 1.4 will show, when the numbers are examined in terms of individual

EU member states, the perception of an 'invasion' of asylum-seekers is not always justified. While examples are drawn from across the Global North, I principally use the EU example here because the case study at the heart of this book is from the Netherlands, an EU member state. There is a significant gap between the public debates and political discourses mentioned earlier and the actual statistics on asylum numbers, as will be shown in the following sections.

1.3.1.1 Political rhetoric and its role in shaping asylum policy

The EU, US, Australia and other industrialised countries from the Global North are democracies, and their governments are expected to respect international rules and laws. Therefore, governments must justify any decision they make or risk being accused of acting against signed agreements and conventions, including the 1951 Refugee Convention. Such governments also have obligations towards their electorates. Because these countries are democratic, not all parties on the political spectrum hold, or are expected to hold, the same political views. That said, in many Western countries since 9/11, restrictive migration policies have increasingly received bipartisan support, with left-wing parties drifting to the right. This means that restricting asylum is not a straightforward decision; neither is maintaining traditional policies.

Restricting access to asylum has been gradual and justified by recourse to 'negative constructions of asylum seekers' (Every & Augoustinos, 2008: 648). It seems that some governments at certain junctures could not but choose to distort the definition of asylum-seekers in order to be able to pass legislation.

Among the negative labels that have been used over the years to demonise asylum-seekers in different countries are: 'potential terrorists', 'economic migrants' (Bohmer & Schuman, 2018: 13–14); 'bogus' (Eades, 2009); and 'terrorists', 'illegals', 'queue jumpers', 'burdensome and threatening' (Every & Augoustinos, 2008: 648). These defamatory practices have existed since the 1990s and possibly before. Individual asylum-seekers have known that their presence was not always welcome. For example, I remember when I applied for asylum in the Netherlands, the country enjoyed a very positive and tolerant image, yet one of the first leaflets I was handed was entitled: 'Nederland is Geen Immigratieland' ('The Netherlands is not an immigration country'). In every Asylum Reception Centre, an announcement was displayed: 'If you wish to go to your homeland, IOM [the International Organisation for Migration] can help'. Asylum-seekers read this and witnessed similar, perceived, deterrent efforts across the Global North in disbelief – efforts described as a 'psychological warfare' (Fernández, 2023).

Politicians' undermining of the support for asylum-seekers takes other forms as well, such as claims that they are economic migrants taking advantage of soft laws (Every & Augoustinos, 2008), that asylum-seeking is an economic or personal choice and that many asylum-seekers are not in 'genuine need of protection' (Neumayer, 2005: 390). There have been calls to restrict the inflow even of genuine asylum cases, as seen in the UK's aforementioned policy towards third countries.

1.3.1.2 Media portrayals of asylum-seekers: Bias and influence

Not all media coverage of asylum-seeking is negative (Kox *et al.*, 2023) but news representations are 'predominantly negative, demonstrating the construction of asylum seekers as threats' (Pantti & Ojala, 2019: 1032). Scholarship 'rightly assumes that [such] news representations contribute to marginalisation and dehumanisation' (Pantti & Ojala, 2019: 1032). In particular, the negative construction of asylum-seeking as an 'economic choice or as an abuse of the Western welfare system' absolves destination countries of their responsibilities and obligations, and even legitimises anti-asylum policies by framing the introduction of increasingly tougher laws as the only way to deal with asylum-seeking.

The impact of media narratives can be clearly seen in the case of Australia, a country in the Global North. In the Australian media, asylum-seekers are represented not objectively but as a large, amorphous, collective group, with a focus on boats and numbers rather than individuals (Bleiker *et al.*, 2013: 398). Instead of representing those seeking asylum as people with personal stories and associating them with a 'humanitarian challenge', they are represented as a threat to 'sovereignty and security' (Bleiker *et al.*, 2013: 398). These 'dehumanising visual patterns reinforce a politics of fear that explains why refugees are publicly framed as people whose plight, dire as it is, nevertheless does not generate a compassionate political response' (Bleiker *et al.*, 2013: 398). This policy, in turn, enforces the 'culture of disbelief', to the detriment of asylum-seekers (Every & Augoustinos, 2008).

How often, and when, this has a direct impact in individual asylum applications cannot be ascertained. In one notable example, however, the Australian media played a dangerous role by misrepresenting an asylum-seeker known as Abyan, a well-known asylum applicant, in a way that undermined her credibility, ultimately raising questions as to journalistic ethics (Doherty, 2015). Misrepresentation of this nature serves to reinforce and contribute to a 'broader discourse that doubts refugees' credibility' (Smith-Khan, 2019a: 404). Indeed, this is far from isolated practice, as 'migration regimes in the Global North commonly use credibility assessments as part of the refugee status determination process' (Smith-Khan, 2017c: 390). A credibility assessment is the process by which an asylum application is found to be 'genuine' or not, and as I will show in Chapter 2, credibility is crucial in the asylum procedure. A similar attack on the credibility was made when Australian media showed an asylum-seeker on a boat, according to politicians, threatening to throw their child overboard (Every & Augoustinos, 2008: 650).

In Europe, similar discursive denigration has occurred in relation to Kurdish asylum-seekers. In a 1998 report referencing Kurdish migration (among others), the Committee on Migration, Refugees and Displaced Persons of the Council of Europe's Parliamentary Assembly referred to clandestine migration as 'one of the acute problems that most of the member countries of the Council of Europe are facing today' (cited by King, 2005: 317). This example is demonstrative of the depth of anti-migration discourse; while at face value a phrase like 'acute problems' may appear to lack any judgement, against a media landscape that reinforces a culture of disbelief such statements may be seen as 'dog-whistle politics', a term used by Bonikowski and Zhang (2023).

The politicised mobilisation of anti-immigrant sentiments is often well timed, as was the case in Australia when on 6 October 2001, shortly before the general election of 9 November 2001, government officials and ministers accused a second boat of asylum-seekers of throwing their children overboard. The claims were later demonstrated by a Senate inquiry to have been based on photographs of asylum-seekers in the sea after their boat had sunk but before they were rescued. However, the proven falsity of these claims did not destabilise the government's agenda and public antipathy towards the asylum-seekers remained high (Marr & Wilkinson, 2003).

Thus, there is a mutual influence between the media, politicians and public opinion. When governments have helped create a negative representation of asylum-seekers in the media, their policies will likely be coloured by those negative images. Moreover, 'suspicion is part of this dynamic', driven not only by 'what asylum applicants say or what documents they produce during the process but also by larger institutional frameworks' (Bohmer & Shuman, 2018: 159). In such frameworks, an innocent asylum-seeker who fears persecution and a fugitive who participated in war crimes may be dealt with by the same ministry, because (in the case of the Netherlands and the UK, for example) the ministries tasked with the security of the country's borders are the ones which also take care of the asylum processes.

The criminalisation of asylum-seekers has 'roots in earlier asylum policies but is intensified in present practices, resulting in vastly different portrayals of asylum applicants either as innocent victims of persecution or as opportunists and potential terrorists' (Bohmer & Shuman, 2018: 159). The suspicion approach is part of the general picture of how asylum-seekers are viewed and treated. Affolter (2021a: 12) says: 'the "fight against abuse" is high on the political agenda [...] Today, asylum determination procedures in the global North are thus structured around a "politics of deterrence" [...] with no country wanting to be more generous in granting asylum and subsidiary protection than others, in order to avoid creating a so-called "pull-effect"'. Deterrence shapes caseworkers' approaches to their role and presents an often-conflicting duality of objectives – assess each case objectively, reduce successful cases to a minimum. This is not to say deterrent policies in themselves directly alter outcomes of asylum applications in the same way a quota might. However, the contradictory aims of helping those who need international protection and avoiding being seen as a source of such protection undoubtedly plays a role in how caseworkers approach their job. Further, when it comes to balancing these two objectives, consciously or unconsciously, the aim of helping asylum-seekers applies less pressure on caseworkers, from the bottom of a significant power differential (in the sense that those most in need of international protection inherently have the least power). On the other hand, public and political pressure to reduce immigration potentially brings significant economic pressure on asylum organisations.

The predominantly negative media portrayals of asylum-seekers not only shape public perception but also influence the broader sociopolitical debates about asylum policies, which are explored in more depth in the following section.

1.3.2 Re-evaluating asylum debates: A sociopolitical perspective

The discussions in preceding sections sketch a landscape of intricate and ongoing public and political debates surrounding asylum. This section contextualises these debates within a broader sociopolitical and historical framework, reflecting on how they extend beyond mere legal or procedural dimensions. Asylum is a complex and interconnected phenomenon, where legal frameworks intersect with deep-seated emotional, cultural and security concerns. Understanding these debates in their full complexity requires an appreciation of their historical roots and the broader contexts of identity and security, as emphasised by Ricatti (2016: 488). This analysis is pertinent to both Australia, the focus of Ricatti's work, and Europe, where my professional experiences as an ex-asylum-seeker and interpreter provide a unique lens through which to examine these issues. By integrating scholarly literature with my personal encounters in asylum settings, this section offers a less polemical and more nuanced exploration of the contentious debates surrounding asylum.

Since the 1990s, and perhaps before, 'party competition in West European democracies [have] all point[ed] to diversification', meaning that the policy concerns of the political parties have not been the only traditional, economic ones (Green-Pederson & Krogstrup, 2008: 610). Indeed, empirical study has shown 'an increasing saliency of immigration issues in the policy agendas of West European parties since the mid-1970s', ever since an '"anti-immigrant turn" of the mainstream Left during the 1990s' (Alonso & da Fonseca, 2011: 880). Political parties seem to be sensitive to 'incentives for different parties in drawing attention to different issues' (Green-Pederson & Krogstrup, 2008: 610), aiming to gain votes in order to be able to gain political power.

Whether certain sections of the European publics have become less welcoming to migrants, and perhaps increasingly 'against immigration', is far from certain, but several distinct trends have been found. These include a sharp increase in the perceived importance of immigration, strong preferences for immigrants who can 'assimilate socially' and a now prevailing association of the EU with poor border control rather than freedom of movement (Dennison & Dražanová, 2018). The salience of these issues, coupled with the growth of anti-immigration parties, can be considered indicative of a general growth in *conservative* attitudes towards migration, here meaning the opposite of *liberal* in the sense of laissez-faire/deregulatory. This conservative attitude applies to the Netherlands as elsewhere, and there has been an intense political debate about how restrictive the state should be in this regard; the mainstream parties feel pressure from the increased success of both extreme right and far left parties, leaving the political landscape polarised (Alonso & da Fonseca, 2011). In the Dutch 2002 general election, the major turn to the right was 'very much the result of the prominent place on the party political agenda accorded to the issues of immigration and law and "order"' (Van Holsteyn *et al.*, 2003, cited in Green-Pedersen & Krogstrup, 2008: 610). More recently in the Netherlands, after the general election of November 2023 the far-right PVV led by Geert Wilders became the largest party in parliament.

While one must always be cautious in attributing any political event to a single cause, in the collapse of the coalition led by the People's Party for Freedom and Democracy (VVD), which led to that 2023 election, migration and asylum politics proved critical. Ultimately, the VVD's coalition partners withdrew over proposed restrictions on asylum, which included limitations on reuniting families and the creation of a tiered asylum system. The party had proposed such measures under significant pressure from the public, from far-right opposition groups and from within the party itself. This recent example of asylum legislation's potentially critical role in modern European politics underscores the need for nuanced and in-depth understanding of the wider phenomenon, something sorely lacking in a media landscape charged with rhetoric.

Television has been linked to an erosion in social trust (Schmitt-Beck & Wolsing, 2010). In relation to immigration more specifically, a 'significant and stable' albeit 'fairly limited' difference has been found between commercial and public service broadcast television in Europe in the form of more negative coverage (Jacobs *et al.*, 2016: 15). Boomgaarden and Vliegenthart (2009) and Schlueter and Davidov (2013) have found that negative stereotypes in news content can reinforce hostile public opinion towards immigration. It should be noted that this sort of media influence is not exclusive to the Global North; in South Africa, Danso and McDonald found news media to be largely negative and 'uncritical', with public opinions correspondingly consistently 'negative about immigrants and immigration and [...] extremely unanalytical in nature' (Danso & McDonald, 2001: 115). This is manifest notably in the uncritical reproduction of statistics and assumptions, a phenomenon significant in its capacity to influence people, including policymakers. In Chapter 4, I will discuss in detail how views of reality come to being and how each individual has a share in forming public opinion.

As well as the media influencing policymakers, politicians influence the media (and public opinion), for instance through unsubstantiated claims. This may be for electoral purposes. Manipulation of facts and misrepresenting them can be a tactic to defame asylum-seekers (Maryns, 2013a: 83). As mentioned earlier in relation to the polarising role of the media, in an attempt to defame asylum-seekers, Australian immigration Minister Peter Reith and Prime Minister John Howard claimed that asylum-seekers from Afghanistan and Iraq threw their children into the sea in order to coerce the navy or coast guard into rescuing them. As Macken-Horarik (2003) argues, the misrepresentation triggered a media and political storm in the lead-up to the 2001 federal election, and the press routinely reframed asylum and migration in terms of illegality, deception and moral threat.

In Europe, anti-immigration policies can be traced back at least to the 1970s, when politicians denied the 'reality of permanent settlement, in line with the new politics of xenophobic exclusionism that went hand-in-hand with economic recession and unemployment ... European political elites began to pander to xenophobic politics – in response to their own declining legitimacy and electoral support – by proclaiming their nations to be "zero immigration" vis-a-vis non-EU nationals' (Luedtke, 2019: 16).

Currently in Europe, the stakes are high for the asylum-seekers, the public, the state and the politicians of the potential countries of asylum (PCAs) in question. While the interrelated issues of national identity, history and security are an integral part of the debate shaping the discourse of today's society, protecting national identity has been considered by some an essential element of managing asylum (Hahamovitch, 2003). Migration and asylum have increasingly been 'converted into a law-and-order question and have become "securitised"' (Trauner, 2016: 313). The triad of politics, public opinion and the media, which provides the podium for the debate and influences it, is interrelated, as each is influenced by the other, as explained above. For the sake of clarity, however, I will separate them temporarily.

Public opinion in countries like the UK, the Netherlands, Belgium, Sweden and Denmark has been critical of the inflow of asylum-seekers. It is possible that the public 'panicked' because their countries were historically more emigration countries than immigration ones. They may have found it difficult to picture their country becoming multicultural. In the media, there is a frequent fixation on the 'other'. The distinct (secular) culture of these PCAs has been presented by politicians such as Wilders in the Netherlands (as well as members of the public) as a reason why their countries should not have 'too many' immigrants. Wilders has even proposed to tax wearing the hijab and talked about the polluting effect of having migrants in the streets.

Migrants from Eastern and Southern Europe, such as Poles, Romanians and Albanians, have been similarly stigmatised in Western Europe. Therefore, the issue is believed to be more of a cultural nature than a racial one, although these concepts can be hard to disentangle. Differences in religion are also presented as a reason why migrants should not be admitted. Across these broad areas of discourse, the 'othering' of migrants is a common denominator. Once, the benefits of immigration were considered to be outweighed by its negative aspects, but the balance has tilted towards a less favourable view of immigration, especially from the 1970s and 1980s, when the identity of the immigrants was no longer the same as before: 'they were increasingly the third world in origin; they had less in common culturally with Europeans than previous asylum movements' (Neumayer, 2005: 390). In addition, the numbers of asylum-seekers (and, more pertinently, their perceived numbers) have increased.

Having examined the background of asylum-seeking and its legal landscape, and demonstrated its interconnectedness to political discourse and public opinion, the final component of the contextual treatment of asylum is the figurative elephant in the room – just how high are these asylum numbers? As the next section will demonstrate, even the statistics of asylum-seeking are subject to political influence and misperception.

1.4 Politics of Perception: Misrepresenting Asylum-Seeker Statistics in Europe

It is crucial to address the persistent perception in the Global North that asylum-seeker numbers are dramatically increasing, leading to widespread calls for restrictive measures across Europe and the First World. This section will critically examine and debunk these anti-asylum claims by comparing them with actual statistics on asylum applications from the 1980s to the present and highlighting the discrepancies.

In all areas of study, when dealing with numbers and statistics one must be cautious about the conclusions drawn. Much depends on which numbers are analysed and how. It is also important to consider both the source of data and who does the analysis. These variables can greatly impact the picture produced. In a notable case in the UK, newspapers widely alleged that the difference between the number of non-EU students who left the UK in 2021 and the who stayed was half a million. Later, when the number was contextualised, it turned out that many of those who had not left were still busy with their studies (BBC, 2017). Also, 'asylum numbers' are not only invariably open to interpretation but are often a means to bolster or diminish arguments for or against asylum and migration. Such statistics demand careful scrutiny and in-depth analysis of the relevant contexts.

In Section 1.2.1, I explained the terminology relating to migration. While the specific meanings of terms such as 'immigration', 'emigration', 'refugees', 'the forcibly displaced' and 'asylum-seekers' may be disregarded in some public discourse, it is remarkable to see how such terms are used interchangeably by people who may be expected to know better. Indeed, politicians have also generated controversy by using the wrong term (e.g. Bolkestein and later Wilders in the Netherlands).

The UNHCR provides an annual *Global Trends* report that gives an overall worldwide figure for the total number of displaced people (e.g. UNHCR, 2021). It divides this number into five categories. In this book, the category under investigation ('asylum applicants') represents only a small percentage of the total number of displaced people. As Figure 1 depicts, in 2023, out of 110 million forcibly displaced people worldwide,

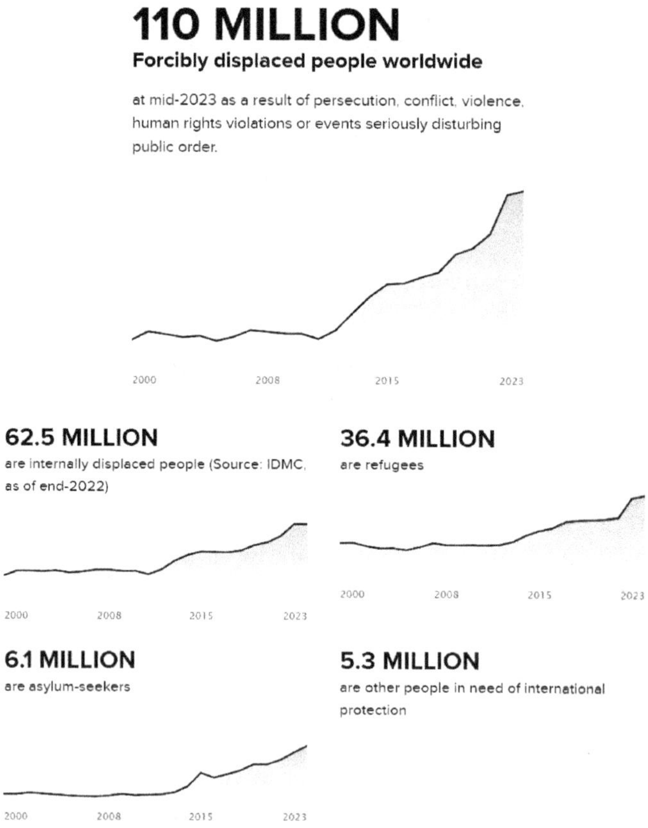

Figure 1 UNHCR Refugee Data Finder global summary statistics (UNHCR, 2023b)

only 6.1 million were asylum-seekers. This categorisation is essential not only for administrative purposes but also for political considerations. It is essential to 'place these numbers in a wider context' as 'Europe is not alone in facing migratory challenges' (Trauner, 2016: 319).

Unspecified, uncontextualised large numbers can scare people into drawing incorrect conclusions. Some right-wing politicians can use them to trigger xenophobic sentiments for political purposes. Such numbers can also lead to unjustified policies on people seeking international protection, as is currently the case in Europe, where refugee policy is often built on the myth of an 'invasion' by migrants from developing countries, with immigration portrayed as harmful for society (van Selm, 2019: 310). Fear is not a good adviser and can lead people to support policies that are not based on facts. Van Selm (2019: 310) reports that '90 per cent of immigrants to Germany are European, and 80 per cent are EU citizens. Of the 10 per cent who are not European, not all are from developing countries, and even of those, not all are refugees or asylum seekers'. Showing the bigger picture like this, contextualising the numbers and using the correct terminology is much more appropriate than vague discussion of 'inflows' and 'influxes', which can give a skewed and incomplete representation of facts.

Uncontextualised 'total numbers' coupled with, for example, the styling of asylum applicants as 'happiness seekers' (*gelukszoekers*) by right-wing politicians such as Wilders and some Dutch media, are particularly detrimental to a functional understanding of the situation posed by asylum application numbers. Figure 2 shows the significant fluctuation in the asylum applicant numbers year by year, reflecting wars, political and economic changes across the globe. The numbers of those in need of international protection worldwide increased significantly in 2014, 2018 and 2022. These peaks coincide with conflicts in the Middle East and Ukraine, and an economic crisis in Venezuela. Conversely, the introduction of travel restrictions in the midst of the COVID-19 pandemic led to

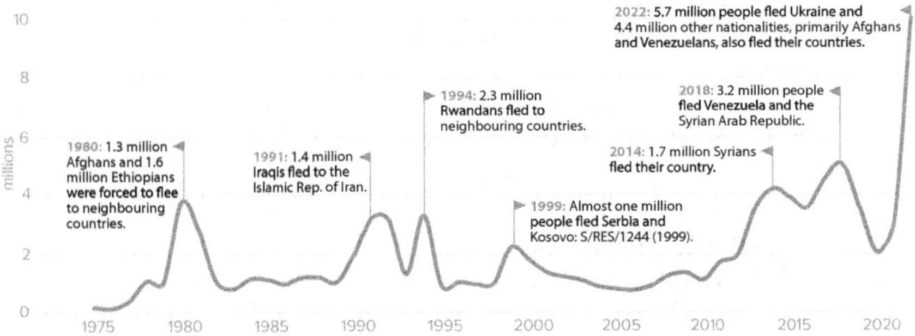

Figure 2 Numbers (millions) of refugees, asylum-seekers and other people in need of international protection displaced each year, 1975–2022 (UNHCR, 2023d)

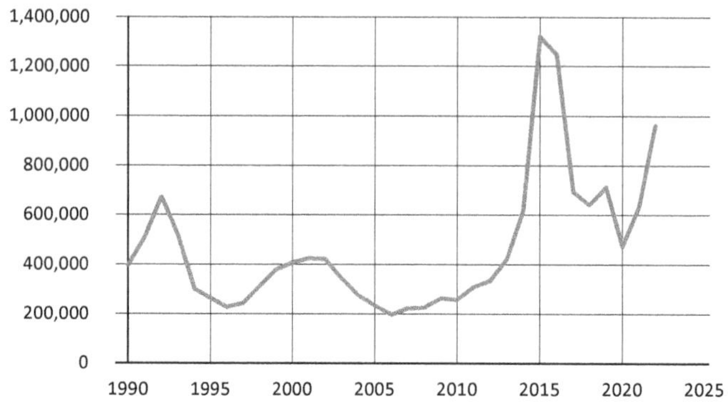

Figure 3 Trends in asylum applications in the EU, 1990–2022 (Council of Europe, 2023, https://www.coe.int/en/web/portal)

sharp decline in asylum applications, as international roads, ports and airways were closed or subject to new regulations, and some countries suspended asylum procedures (Ghezelbash & Tan, 2020).

As Figure 3 depicts, such fluctuations in global numbers of displaced people can have a significant impact on the numbers of asylum applications filed within the EU. Critically, however, as a comparison between Figures 2 and 3 reveals, this is not always the case. In 1994, for instance, the flight of 2.3 million Rwandans had little effect on EU numbers. Figure 2 also shows a small decline in global numbers after a peak in 2014, which was then followed by a peak in 2018. Figure 3 shows that, in the EU, the 2014 first peak was seen acutely but the 2018 peak translated into only a small increase.

To enrich this contextualisation, Figure 4 shows the percentage of Venezuelan asylum-seekers 'hosted' by different developed and developing countries. The vast majority of Venezuelan asylum-seekers not only remained in developing countries, but, as seen in Figure 5, principally in neighbouring countries. Thus, uncontextualised figures can present a misleading image of asylum-seeking and global changes are not felt evenly across regions.

It is also clear that continents other than Europe receive a large portion of asylum applications. While Europe received the majority of asylum applications in some of the years spanning 2013–2022 (Figure 6), this was far from a uniform trend. Note, I am talking about asylum-seekers, not forcibly displaced people. The latter percentage in Europe is much less than in other regions: there were 110 million forcibly displaced people in the world in 2023, the majority of whom were internally displaced, and many of the remainder fled to neighbouring or developing countries (UNHCR, 2023d). Further, Figure 6 shows that the Americas took an increasingly large number of applications.

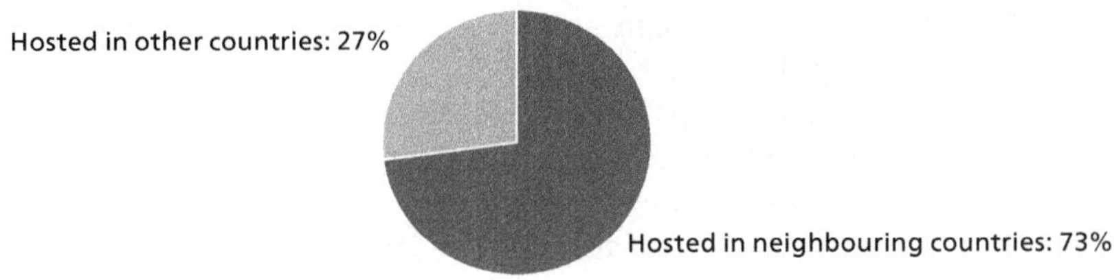

Figure 4 Numbers of Venezuelans displaced abroad in developed and developing countries (UNHCR, 2021)

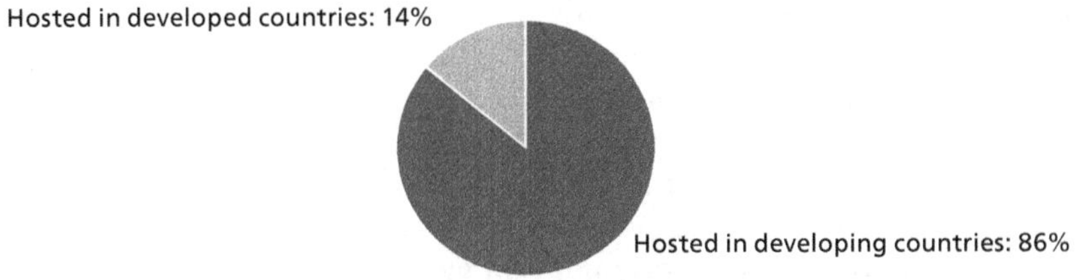

Figure 5 Numbers of Venezuelans displaced abroad in neighbouring countries (UNHCR, 2021)

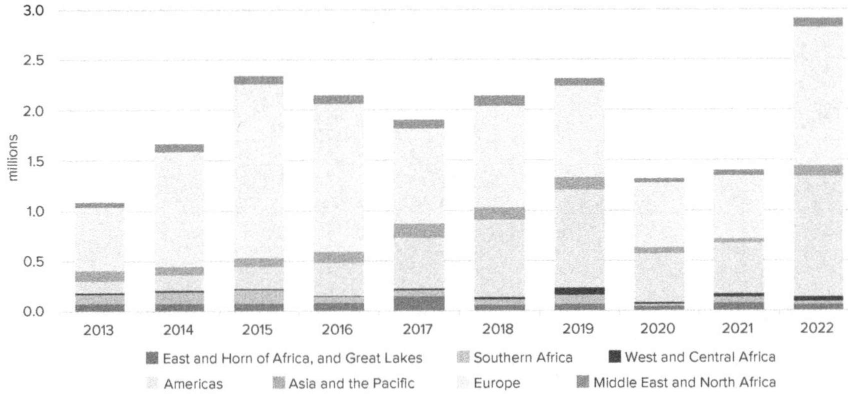

Figure 6 Individual asylum applications registered by region of asylum, 2013–2022 (UNHCR, 2023d)

Notably, and to demonstrate further the malleability and potential misleading nature of uncontextualised statistics, these numbers may contain a significant number of repeat applications (UNHCR, 2021) because some asylum-seekers may end up lodging more than one application or may apply in more than one country. Even when examining a single year in isolation, context proves key in deriving meaningful conclusions from numbers.

The (dis)connection between statistics and public perceptions also applies within regions. In the case of the EU, as alluded to above, hyperbole often abounds in terms of media representations of asylum-seeking. One aspect of this is the question of the relative distribution of applications between member states. A contextualised examination of statistics reveals that Germany receives the most applications among EU member states, followed by France, Spain, Greece and Italy (Figure 7). Given that the last three of these countries are points of entry to the EU and that many asylum-seekers will travel on to reach other states, the actual number of asylum applicants could be significantly smaller. Many asylum-seekers are fingerprinted and are considered asylum applicants in one country even though many then move northwards to other countries, where they are again registered as asylum-seekers.

The Netherlands ranks eighth among EU member states in terms of numbers of asylum applications received, despite commonly being portrayed by the Dutch media as one of the leading countries in this respect. In Eastern European countries, asylum applications have also become a politicised issue in several recent elections (Santana *et al.*, 2020), and yet 80% of applications in the EU are filed in Western rather than Eastern European member states. In many such states the politicisation of immigration has often been 'packaged' with long-held ethnocentric concerns about large historical minorities (Russians in the Baltic states,

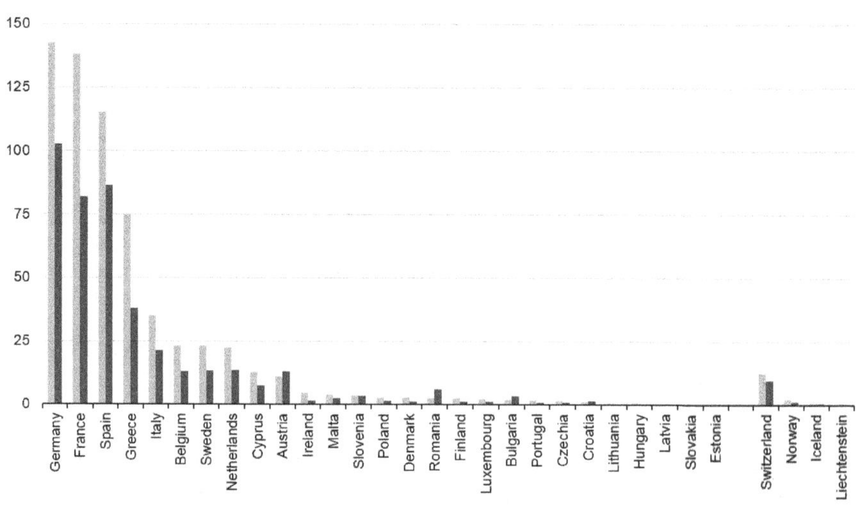

Source: Eurostat (online data code: migr_asyappctza) eurostat

Figure 7 Number (thousands) of first-time asylum applicants (non-EU citizens), 2019 and 2020 (Eurostat, https://ec.europa.eu/eurostat/statistics-explained/index.php)

the Roma in Central Europe), 'traditional values' and economic strands of EU scepticism. In such efforts, the presentation of 'European' statistics may be leveraged to dramatise the levels of migration posed by such countries even though they themselves were net emigration countries in latter part of the twentieth century (Okólski, 2012).

It is essential, then, to interpret statistics with caution to avoid overplaying, or underplaying, the situation in a given state. For instance, the number of applications to a given country should be set in the context of the size of the national population. In addition, it is not the case that those who arrive in a destination country will automatically be allowed to stay.

1.5 Conclusion

This chapter has charted the evolution of asylum from its historical origins to the contemporary landscape, underscoring the critical role of statistics in shaping both public perceptions and policy decisions regarding asylum-seekers. By dissecting how data are presented and manipulated, the chapter has illuminated the complexities that frame the contemporary asylum discourse – where numbers not only inform but also mislead.

The exploration has revealed the intricate interplay of legal, political and social dimensions that govern asylum processes. This multifaceted approach sets the stage for a detailed enquiry in the rest of this book, starting with an investigation into the dual nature of asylum procedures in Chapter 2. These procedures are not merely legal processes but are imbued with political motivations that can significantly impact their fairness and transparency. The design of these procedures often compromises the quality of communication – a central theme this book addresses through its focus on dialogue and information flow within asylum consultations.

2 Navigating the Nexus: Language, Law and Politics in Asylum Procedures

> One of the major sources and objects of power and inequality is symbolic and revolves around the use and abuse of language and discourse.
>
> (Blommaert, 2001a: 13)

2.1 Introduction

This chapter builds on the analytical foundations laid in Chapter 1 and delves deeper into the complexities of asylum procedures. It not only highlights the legal and political dimensions of such procedures, but also examines the intricate interplay between these elements and their impact on procedure design, and in turn on the communication practices during interpreter-mediated encounters. Chapter 1 provided the historical backdrop of the origins and evolution of asylum-seeking and asylum procedures. Chapter 2 dissects how political contexts and agendas shape the design and function of asylum procedures and, importantly, influence communication dynamics, particularly in interpreter-mediated hearings and legal consultations. It demonstrates the importance of engaging with both explicit and implicit communication practices to ensure fairness and transparency in asylum adjudication.

For asylum-seekers, the decision to grant international protection rests entirely with the potential country of asylum (PCA). As the guardian of that international protection, the United Nations, represented by the UNHCR, has, in the main, an advisory role.[1] As highlighted in Chapter 1, no unitary asylum procedures and/or regulations govern how asylum applications are dealt with in different countries. The UN does not impose regulations on how to apply the 1951 Refugee Convention but only general rules. What has emerged since 1951 is an institutional and legislative

1 An exception to this is found in some developing countries, where the UNHCR does carry out asylum procedures, when local governments do not. The UNHCR usually does this as a preliminary step towards identifying refugees to be resettled in third countries in the Global North. As the focus of the case study at the core of this book is on the Global North, specifically the Netherlands, such work by the UNHCR will not be investigated further.

landscape that has been described as 'nested' (relevant institutions may occupy positions in wider frameworks), 'parallel' (commitments and obligations pertaining to asylum may contradict those in other areas) and 'overlapping' (institutions may share responsibility of aspects of asylum and refugee regulation). This is the 'refugee regime complex' (Betts, 2010: 19). A full exploration of the variety of regional regimes and treaties, and the even more diverse political influences on them, is beyond the scope of this chapter, and even this book. Chapter 1 introduced the Common European Asylum System (CEAS), the most relevant regional regime to the case study at the core of this book (see Section 1.2.3) and outlined its relationship to the 1951 Convention. Within the global refugee regime complex, a myriad of political pressures are, legitimately and less so, at play in a given PCA, procedure and even case. On the whole, however, it maybe surmised that local and international politics influence the design and outcomes of asylum procedures, as documented by Schittenhelm (2019), Winn (2020), Cucu and Panon (2023) and Zaun *et al.* (2024). Moreover, the daily practices within asylum processes are profoundly shaped by local political, social and economic influences (Fontanari, 2022).

This chapter principally investigates how politics directly influences a procedure's design and implementation. At the most fundamental level, the communication aspects of such procedures are regulated and directly influenced by, among other things, the language ideologies of the relevant authorities. 'Ideologies' refer to how authorities perceive a phenomenon and think it operates. By exploring how these political influences affect the technicalities of the procedure, I show that they may alter the chances of an asylum-seeker getting international protection and that the theoretical basis of this procedure may not be as solid as the authorities think. I question how sense-making and meaning-making are conceptualised during the procedure and call for complementary tools, principally in the form of interviews after the interpreter mediated encounter (IME), to make the procedure fairer.

The rest of this chapter is organised as follows. First, Section 2.2 provides a general introduction to asylum procedures in the Global North, followed by a detailed account of the procedure in the Netherlands, given its salience to the case study presented in Chapter 3. These procedures are then engaged with critically, first by unpacking the problem areas in their fundamental design (Section 2.3). At the heart of this analysis is an account of how the politically motivated choice of language ideology directly engenders deficiencies in the procedures (Section 2.4). Section 2.5 begins the work that forms the core purpose of this book: identifying the avenues for improvement from which recommendations may be formed to alleviate these deficiencies in the design of asylum procedures. Section 2.6 builds on this, by locating and grounding these areas for improvement in the specific roles of the key parties to asylum procedures in the Netherlands, as a representative example of the Global North in general. Finally, Section

2.7 concludes by collating remarks and reflections on the book's core message – that the design of asylum procedures in the Global North are both politically motivated and flawed, and that this need not be the case.

2.2 Navigating the Asylum Pathway: Legal Hurdles and Cultural Climates

It is imperative for asylum applicants to substantiate claims of persecution or the legitimate fear thereof. This persecution may be inflicted by state authorities or non-state actors within their country of origin,[1] as delineated by the 1951 Refugee Convention. In addition, they also have to satisfy the rules and requirements of the PCA. Since the 1980s, the burden of proof for a given application has increasingly shifted to the applicant, as a culture of disbelief has become more established in the Global North (Dempster & Hargrave, 2017). Many asylum applications are rejected 'not because their claims do not fulfil refugee status requirements, but rather because they are not perceived as being credible, which is a legal precondition for being recognised as a refugee' (Affolter, 2021a: 2). Further, applicants must prove there is a discriminatory motive behind this persecution (Binder, 2001). Then, even if the application is found to be credible and has satisfied all these demands, the outcome of a given case remains far from certain, as this chapter will show. Moreover, the application is conducted in a procedural climate where the applicant is often not welcomed. Indeed, calls have skyrocketed in many countries to stop migrants from entering, as Chapter 1 explored. For example, even though over 90% of those applying for asylum in the UK are found to be genuine asylum applicants, there are still many calls to stop the 'invasion' of 'migrants', whether by politicians, members of the public, or both (Dempster & Hargrave, 2017). In other words, there is a genuine intolerance of refugees in many countries in the Global North.

To adequately explore these issues, it is pertinent first to outline the process of an asylum procedure. As noted in Chapter 1, the legal framework gives PCAs the ability to set their own procedures, and variation naturally follows. In Section 2.2.1, the asylum procedure is introduced in the context of the Netherlands, where the case study is set, but much of the ensuing critical discussion is applicable to other EU member states due to the CEAS, and indeed across the Global North, given the propensity to glean insights from other countries' procedures. For instance, Dutch politicians have drawn from other countries' asylum procedures while the Conservative government in the UK sought inspiration from the Australian model of 'offshoring' (Matera *et al.*, 2023). Nevertheless, asylum procedures

1 For example, Syrians seeking asylum in the Netherlands were often granted protection even if they had not directly lived under the control of the Assad regime but had instead fled from non-state military groups such as the Al-Nusra Front or ISIS.

are not static entities, but change and adapt in response to political and administrative considerations. Numerous changes to the Dutch asylum process occurred between the study in 2014 and the writing of this book. Where relevant, these have been noted in the section below. The procedure is complex and the section is intended to be only a general introduction.

2.2.1 The asylum procedure in the Netherlands

When asylum-seekers arrive in the Netherlands, they are required to register their arrival and submit a request for international protection (Immigratie- en Naturalisatiedienst, 2023a, 2023b). The INS (Dutch immigration service) is responsible for handling this process, during which the asylum-seeker is subjected by the authorities to a procedure designed to determine whether or not there is legal ground for entitlement to international protection, based on the 1951 Convention and its 1967 Protocol, as well as national laws. The Convention is the basis upon which the authorities determine whether or not an asylum-seeker satisfies the definition of a refugee. The determination of refugee status is influenced by how asylum-seekers articulate their reasons for seeking asylum and present their personal histories, all evaluated from the viewpoint of the authorities (Bögner *et al.*, 2010: 519). The credibility of these accounts, as judged by the INS, is crucial to the outcome of the application (Jacquemet, 2011: 482).

Following the registration and after the first hearing (*aanmeld gehoor*), the asylum-seeker is given six days to rest and to prepare for the official procedure. The six-day 'rest-and-preparation period', which precedes the detailed interview (*nader gehoor*), often lasts much longer due to backlogs at Ter Apel, with some waiting months before the formal procedure begins. During this 'rest-and-preparation period' (Immigratie-en Naturalisatiedienst, 2015), the asylum-seeker is given information on the procedure by the Dutch Council for Refugees (DCR) and by an asylum lawyer (VluchtelingenWerk Nederland, n.d.) and is also seen for a medical interview by the medical centre (medTadvies) to find out if he or she has any mental and/or physical condition which the INS must take into account. Since late 2022, this initial process has also entailed pre-registration (i.e. before the submission of the asylum application) of basic information by the INS. This step is an administrative step prior to the formal asylum application and does not constitute the legal beginning of the asylum procedure. This process emerged in response to capacity problems, particularly at Ter Apel, the country's largest asylum reception centre, in terms of both application processing and housing conditions. Ter Apel, located in the north-east of the Netherlands, is operated by the Central Agency for the Reception of Asylum-Seekers (Centraal Orgaan opvang asielzoekers, COA). It serves as the primary entry point for asylum-seekers, where they undergo essential initial processes like identification and registration, overseen in collaboration with the INS and local police. This facility is a critical component of the Dutch immigration system, and the challenges faced by it reflect broader challenges in global migration and asylum policies.[1] Conditions at Ter Apel became so dire that legal action was taken against the state and the COA (VluchtelingenWerk Nederland, 2023).

Since the implementation of the EU's Dublin III Regulation in 2013, at this initial stage of the asylum procedure it is established if another country is responsible for a given application (VluchtelingenWerk Nederland, 2023). After this period, the 'Algemene Asielprocedure' (AA), or 'General Asylum Procedure', starts (Immigratie- en Naturalisatiedienst, 2023a, 2023b). Once it commences, this procedure normally lasts eight days but may be extended to 14 days in exceptional cases. The application is either accepted or rejected. If rejected and not overturned on appeal, the asylum-seeker may be transferred to a return facility (Vrijheidsbeperkende locatie) while their departure to their country of origin is prepared. The asylum-seeker is entitled to lodge an appeal under the General Administrative Law Act (Algemene wet bestuursrecht, Awb) before the Regional Court, or, later, at the Council of State.

This General Asylum Procedure starts with an asylum hearing (initial or verification interview) which is conducted by an INS employee, during which questions are asked about the nationality, identity and travel route of the asylum-seeker. Where the asylum-seeker does not speak Dutch to a sufficient standard – which is usually the case (Doornbos, 2006: 22) – communication is mediated by an interpreter, who is provided by the state.

An independent lawyer is assigned to discuss with the asylum-seeker the content of this first hearing, and both parties are given a written report of the hearing. This meeting can be used, where relevant, to prepare the asylum-seeker for a second hearing (called the 'nader gehoor', or 'detailed hearing'). In some cases, the INS may decide to postpone this detailed hearing and hold it in the 'Verlengde Asielprocedure' (VA) (the Extended Asylum Application) if it thinks it needs more time to investigate the case (Immigratie- en Naturalisatiedienst, 2023a, 2023b).

During the detailed hearing the applicant is asked why they have applied for asylum in the Netherlands (Doornbos, 2006). This hearing used by the INS to make its decision. The Dutch Council for Refugees (DCR) may attend the hearing upon request of the lawyer or applicant (VluchtelingenWerk Nederland, 2023). Minors are accompanied by NIDOS during these hearings.

The day after the detailed hearing, the lawyer discusses the report of the hearing with the client. Corrections and/or additions can be made to

1 For more detailed information on the asylum procedures and the role of the Ter Apel centre within the Dutch immigration system, visit the Central Agency for the Reception of Asylum Seekers (COA) website, https://www.coa.nl/en.

the report, which is then passed on to the INS to decide what happens next. There are three possibilities:

(1) The applicant will be granted international protection. In this book's case study (Chapter 3), the applicant had been attempting to obtain this permit after having been previously denied and instead had been granted a less stable permit ('Subsidiary Protection').
(2) The INS believes that more research is needed, it will refer the applicant to the Extended Asylum Procedure. The applicant will be provided with a report of the detailed hearing and will be rehoused in an asylum-seekers' centre (ASC).
(3) If the application does not satisfy the requirements for asylum according to the INS, then the asylum-seeker will receive the so-called 'Intention to Reject' paperwork ('Voornemen tot Afwijzing'). In this, the INS explains that it intends to reject the application and presents the reasons. The applicant will be given the opportunity, with the assistance of their legal advisor, to make corrections and additions and to respond to the Intention to Reject.

When the INS receives a response of the applicant to its Intention to Reject, it has three options (Immigratie- en Naturalisatiedienst, 2023a, 2023b):

(1) The applicant will be nonetheless granted an asylum residence permit.
(2) If the INS decides that more time is needed to conduct research, then the application will be referred to the Extended Asylum Application, in which case the applicant is then rehoused in an ASC.
(3) The application is rejected, which means that the applicant will be expected to leave the Netherlands. At this point the applicant can decide to lodge an appeal. This appeal is filed under the General Administrative Law Act (Algemene wet bestuursrecht, Awb) before the Regional Court.

In summary, then, the basic sequence of the procedure is: screening by the police; initial hearing at the INS; detailed (or substantive) hearing, also at the INS; decision. Alternatively, there can be an Extended Asylum Procedure before the decision when the INS considers that more time is needed to investigate the case further. At the time of case study, the Extended Asylum Procedure usually had a designated length of six months but in September 2022 this was extended to 15 months, and up to 21 months in some cases (Vluchtelingenwerk Nederland, 2023). (These timelines reflect practice under backlog conditions and are not fixed statutory limits.)

During the Extended Asylum Procedure, as in the case of the preceding General Asylum Procedure, the INS can grant the applicant international protection or can decline the asylum application. In the latter case, the applicant will firstly receive a letter in which the INS explains its intentions. This is again called an 'Intention to Reject' (Immigratie- en Naturalisatiedienst, 2023a, 2023b). If the applicant is not prepared to accept this decision, they can discuss this with their lawyer, who can submit a 'Zienswijze' (lawyer's response) to the INS explaining why they do not agree with the Intention to Reject. The INS may reconsider or reaffirm its decision. It then sends the applicant the official decision, and an explanation of its motivations and the consequences of this decision (Spijkerboer, 2010).

If the asylum-seeker rejects this decision, then they can go to court (Immigratie- en Naturalisatiedienst, 2015). The judge decides: (1) whether the INS dealt with the application in a careful manner, (2) whether its decision conforms with Dutch laws and regulations and (3) whether the decision conforms to international treaties.

In its decision to reject, the INS indicates the time by which the applicant is required to have left the Netherlands. Thereafter, they are not entitled to reside in an ASC (Immigratie- en Naturalisatiedienst, 2014). Failed applicants are responsible for arranging their own return to their homeland and risk being deported (often escorted) if they do not.

If an appeal is rejected by the court, the asylum-seeker is entitled to lodge a higher appeal at the Administrative Jurisdiction Division of the Council of State (De Raad van State, 2020), which is the highest administrative judicial authority in the Netherlands. If its decision of the is in accordance with that of the lower judge, then the asylum-seeker can take their case to the European Court of Human Rights.

The Temporary Protection Directive (TPD), a result of the EU's Council Implementing Decision (EU) 2022/382, is a more recent measure, developed in response to the high numbers of applicants resulting from the war in Ukraine. It allows the INS to file, but not process, any asylum application for the duration of the period of temporary protection. It confers lawful residence and a number of social rights during the protection period, though it is not equivalent to refugee status or a regular asylum permit (AIDA, 2022).

2.3 Asylum Procedure Design

Having provided a detailed account of the asylum procedure in the Netherlands, this section focuses on how political agendas influence the design and function of such procedures (specifically in the Netherlands but also more widely), particularly in relation to communication dynamics (e.g. during hearings and legal consultations). This analysis, transcending politics and law, sets the stage for the case study in Chapter 3.

As noted in the preceding section, an asylum application hinges on its perceived credibility. Sections 2.3.1 to 2.3.5 will critically examine how the legal frameworks and operational protocols within the asylum process in the Netherlands (and by extension the Global North) scrutinise and shape the narratives of those seeking refuge. They explore the dual hearings structure, the rigorous vetting of asylum claims and the pivotal role of legal representation. Each aspect reveals the layered and often contentious nature of determining credibility and the outcomes of asylum applications.

2.3.1 Hearings: Interrogating credibility

Authorities consider hearings crucial, as asylum applicants often bring only their narrative of escape. In such cases little factual evidence is available (Eades, 2005; Van Veldhuizen, 2022). Caseworkers look for clues in the applicant's backstory to judge the credibility of their claim. In the Netherlands (and elsewhere in the Global North), the applicant is given time at the start of the hearing to tell their story (van der Kleij, 2015: 11), not only to explain the reason for their flight but also to allow the authorities to detect possible weak points or falsifications and begin asking scrutinising questions.

In fact, after screening (*politie*) there are two hearings (initial followed by detailed/substantive). The screening involves a police interview, with brief questions about identity, travel route, and reason to apply for asylum. The initial hearing is more detailed regarding more or less the same matters. At the second hearing applicants are asked in much more detail about why they fled their country and cannot go back home. The initial hearing is to assess the admissibility of the application and, as Maryns (2005: 300) notes, 'at this stage it is decided whether or not the application is under consideration for further investigation'. More pointedly, the hearings are meant to 'differentiate between economic migrants and legitimate political asylum seekers' (Bohmer & Shuman, 2010: 212) and 'to discern the truth and to differentiate between legitimate and fraudulent applicants' (Bohmer & Shuman, 2018: 160). They are designed to 'negotiate institutionally acceptable identities' (Kjelsvik, 2014: 93). The INS wants to draw a picture of the identity of the applicant and their claim. The applicant answers questions put forward by the INS according to the latter's own rules. From the moment the application has been made, a record is kept that includes the INS's questions and the applicant's answers. These 'entextualised' pieces of talk are used and reused during the different phases of the application. The texts are retained and may be consulted later in the applicant's life, when the authorities want to create a profile for the person in question (see Gallez & Maryns, 2014).

During the hearings, the caseworker scrutinises the story of the applicant. 'Digging deep' is a 'routinised practice' for migration institutions in the Global North, such as the INS (Affolter, 2020, 2021a). Digging deep means decision-makers 'interrogate asylum seekers during asylum interviews in a way that is aimed at "discovering" indicators of so-called non-credibility' (Affolter, 2021a: 9).

The fundamental premise is generally that the INS should disbelieve applicants (Affolter, 2021a). The caseworker will search for contradictions in the story. An important indicator of credibility is whether asylum-seekers can speak in detail about 'events' relevant to the asylum claim (Affolter, 2021a). Caseworkers will check elements of the narrative (e.g. the names of landmarks) with a view to verification. The material collected by the caseworker is placed into a file. This process of entextualisation has attracted much criticism. In essence, it is a mechanism through which verbal discourse is rendered into a written format to facilitate its dissemination. This transformation inherently involves the reinterpretation and recontextualisation of the original spoken content, tailored to fit new discursive contexts (see Blommaert, 2001a, 2001b). In sociolinguistic research, the process of entextualisation is examined as the extraction and subsequent embedding of spoken discourse from an environment replete with non-verbal cues and contextual understanding in a new, textual realm. The resultant text, though stable, typically lacks the contextual richness of its original and undergoes modifications to conform to textual norms (Blommaert, 2001a, 2001b).

Scholars underscore a pivotal dimension of entextualisation, particularly its potential to substantially alter the meaning and implications of the original discourse. As oral communication is transposed into text, it often becomes simplified, standardised, or otherwise modified to meet the demands of new environments. These alterations can shape interpretations of the text, particularly in legal contexts or administrative settings (Maryns, 2006). Moreover, entextualisation is intricately linked to dynamics of power. Control over the transformation of speech into text often gives control over the narrative, for instance which elements of the original discourse are emphasised and which minimised. This is crucial in asylum hearings, as the stakes for participants are so high. Entextualisation can either reinforce or challenge power structures (Blommaert, 2001a, 2001b). In sum, it represents a complex, critical process that profoundly affects how information is conveyed and perceived across various social and institutional frameworks. Its impact on discourse and power dynamics underscores its importance within sociolinguistic studies, especially in understanding how language functions within different forms of social organisation and control (Blommaert, 2001a, 2001b; Maryns, 2006).

In light of the aforementioned lack of hard facts in the narratives of many, if not most, asylum applicants, 'institutional representatives [...] have to turn to the visible but often very minimal cues in applicant performance' (Maryns, 2013a: 87). In addition, these minimal cues 'often become indexical of issues as crucial as speaker identity and credibility' (Maryns, 2013a: 87). This can lead to tragic outcomes for asylum applicants, as we will see later, for, often, asylum applicants' linguistic repertoire and world views may not be compatible with the INS's (Blommaert, 2001a, 2001b). Additionally, the traumas some applicants have been subjected to may heavily affect their ability or willingness to recall and/or dwell on certain elements of their story.

In conclusion, asylum procedures frequently employ what amounts to interrogation as a strategic deterrent (Bohmer & Shuman, 2007).

2.3.2 Navigating the labyrinth: The complex dynamics of credibility and legal representation in the Dutch asylum procedure

This section examines the adjudication challenges applications face. It explores how the structure of the asylum procedure, limited legal assistance and complex communication dynamics influence outcomes. During the hearings, 'some forms of inquiry, especially those designed to identify minor discrepancies in an application, can obfuscate rather than clarify' (Bohmer & Shuman, 2018: 160). So, while it may seem inherently good that the applicant is allowed to tell their story, conversely the caseworker is allowed to ask questions that uncover weak spots in the applicant's account. Moreover applicants have only a limited amount of legal assistance, because the state tries to keep lawyers' interventions, and those of the Dutch Refugee Council, to a minimum.

This is manifest in some of the procedure's elements and regulations. For instance, meetings between lawyer and client take place before the substantive hearing, not the initial hearing. This leads to a gap in the legal preparation and advice available to asylum-seekers at critical early stages, especially the initial screening by the police, at the start of the procedure. This screening investigates the applicant's identity, nationality, travel history and other factors that could affect the validity of their asylum application. The absence of legal counsel during this crucial period raises questions about whether this is due to a formal rule or merely customary practice.

In response to these limitations, the Dutch Refugee Council sometimes prepares applicants for their first hearing. Although the Council's involvement is valuable, it does not fully compensate for the absence of early legal counsel and often lacks depth. Lawyers are not expected to attend asylum hearings and are not permitted to intervene if they do so (Jacobs & Maryns, 2021). Similarly, the Dutch Refugee Council can attend hearings but not participate. Lawyer and representatives of the Council can talk to the applicant only during breaks.

The minimisation of lawyers' involvement results in caseworkers having a large role. While lawyers can review INS reports and offer legal advice and make additions or corrections, their ability to affect the proceedings is limited. They can respond only if the INS declares its intention to refuse the application and if it later makes a negative decision. This is partly due to the communication and language policies established by the INS, which dictate the nature of interactions between asylum-seekers, their legal representatives and the INS. Even when an appeal is made against the INS's decision, it is usually at an advantage through its involvement in the previous stages of the process. In contrast, the lawyer remains in a more constrained position, limited by the same lack of influence at those earlier stages. In effect, lawyers can offer guidance and counsel, but INS protocols and rules limit their influence. In addition to their limited legal support, during the hearings it is caseworkers, rather than applicants, who control the flow of the conversation. At the start of the second, substantive hearing, as mentioned above, the applicant is asked to state the reason for their flight in what the INS calls their own words. In addition to any questions arising, the caseworker takes out a list of prepared questions to examine the credibility of the applicant's backstory (Van Veldhuizen *et al.*, 2018), crafted to identify potential fraud. Caseworkers are required to scrutinise the narrative, not merely document it; that is, even the most neutral caseworker is obliged to cross-examine, challenge and attempt to pick apart an applicant's narrative. While scrutiny at the evaluation stage of a procedure is undoubtably necessary, the atmosphere of critical scepticism accompanying entextualisation engenders a risk of unduly weakening applicants' narratives.

Even if an applicant meets the criteria for international protection under the PCA, this does not guarantee a successful outcome (Neumayer, 2005: 390). Procedural features of the asylum system can still lead to unfair decisions. For instance, applicants are expected to present a detailed and coherent account, yet interpreter-mediated communication may distort meaning, resulting in their story being perceived as incoherent. During the hearing, restrictions imposed by the caseworker may further prevent applicants from expressing what they would have said if they were able to speak directly.

The applicant's manner of expression during hearings can subtly influence INS credibility assessments, with perceived inadequacies often leading to responses being framed as vague or inconsistent (Coffey, 2003). The techniques and tactics of unmasking a fraudulent applicant are based on theoretical foundations that may sound logical and fair but are not, as we will see later in this chapter. At times, embedded assumptions in the asylum procedure that are considered logical by the authorities may not be so from the applicant's perspective. For instance, people in danger are expected to 'take prompt and effective steps to save themselves and will never willingly put themselves at risk' (Cameron, 2008: 567). In practice, many other considerations can influence the decisions of asylum applicants when they flee danger in the complex reality of their social and political situations (to say nothing of the relativity of definitions of 'danger' and 'common sense' across cultures, professions, lifestyles, social strata etc.). Other assumptions are partly found in language ideologies currently discredited by communication scholarship (see Section 2.5).

Even when an applicant's narrative fulfils the credibility requirements, further requirements are made as to how this content is presented. For instance, as part of the internal credibility of the applicant's account, the applicant is expected to put forward any information that is relevant to the case during the hearing. Many of the decision-makers who participated in the research by Baillot *et al.* (2014: 118) were 'adamant that delay in disclosing a key aspect of the asylum claim, or even delay in making a claim itself, would (and for many, should) reflect negatively on a claimant's credibility'. When there are inconsistencies, whether real or perceived, it becomes difficult for asylum-seekers to establish their credibility (Baade & Gölz, 2023), as decision-makers perceive inconsistencies as a sign of dishonesty (Herlihy *et al.*, 2010).

The demeanour of the applicant during the hearing can also influence whether the story is found credible, even though it is unlikely to be explicitly given as a reason for an adverse decision; rather, it may influence the outcome 'in unacknowledged ways, such as framing the applicant's responses as "vague, lacking in detail, inconsistent or tentative"' (Coffey, 2003, cited in Smith-Khan, 2020: 4). The evaluation of demeanour reflects and amplifies the inherent biases and procedural challenges discussed in this section, impacting the fairness of asylum outcomes. Demeanour 'includes a wide range of behaviours, including body movements, facial expressions, disposition and attitude, tone, volume and pace of speech, externally observable emotional state, and level of articulacy', but 'cultural variances in applicants' styles of narration and emotional presentation, as well as the traumatic nature of the events alleged, and the mediating presence and role of an interpreter, can render demeanour ever more ambiguous' (Baillot *et al.*, 2014: 123).

The UNHCR states that, 'since asylum decision-makers are evaluating a subjective fear of persecution, 'determination of refugee status will therefore primarily require an evaluation of the applicant's statements rather than a judgement on the situation prevailing in his country of origin' (UNHCR, 1992, cited in Baillot *et al.*, 2014: 125). However, the applicant's fear must be well founded for the application to be successful. That is, it must be grounded in the objective situation in their home country, and it is here is where the 'external aspect of credibility [...] comes into play, with the pursuit of corroboration being a key objective' (Baillot *et al.*, 2014: 125). Examples of supporting evidence are medical or other expert reports and country-of-origin reports (produced by the Ministry of Foreign Affairs).

Further, while an applicant's narrative needs to be coherent and plausible, it also needs to coincide with the 'expectations of the decision maker' (Smith-Khan, 2017c: 392; Herlihy *et al.*, 2010). Further, the 'fluency of the testimony (that is, the incidence of hesitation), as well as its clarity and detail' can play a role (Maryns & Blommaert, 2002: 18). A narration of a credible story is characterised as 'smooth and uninterrupted, preferably rendered in a coherent national language' and it is expected that 'narrative rationality and embodied emotion to meet the required subjectivity of probable and credible performance' (Maryns, 2013b, referring to ideas from McKinnon, 2009).

In summary, the design of the hearings presents significant challenges to an asylum applicant. Rather than being impartial, the process is interrogative and sets high thresholds for credibility (subjective and objective), against a backdrop of societal aversion, as well as significant linguistic, bureaucratic and procedural barriers to understanding.

2.3.3 Constructing reality: Monologism and dialogism in asylum procedures

Generally, how language is theorised affects how communication is understood and employed. Consequently, this will impact how the role of each interlocutor is theorised. In any communicative framework, it is possible that a certain understanding of language is chosen in order to achieve a certain goal, not necessarily because it is the only theorisation available, as understood by the party making the decision. This is to say, at the level of an individual or an institution, the choice of language theorisation is instrumental. To provide a simple but illustrative example, consider the effect on an interaction of choosing to interpret a conversation partner's words as literally as possible. It is not difficult to imagine a scenario in which adopting such a conceptualisation of language use may afford a listener the opportunity to find offence or deceit in another interlocutor's speech which might otherwise be mitigated; consider, for some very direct examples, the phrases 'break a leg' and 'I'll be there in a minute'. To provide another example, in a multicultural setting, an interlocutor from a culture that values direct communication may (knowingly or unknowingly) interpret another interlocutor's indirect (and to their mind polite) request as an optional suggestion, rather than an urgent task. These simple scenarios illustrate how the choice of language theory (or ideology) can serve a specific communicative goal – vitally, one that may not be shared, or even apparent, to other interlocutors.

In the case of the asylum procedure in the Netherlands, the INS, the organisation that processes applications, may be reasonably assumed to wish to exercise control over the communicative event during interviews with asylum applicants, for the reasons discussed in Chapter 1. As such, the INS may choose a certain traditional understanding of language even though there are indications that such an understanding is outdated. In light of this, it is very likely that the INS's monological theorisation of language is not a coincidence; it has a strategical function. Monologism and dialogism will be discussed detail in Chapter 4. Briefly, however, those who adhere to the monologic theorisation of language posit that reality is a solid entity, separate from the actions of individuals. If this reality represents meaning, then it is considered to be the sole production of one mind. Dialogism, on the other hand, theorises reality as co-constructed.

Reality is not the offspring of one brain: it comes into being during the communicative event in which individuals are engaged. All interlocutors share in the construction of meaning.

In light of this, it may be argued that the INS seeks to make its own asylum procedure as easy as possible for it to administer, and so will want to 'isolate' the applicant's story to facilitate the application of the relevant credibility criteria. The 'sole-authorship language ideology'[1] (Smith-Khan, 2019b: 423) adhered to by the INS (which falls under the monologic theorisation of language) makes this control possible and defendable. It conceptualises meaning-making as the production of one mind. In this context, it is evident that the INS's adherence to a monologic interpretation of language strategically streamlines the process of narrative control within asylum proceedings. This choice is designed to render the decision-making process both more manageable and more predictable, by ensuring that narratives conform neatly to predetermined legal and procedural contours. However, scholars of language, communication and sociolinguistics have heavily criticised this understanding (see Chapter 4).

In terms of monologism's utility, asylum procedures are designed in such a way that different decision-makers are guided and controlled such that they would reach a similar judgement if they all separately dealt with a given case. Based on the monological way of theorising reality and the resulting 'sole-authorship language ideology', it is deemed possible to 'completely control or neutralise the impacts of interlocutor interaction, linguistic choices and social dynamics, and thus somehow distil asylum seeker communication from social interaction in a true or pure form' (Smith-Khan, 2019b: 423). The trouble with this underlying theoretical foundation is that it produces a concept of meaning which is inherently flawed. The monological theorising of reality and the associated production of meaning and sense-making within asylum procedures engender the risk of wrongdoing to asylum applicants and those who work with them, such as their legal representatives.

The possible influence of the other participants in the asylum procedure, such as the legal representative and the interpreter, is given little consideration within national conduct guidelines. For example, in Australian guidelines, the applicant is considered the narrative's primary, almost sole creator (Smith-Khan, 2017b, 2019b). The interpreter is treated as a 'mere machine, capable of faithfully reproducing verbatim the utterances

1 Sole-authorship language ideology suggests that, in formal settings like asylum hearings, the person telling their story is solely responsible for its content, but this overlooks how interpreters and cultural contexts can influence the narrative. This concept, highlighted by scholars such as Jan Blommaert and Susan Ehrlich, points to the complex nature of language use in legal environments. The ideology assumes that inconsistencies in a person's story are evidence of dishonesty, rather than considering natural variations in how stories are told or potential errors in translation. This oversimplified view can lead to serious misunderstandings and incorrect legal judgements.

of the speaker' (Smith-Khan, 2017b: 529). This ideology does not consider the 'possibility that there may not be a perfect alignment of terms across languages or that different interpreters or translators may make different lexical choices' (Smith-Khan, 2017b: 529). That legal representatives are seldom mentioned in the guidelines underplays the 'valuable and complex contributions that legal representatives make to applications and appeals, and more specifically the way they shape how claims or responses to adverse information are communicated' (Smith-Khan, 2019b: 414–415). The specific roles of legal representatives, caseworkers and interpreters are considered at length in Section 2.6. In terms of this discussion of procedure design, it is sufficient to conclude that the lack of recognition of their roles, in part a direct consequence of a monological approach to the theorisation of language, is significantly to the disadvantage of applicants insofar as it assigns them full responsibility for the content of their case. This procedural design element is mirrored in the approach taken in relation to evidence, discussed in the section that follows.

2.3.4 Burden of proof: Credibility and evidence in asylum hearings

While authorities want to receive well-documented asylum applications, applicants 'rarely have documentation to prove they are whom they say they are or that the atrocities they have experienced really happened' (Bohmer & Shuman, 2007: 604). Many have escaped their country with 'few possessions or documentation of their claim', for different reasons (Stobb, 2019: 197) and 'rarely have enough evidence to conclusively "prove" their claims' (Kagan, 2003: 414–415, cited in Stobb, 2019: 201). In the absence of physical evidence, immigration authorities rely heavily on their ability to assess the credibility of asylum seekers, making such judgements central to the decision-making process (Granhag *et al.*, 2005). These institutions do not often give applicants the benefit of the doubt when they deal with their statements but are perceived as 'guilty until proven innocent' (Bohmer & Shuman, 2018: 80). Authorities think that when applicants cannot produce documents, 'it would be possible for them to make false claims in order to enhance their application for asylum' (Eades, 2009: 31).

Indeed, because 'persecution often leaves victims without the means to prove their identity' (Bohmer & Shuman, 2007: 604), some applicants may find themselves in a situation where they have to resort to using false documentation to be able to go to their asylum destination or even to be able to flee their home country. As such, they may find themselves using false identity papers upon arrival in the PCA.

Some applicants actively try to frustrate interrogation at their asylum destination, knowingly, unknowingly or under bad advice. Motivations for this include fear of deportation or punishment, or simply the learnt behaviours of individuals who have been at the mercy of unjust authorities in the countries from which they have fled. From my own experience as an interpreter, many applicants mention that their travel agents have ordered them to get rid of their papers, or are just too scared to keep their documents because of the fear that they may be used as grounds for their forced return.

This lack of evidence and formal documentation means that applicants largely rely on their stories and testimony during the hearing. Therefore, their narratives are the 'cornerstone of political asylum cases' (Bohmer & Shuman, 2018: 166). The credibility of the narrative is thus the crux of the application (Baillot *et al.*, 2014), because it is often the only evidence on which asylum authorities can base their judgement (Stobb, 2019). Applicants who are found incredible or fraudulent face 'considerable obstacles in restoring their credibility' (Coffey, 2003: 377). Even a small lie that lacks relevance can lead to refusal (Bohmer & Shuman, 2018). In short, the credibility assessments designed and implemented by asylum institutions are not a scientific or impartial truth-seeking practice (Schneider, 2019); rather, they are a face-to-face questioning session or formal oral procedure (Kälin, 1986).

Conversely, despite the clear and specifically designed power imbalance inherent in the hearings, applicants may achieve credibility even if they fail to provide any independent, corroborative evidence to support their claims, provided their account is coherent, consistent and plausible (Melloy, 2007). That is, 'assessing credibility is not an exercise in establishing the truth, but about "making findings of fact that are reasonable and open on the evidence"' (Baillot *et al.*, 2014: 112, quoting Norman, 2007: 291).

2.3.5 Filters of credibility: Navigating institutional challenges in asylum procedures

This subsection critically examines credibility during the procedure and highlights how its assessment is intricately shaped by complex interplays of institutional practices, political pressures and procedural designs. As outlined, asylum applicants face two key hurdles: they must 'fulfil refugee status requirements' and establish credibility (Affolter, 2021a: 2; see also Affolter, 2021b).

Applicants' statements during hearings are recorded by the caseworker and placed in a dossier, which is subsequently forwarded to a decision-maker. This written record does not necessarily capture all the detail of every comment, nor does it strictly adhere to the interpreter's translation. Instead, the content of the file depends primarily what the caseworker thinks essential, guided by the regulations and instructions of the INS. These notes also depend on what the caseworker believes has been communicated by the asylum applicant, as translated by the interpreter. This means that what the applicant actually says goes through at least two filters before it is recorded in the file: those of the interpreter and the caseworker. Consequently, the resultant text reflects what these two individuals have made of the applicant's various statements. Even then, the filtered meanings of the interpreter and the caseworker go through a third filter: it has to be recorded on pre-designed forms. This last process is known as entextualisation.

In conclusion, credibility assessments in asylum procedures are highly complex evaluations that extend beyond mere factual presentation. The testimonies of applicants undergo multiple subjective interpretations – on the part of interpreters and caseworkers – and are then further complicated by procedural entextualisation. These layered processes can significantly distort original narratives. This underscores the need for a critical reassessment of practices to ensure fairness and accuracy in asylum adjudications.

Having established the core problematic areas in the fundamental design of asylum procedures, the following section steps back to assess their origins and explores the interplay of political rhetoric, bureaucratic pressures and linguistic ideologies to show how these factors collectively influence the fairness and effectiveness of asylum evaluations.

2.4 Navigating the Complexities: Political, Bureaucratic and Linguistic Influences on Asylum Procedures

The following sections explore the intricate dynamics at play within asylum procedures, focusing on the pivotal role of political rhetoric, bureaucratic influences and the impact of linguistic ideologies. They examine how political decisions and legislative frameworks shape the administrative landscapes of asylum across different jurisdictions, revealing the complex interplay between national policies and their practical implementation. This discussion not only highlights the challenges faced by caseworkers but also scrutinises how institutional practices and language ideologies affect the outcomes of asylum applications. Through this comprehensive analysis, I aim to provide a nuanced understanding of the factors that influence the fairness and efficacy of asylum procedures and to emphasise the need for an informed approach to policy design.

2.4.1 The politics of protection: National influences on asylum procedures within the EU

In Chapter 1, I explained that political asylum attracts much contention in politics and broader society. While international protection has its origins in international relations, national politics plays a central role in deciding how a given asylum procedure is set up and implemented. Within the EU (see Section 1.2.3) the Common European Asylum System (CEAS) stipulates common standards across a number of areas ranging from the reception conditions of asylum-seekers to establishing which state is responsible for a case under the Dublin III Regulation. Nevertheless, many of the particulars of a given state's asylum procedures remain the purview of nation policy.

National politics have increasingly brought about a legislative tightening of the legal requirements for demonstrating a need for protection and also how courts can review asylum decision-making (see Section 1.4). In the case of the Netherlands, the courts' main function has become to review if the INS has applied the rules and legislation properly. This approach is not used everywhere in Europe. The UK system of appeals, for instance, has two tiers, with the first-tier tribunal (Immigration and Asylum Chamber) hearing appeals in asylum and citizenship cases. This 'tribunal is independent of government. A judge will listen to both sides of the argument before making a decision' (Ministry of Justice, 2023). The second tier, similar to judicial review in the Netherlands, hears cases where there is as question as to the lawfulness of the case itself and/or the conduct of a participant institution.

Even where the judicial review is robust, asylum processes are still subject to political pressure. In the UK, politics has been playing an increasingly decisive role. There have been calls for a tougher stance on who can be defined as a refugee. During the Conservative Party's leadership hustings in 2022, Rishi Sunak, a contender who later became Prime Minister, called for a narrower definition of a refugee (Badshah, 2022). Similarly, there have been calls for restrictive and tougher asylum policies in the Netherlands since at least the 1990s. Bolkestein, a former prominent Dutch politician, called for 'het kaf van het koren scheiden' ('separating the wheat from the chaff'), having endlessly argued that most of those who apply for asylum in the Netherlands are 'gelukzoekers' ('happiness-seekers'), not genuine asylum-seekers. He also blamed successive Dutch Labour cabinets for the visible presence of foreigners in the big Dutch cities.

The political pressure on asylum institutions more generally has been covered in Chapter 1. However, it is essential to consider such pressure when reviewing the design of asylum procedures in the Global North, not only because it has a direct influence on the leniency or lack thereof in definitions of a refugee, but also because political influences are amorphous and have potentially hidden social effects. These are closely related to the issue of caseworker pressure, which is discussed below.

2.4.2 Contextual dynamics: Influences on the outcomes of asylum procedures

Asylum procedures of any design do not take place in a vacuum and are subject to indirect political influences. These range from the impact of persons and personalities to organisational factors such as budgetary constraints and working conditions. To begin at the level of individuals, decision-making in asylum determination is complex and highly politicised (Baillot *et al.*, 2014; Van der Kist *et al.*, 2019). It follows that caseworkers, who implements the policy on the ground, may be pressured into taking restrictive decisions. On the one hand, they are expected to decide asylum applications 'on a case-by-case, merits basis'. On the other hand, they are the 'primary organ of the state responsible for "protecting" (read "containing") borders' (Baillot *et al.*, 2014: 129). Caseworkers naturally have different personalities, understandings and behaviours and leave their own mark on how the hearing is conducted, which undermines the notion of standardisation, which aims at a certain level of impartiality and fairness.

At the organisational level, 'institutional cultures, resource constraints' and sociopolitical forces coalescing around migration and asylum (Baillot *et al.*, 2014) have a bearing on decision-making. The INS, for example, has had resource problems for years. At the time of writing, the Netherlands faces major problems with processing applications and housing applicants, as widely reported in the Dutch media. This is something I hear daily in my work as an interpreter. Applicants must wait months for their initial screening hearing with the police, which is a very short encounter wherein the applicant must answer questions about why they have come to the Netherlands and how they have arrived there (see Section 2.2.1), even before the start of the INS hearings. Some applicants end up sleeping rough because of a lack of accommodation (Aljazeera, 2023). Doctors Without Borders has had to intervene because medical care was lacking (NOS, 2022).

This problem is not uniquely a Dutch one and is not new. The INS may have deliberately kept the number of decisions low to create a 'hostile environment' – a term used by Theresa May during her time as the UK's Home Secretary (before she became Prime Minister) – in order to deter asylum applicants. For 30 years, the INS has had too few caseworkers and too few housing resources in the asylum centres. It is remarkable that a rich country like the Netherlands has to house applicants in inhumane conditions.

The problems with asylum procedures go beyond the physical. Applicants, by definition not being from the PCA, might lack the knowledge that might be expected of individuals from the PCA. The knowledge they do bring with them is called 'speaker pretextuality' in the literature. It is a 'package of socially preconditioned knowledge articulated in speakers' personal baggage and assessments of what is meaningful in the interaction combined with their capacity to anticipate what is required and hence will be recognised as meaningful in the ongoing text trajectory' (Maryns & Blommaert, 2002: 13). The pretextual gap refers to knowledge the applicant does not have. A lack of knowledge of bureaucracy, law and the workings of the social services can have negative consequences for an applicant that range from the banal or frustrating to the disastrous in terms of their recognition of a right to international protection. The following chapter shows how crucial these aspects of applicants' knowledge are for understanding how sense-making and meaning-making are created, evolve and unfold.

2.4.3 Over-standardisation and language ideology

Asylum institutions are motivated to seek a standard, objective approach to asylum applications, but any claim that this has been achieved is 'challenged by statistics that demonstrate large variances in success rates between different immigration offices and individual decision-makers' (Smith-Khan, 2017b: 522). Simeon (2010) similarly raises concerns about the variability in decision-making. Further, as found in the field of judicial fact-finding more widely, decision-making conceals 'a plethora of motivations such as policies, principles, personal idiosyncrasies, ideologies, and standards of morality' (Smith-Khan, 2017b: 522). It is impossible to assume these are the same for each individual responsible for making decisions. The practice of determining credibility is highly subjective. Decision-makers exercise considerable discretion in interpreting data, and often focus on finding inconsistencies or contradictions in asylum-seekers' narratives (Nielsen & Møller, 2022). This insufficiently critical attitude is at odds with the scrutiny levelled at applicants. Nevertheless, asylum agencies often consider the applicant's entextualised story (as told during the hearing) as an objective reflection of reality, which would produce similar outcomes for the applicant were other individuals involved in the procedure. There is a misplaced perception that the applicant 'constructs the official narrative that comes out of the application and appeals process' (Smith-Khan, 2017b: 531). As such, much of the responsibility for what is laid down on paper is assigned to the applicant. The decision-maker, on the other hand, is represented as 'playing an important role in *thinking and questioning*, their role as narrative co-constructor is minimised' (Smith-Khan, 2017b: 531, emphasis added).

Caseworkers and decision-makers are assigned actions that relate to cognitive processes, such as 'receiving and testing texts', but their share in and influence on meaning-making is generally ignored (Smith-Khan, 2019b: 414). This is a fundamentally faulty premise, for sense-making and meaning-making are a shared endeavour (see Chapter 3): meaning is negotiated and collectively made during interactions such as hearings. Caseworkers and decision-makers are considered by the INS as being capable of objectivity and neutrality when assessing the credibility of an asylum application (Nielsen & Møller, 2022) even though research has shown they rely heavily on their subjective judgements about human behaviour (Herlihy *et al.*, 2010). Their influence as co-creators of texts is almost wholly erased. Caseworkers' sense-making actions, such as 'their control over the hearing process as a whole, including who can participate and how, and their roles in questioning and in reformulating communication into a final written decision record' (Smith-Khan, 2019b: 214) is excluded from the evaluation of the application. In contrast, applicants are perceived as 'subjective beings' (Smith-Khan, 2017b: 531), whose participation in meaning-making is coloured by subjective conclusions which do not necessarily align with objective truth. While this selective recognition of subjectivity does, in the loosest possible sense, go some way to achieving standardisation in asylum procedures, it amounts to tackling a problem by refusing to record it.

This pursuit of standardisation, in no small part through language ideology, is far from apolitical. Inevitably, where decisions are to be made on how the procedure is to be designed, many seemingly unpolitical technicalities will show political influences if examined closely. Political authority, represented by immigration services, designs procedures where applications are examined so that fraudulent applications are filtered out (Bohmer & Shuman, 2018). For this to happen in the Netherlands, a representative of the INS must talk to the applicant, usually during an interpreter-mediated hearing (an interpreter-mediated encounter, or IME). Given that the procedure is not a purely judicial or administrative process, communication tools and practices play a prominent role in it. These tools are based on language ideologies and understandings. The INS could not design such a procedure without taking a stance (at least tacitly, perhaps even inadvertently) regarding which language ideology. Certainly, the procedure was not designed by one individual, but by an organisation (the INS). While it is true that not every individual within the INS who had an input into its design consciously engaged with language ideologies, it is a fact that the work of the INS as an organisation is not based on intuition or purely on common sense. It is tasked with objectives within a legal framework, but the INS is not a purely legal entity: it is a legal tool of a political entity, the government – and governments do not work purely based on intuition.

2.4.4 Monologism manifest: Textual ideology in asylum procedures

The asylum procedure involves a 'deeply rooted nationalist idea of language – an ideology that probably endures for longer in institutional domains than in other, less hegemonically structured facets of society' (Maryns, 2013a: 87). This ideology 'causes the performance of clients to be measured against hegemonically organised regimes of language that impose a textualist standard that serves as a functionally differentiated norm against which all language use is measured' (Maryns, 2013a: 87). This ensuing textual ideology leads to talk being treated as a written form of language: the criteria of textuality 'consistency and factuality expressed in a monolingual standard code [...] are considered the most objective and reliable means of performance in institutional processes' (Maryns, 2013a: 87). As a result, the '[c]ontextual salience is overshadowed and suppressed by the imposed criteria of textuality, both in interaction (performance) and in the subsequent entextualising or "writing up"' (Maryns, 2005: 314). The procedure is designed to conform to assumptions about how language is understood and, given that it is heavily influenced by language, it is inevitable that those assumptions will colour the procedure's outcomes. Even though language 'plays a critical role in the construction of institutional identities', research has shown that there are remarkable 'uncritical assessments of the relationship between language and identity' (Maryns, 2013a: 88). This is arguably a major flaw in the asylum procedure, for, as mentioned earlier, it is essentially a communicative event in which language is of major importance. I am not talking about language as an abstract concept; rather, language, whether in written format or oral format, is mainly about sense-making. The textual ideology and practice benefit the institution more than the applicant. Language is treated as a 'transparent referential vehicle', that is to say, a 'neutral and objectifying tool to represent facts, events, and identities in the institutional space' (Maryns, 2013a: 86). Much of this understanding prominently features in the manner in which the applicants' backstories are treated and understood. Those backstories 'inevitably undergo all sorts of filtering and transformation in order to achieve the preferred textualist standards, [and] the neutrality of representation is still taken for granted' (Maryns, 2013a: 87).

It can be posited that the architecture of asylum procedures may indeed reflect a nuanced understanding and expectation on the part of policymakers regarding its disempowering impact on applicants, in response to political pressure. This raises the possibility that certain procedural elements have been intentionally crafted to present challenges and so reduce applicants' ability to present their narratives. Nonetheless, it is imperative to distinguish between the systemic design and the intentions of the individuals executing these policies. To enrich our understanding of the complex interplay between policy design and the empowerment of applicants, further empirical research is necessary to probe the depth of awareness and deliberate intent on the part of the architects and administrators of these procedures. The INS must have come to realise that applicants, when producing their 'home narratives', 'typically attempt to provide significant background information on people, places and events in the home country' (Maryns & Blommaert, 2002: 16). Home narratives are sub-narratives in which details of the applicant's refugee experience are sketched and documented. They often fulfil 'crucial contextualizing functions in the stories: without them, a precise understanding of the causes and motives for the escape cannot be reached' (Blommaert, 2001a: 22). They can be considered the most prototypical example of the contextualising observable in asylum-seekers' overall narratives. Although home narratives typically attempt to provide important background information on people, places and events in the home country, asylum-seekers are often not given a chance to tell these stories in the procedure: due to time limitations, officials expect unequivocal questions to be followed by unequivocal answers. As a result of this combination of such practical considerations and reasons related to the language ideologies to which the authorities subscribe, too often important contextualising details are not included in the asylum reports. Contextualising accounts tend to be considered unimportant and, therefore, can end up being kept out of the entextualised text.

A further problem with these home narratives is that although they often allow applicants to make points, they often fail to meet procedural-discursive expectations in the asylum procedure (Maryns & Blommaert, 2002). Pretextual gaps between what is recognised and what can be produced manifest themselves in three different aspects of discursive practice:

> Whereas the home narratives were shown to have a localizing function – personalizing the story and anchoring it in particular spatial and deictic frames – the highly modified versions of the story we find in the letters from the authorities show a completely different contextualization of the story: away from the local, away from the experiential, the affective, the emotional, the individual positioning of people in conflicts, towards generalizable categories and space-time frames. (Blommaert, 2001b: 442)

Often applicants do not get the chance to tell their story fully and adequately, as the stream of thought (the internal dialogue in the mind) during the process of sense-making is often interrupted. Moreover, the caseworker does not have the freedom to let the applicant do so because of the entextualisation of talk and all the restrictions that come with it. Applicants are thus deprived of the opportunity to bring forward information they would have wanted to be included in the report. Additionally, the caseworker may not have time to address every important detail during the asylum hearings: '[d]ue to time limitations, officials [...] expect unequivocal questions to be followed by unequivocal answers[...]. Contextualising accounts tend to be considered a waste of time and are therefore kept out of the procedure' (Maryns & Blommaert, 2002: 16).

2.4.5 Influence of textual ideology on narratives

In addition to the broader influence of textual ideology on the asylum process, the specific influence of textual ideology on narratives is worth examination. While suitable in certain institutional encounters, the textual ideology and the ensuing practice of entextualisation of talk cannot be adhered to and applied in interpreter-mediated encounters without questions being raised. Even though the 'textual standard may equally be imposed on all institutional clients, the resources needed to meet this standard are not equally accessible to all of them' (Maryns, 2013a: 87). Sociolinguists have long opposed this approach to talk in an interpreter-mediated encounter.

They affirm that 'language should not be treated as an abstract category [as is done by the INS] but as a socially anchored and deeply contextualised phenomenon' (Maryns, 2005: 300). It is unfortunate that 'precisely in a language situation as multilingual as the asylum application procedure [...] the idea of language in terms of a subdivision into different varieties still has to be accepted' (Maryns, 2005: 300).

2.5 Critically Interrogating Asylum Procedures: A Dialogical Perspective

Having observed the shortcomings of the Dutch asylum procedure, as representative of such procedures across the Global North, the previous section evaluated the driving factors behind the designed-in shortcomings. The following sections re-engage with the asylum procedure critically.

2.5.1 Decoding narratives: How interpersonal dynamics shape decisions on refugee status

Decisions on refugee status 'rely heavily on judgments about how individuals present themselves and their histories' (Bögner *et al.*, 2010: 519). When the (verbal) actions of the applicant do not align with the INS' expectations, for example if they are late in disclosing sensitive personal information or fail to disclose it, the INS may assume the applicant's story is fabricated (Bögner *et al.*, 2010). This does not necessarily have to be the case; for example, the applicant may have felt that disclosing personal information was simply unnecessary, or they may have been too traumatised to be able to relate particular, especially, personal, elements of their story. Additionally, caseworkers may fail to ask the applicant the relevant questions or may fail to include the applicant's answer in the report. Disclosing information or not doing so should not be understood as solely the personal decision of the applicant (Bögner *et al.*, 2010). Factors related to 'interpersonal, situational and contextual' aspects of a narrative can and will impact how applicants present their story (Bogner *et al.*, 2010: 522). An uncritical attitude towards this fundamental phenomenon is a potential source of significant miscommunication. For instance, every (verbal) action the interpreter makes influences how the interaction proceeds. The applicant and the caseworker internalise these (verbal) actions and any following (verbal) action on the part of either of them is thus subject to influence by the interpreter's prior contributions. This is discussed in full in Chapter 4, which explains how meaning-making is shaped during interpreter-mediated interactions.

These unrealistic expectations also impact how the applicant's story will look once written in the asylum report. In this respect, the attitude of the INS is too uncritical of the stories of asylum applicants. I am referring here to its attitude to how meaning-making and sense-making take place during the interpreter-mediated encounter (for reasons related to the language ideology adhered to by the INS) and political considerations. If the applicant's story does not fully align with the expectations of the INS, the narrative is quickly characterised as a bad story (Blommaert, 2001a). This is particularly worrying when caseworkers fail to appreciate that their presence – and that of the interpreter – does influence the applicant's performance, as it certainly does. All interlocutors, regardless of context, influence and sometimes condition how interactions unfold and which direction they take (see Chapter 4). If the INS does not appreciate this and theorises communication from a monological point of view instead of a dialogical one, the influence of the other interlocutors will be left out. Whatever comes out of the mouth of the applicant will be seen as solely their own production. Without taking into account the influence of the other interlocutors and without taking into account any pretextual gaps, the INS is likely to find the story non-compliant with its expectations. Scholarship has shown that what the INS considers a disjointed or rambling story is quickly 'qualified as "unreliable" or full of "unclear elements" and "contradictions"', and parts of the stories that are 'difficult to understand during the interaction are often not understood at all' (Blommaert, 2001a: 23). Consequently, credibility may be undermined, especially if the group to which the applicant belongs is not deemed to have a good chance of receiving international protection.

2.5.2 Assessing credibility: The role of communication resources in asylum hearings

If the personal resources of applicants, such as their communication skills and those related to their knowledge of the world, are insufficient to deal with the questions during the hearings, or to tell the story in a manner that the INS expects, then their credibility may be considered doubtful. The caseworker may think, based on their monological view of how language works, that they should not intervene in any way while the applicant is telling their story; that the applicant will understand the questions in the way they are formulated and understood by the caseworker; and that the applicant will produce an answer which can be assessed according to the monological criteria of the INS. When the applicant 'fails' to meet these expectations (i.e. to present their story as expected by the INS), their story may be considered weak or fraudulent, or both.

Contrary to this monological perspective of language, communication scholars (e.g. Blommaert, 2010) emphasise the interactional nature of communication in which the criteria for the credibility of the account take into consideration:

> [...] internal consistency, or whether a particular text exhibits an 'appropriate' level of detail, [which] depends on (socio)linguistic factors, like

> decision-maker questioning style [...], interpreter choices and identity [...], and, where present, the contributions of a legal representative in the creation of both spoken and written texts. (Smith-Khan, 2021: 2)

Further, 'rather than being neutral, making judgements about external consistency and demeanour are subjective, evaluative processes, informed by decision-makers cultural and social perspectives' (Smith-Khan, 2021: 2).

Institutional discourse, like that of the INS, is not known for its accessibility to outsiders, even for the native speakers of the PCA, let alone for a foreign applicant. Further, different cultural understandings and expectations about credibility can complicate communication during the procedure (Jacobs & Maryns, 2023). The institutional discourse, guided by formal, legalistic and procedural norms, often clashes with the 'experiential discourse' of asylum-seekers, shaped by their personal experiences and sociocultural backgrounds (Nikolaidou *et al.*, 2023).

The applicant's linguistic repertoire plays an important role in the asylum procedure (Kjelsvik, 2014). So, when caseworkers engage with the applicant during the hearing, the latter is already suffering inequality, insofar as they come from a different part of the world and lack the information that is at the disposal of the caseworker. The 'unequal communicative resources' of the applicant have a direct bearing on the latter's position during the hearing, which brings directly into question the procedural fairness of asylum applications, because the 'under-resourced' applicant will find it difficult to 'construct their own credibility' (Smith-Khan, 2019a: 404). In addition, as previous scholarship, including my own (Mizori, 2017), has shown, the applicant too often may not have a clear idea of the roles of the different individuals and institutions they deal with during the procedure. It is not unheard of for the applicant to think that their legal representative is connected to the immigration department.

2.5.3 Unveiling internal dialogues: The entextualisation of asylum hearings

When human beings make sense during an interaction, such as an asylum hearing, they engage not only with the interlocutor and the context at hand but also with their own past experiences. They interact with the other interlocutor(s), evaluate what they say and then re-evaluate their own positions and thinking. This 'internal dialogue' is discussed in the following chapters.

Likewise, caseworkers not only evaluate what the applicant actually says but also engage with their own personal experiences and information. What eventually ends up entextualised is thus not only what the applicant has said but is what the caseworker has just heard, or seen, or both, and what they made of it based on their own past experiences and information. The INS reports fail to record this internal dialogue on both sides.

Given that the INS views interpreter-mediated hearings from a monologistic perspective, it is not surprising that the INS report presents only a 'skeleton' of the decision-maker's internal dialogue. More generally, human beings simply do not fully disclose the contents of their internal dialogues, and decision-makers do not fully report the reasons that led them to make negative decisions or to find a story incredible, in part because they think that certain aspects of the decision-making process need to remain opaque in order to protect the integrity of the process (Schneider, 2019). Given that decisions are made about what is entextualised and what is not (see Chapter 4), it is not surprising that an asylum case can end up being rejected due to missing parts of the story or misunderstandings on the part of the caseworker. The solution to this, as I argue throughout this book, is to adopt a dialogistic approach to such interactions.

2.5.4 Power dynamics and justice: Challenges in refugee hearings and beyond

Even though applicants have the opportunity to revisit the report of the substantive (second) hearing and make additions and corrections, decision-makers primarily assess credibility based on the information presented during the hearing itself, rather than on post-hearing reports. After reviewing any corrections or additional information submitted by the applicant or their lawyer, a decision is made in accordance with the asylum criteria. If the INS intends to grant international protection or subsidiary protection, this is communicated directly to the applicant and their lawyer. If the INS intends to deny international protection or subsidiary protection, a preliminary decision is issued to the applicant and their lawyer. This draft outlines the reasons for the intended refusal – often due to the perceived incredibility of the account or insufficient information presented at the hearing – and offers the applicant an opportunity to respond (see Section 2.2.1).

Clarifications submitted through the lawyer following the substantive hearing are often rejected, particularly when the applicant belongs to a group that is generally viewed as undeserving of protection. The introduction of new information at this stage is frequently found to be incredible (Smith-Khan, 2020). Decision-makers often argue that such material should have been presented during the hearing, disregarding explanations from the applicant and their lawyer as to why this did not or could not occur. Explanations related to the applicant's conduct during the events described in their account, or their behaviour outside the hearing itself, are especially unlikely to be accepted (Smith-Khan, 2019b: 421).

As discussed earlier, lawyers have limited power during the initial stages of the procedure, including the substantive (second) hearing. In the Netherlands, applicants are prepared through brief pre-hearing consultations with both the DCR and their lawyer. Although lawyers are permitted to attend the hearing, this rarely happens due to scheduling constraints. Even when they do attend – as is the case in Belgium and Australia – they have no power to influence the dynamics of the interaction (Jacobs & Smith-Khan, 2021). Lawyers may only communicate with applicants during short breaks, as discussed below.

While a lawyer's real influence begins in post-hearing consultations and during judicial review, this may be too late in the case of some applicants. Substantive interventions from the lawyer are often frowned upon and may even be regarded with suspicion. This procedural shortcoming appears to be in line with the fact that the 'guidelines' instructions regarding the social and cultural background of the applicant almost exclusively focus on their conduct in the hearing, and neglect to address the way social and cultural factors may lead to different perspectives and behaviour in their refugee narratives and outside life' (Smith-Khan, 2019b: 421).

As discussed in the previous section, interlocutors do not only engage with what is said during the interaction itself. Pre-hearing information is an inherent part of the material introduced in the hearing. When the INS fails to consider information that is inherently connected to the applicant's cultural background and personality, the quality of the decision is compromised. Furthermore, the influence of other interlocutors – in this case, the interpreter and the caseworker – must be addressed as part of the sense-making and meaning-making process. Any attempt to ignore these influences will degrade the quality of the report and, subsequently, that of the decision. I present solutions to these challenges in the following chapters.

2.5.5 Communication dynamics: Empowering and disempowering voices in asylum hearings

The monological conceptualisation of communication, as exemplified by the INS hearings, has been consistently refuted by scholars in the fields of communication and interpreting for several decades. Communication is seen and theorised as a group activity whereby each interlocutor influences how each and every other interlocutor makes meaning, and they themselves are also influenced by this process, even when they are silent (see Chapter 4). It is also accepted by communication and asylum scholars that applicants are disempowered on different levels and for different reasons. This disempowerment stems from procedural intricacies, linguistic barriers and cultural misinterpretations that systematically marginalise applicants, underscoring the need for dialogic reforms that enhance fairness and responsiveness in the asylum process.

The applicant is not accommodated in a way that reflects a realistic understanding by the INS of the disempowered position of the applicant. While applicants are indeed granted legal assistance, they are largely on their own during the actual hearings. The INS expects interpreters not to intervene during the hearings. It is impossible to know how often INS interpreters would interfere when they thought the applicant was disempowered during the interaction if they did not fear losing their assignments – they depend on the favourable feedback of caseworkers for their further employment. I argue that to empower applicants, interpreters must not fear such repercussions from the INS. Assigning interpreting jobs through an independent body could mitigate this issue.

2.6 Navigating Complexities: Actors and Dynamics in Asylum Procedures

Asylum procedures are complex, dynamic processes shaped by a multitude of factors, including political influences, legal frameworks and communicative practices. This section focuses on three pivotal actors within these procedures: interpreters, caseworkers/decision-makers and lawyers. These individuals play crucial roles in shaping the narratives and outcomes of asylum applications, yet their contributions and the perceptions of their roles are often fraught with misunderstandings and underestimations.

2.6.1 The Interpreter: Bridging gaps and confronting misconceptions

Interpreters are essential in bridging communication gaps but there are frequently misperceptions of their neutrality and the scope of their duties. It is difficult to imagine an asylum procedure without interpreters (Bohmer & Shuman, 2007) but in some countries it is not mandatory to engage an interpreter when the applicant has learned the national language of the PCA or a lingua franca. The asylum procedure is, among other things, a big communication event consisting of smaller ones, such as hearings and legal consultations. The overall procedure is about sense-making between the applicant, the PCA's immigration service (in this case the Dutch INS) and the lawyer (see Chapter 4).

Unlike the work of a shopkeeper, a lawyer or a taxi driver, say, the interpreter's role and task are not always clear to the public, or sometimes even to those who work with them. Even different interpreters view their tasks differently. Often, the interpreter's actual responsibilities are unclear. Their work and roles are understood and theorised differently by different people because of their different expectations and backgrounds (see Chapter 6). For example, some users of interpreting services may have no knowledge of interpreters' 'conventional role or ethical obligations, expecting them not only to interpret but also to provide assistance, advice, and moral support' (Cheung, 2018: 234). These roles and expectations, however, can be rejected by the police and judiciary.

This lack of clarity produces in some applicants a suspicion that interpreters side with the 'other', that is, with the police or the INS, because the interpreter speaks their language and conforms to the procedure. The INS itself may have the same suspicion that the interpreter is siding with the 'other', and may be wary of an interpreter affording an applicant undue (in its view) assistance, or even may be 'coaching' a witness. The INS counters this by involving only officially certified interpreters, who are required to adhere to professional ethical obligations.

The party that pays for the interpreting services may think that the interpreter ought to be on 'their side'. I remember a training session for interpreters attended by a police officer who was very surprised when the attendees said they were neutral and did not take sides in criminal cases. Interpreters may even be asked to comment on the applicant's dialect or language use more broadly (Drugan, 2020: 316), as has happened to me and many interpreters I know. Interpreters working in immigration settings can be asked to comment on the 'likelihood of an interviewee being a native speaker of a particular language or dialect, or to make a judgment on the authenticity of an interviewee's accent' (Drugan, 2020: 316). Even more surprisingly, Elias-Bursać (2015: 86) notes one example of a 'judge directly questioning a court interpreter regarding the veracity of a witness's claim in the courtroom'. This has happened to me and many interpreters I know. Research also shows that interpreters are expected by some service users 'to be proactive and sympathetic' (Cheung, 2018: 234). I once was ordered by a judge in the UK to 'only translate' what was said by the applicant. I was 'not there to give evidence', he said. The judge had misinterpreted my request to correct a mistake in my translation.

How interpreters and their work are understood or theorised varies across countries and even within a single institutional culture. Some of those who have not worked with interpreters, and also many who have, still think that interpreters should produce word-for-word translations. Such preconceptions fuel the erroneous assumption that communicating through an interpreter reproduces how interlocutors speak directly to each other, and the interpreter is in effect 'a mechanical conduit and simply pass[es] messages back and forth' (Roy & Metzger, 2014: 160), even though this has been long discredited (see Chapter 4). This misconception of interpreting backgrounds the 'plethora of linguistic choices interpreters make and the impact these have on text production' (Smith-Khan, 2019b: 215). Research has shown that the interpreter, 'rather than being a neutral conveyor of messages, is an active participant [in the interaction] who can potentially influence the direction and outcome of the event' (Roy & Metzger, 2014: 161). This is not necessarily intentional but is an aspect of how human sense-making and meaning-making occur (see Chapter 4). When human beings interact, they influence how others make meaning and are influenced themselves by what others say. This mutual influence takes place during interpreter-mediated hearings and legal consultations.

In many countries interpreters are expected to have relevant qualifications, to be members of professional bodies and to adhere to a code of ethics. In the Netherlands, where I remotely work, requires them to undertake so-called 'continued learning' and registration is ended unless the interpreter has followed courses during a period of five years. They must be sworn in by a judge and are required to follow the rules a major professional body sets. Similar rules apply in Australia, where 'Legal Aid NSW requires that interpreters should have NAATI accreditation (Legal Aid NSW 2014)' (Xu, 2020: 8).

Sentiments towards interpreters also vary considerably. Some people greatly appreciate their work, while others dislike their very existence. Some hate their 'intrusion' and others might think interpreters are 'too present' and do what they should not. It is not unheard for an interpreter from the same country as the applicant to be 'suspected of correcting or improving the applicant's testimony, or [of being] collaborators with the applicant's enemies' (Bohmer & Shuman, 2007: 606).

Even those who speak the PCA's language may decide to use an interpreter despite these misgivings. The presence of an interpreter can afford some applicants an advantage over others, depending on the languages understood. For example, in English-speaking countries an interpreter may provide 'strategic advantage for applicants who understand English: it gives them more time to formulate their responses when they hear both the original and the interpreted versions' (Smith-Khan, 2020: 123).

2.6.2 The caseworker/decision-maker: Co-constructing narratives and outcomes

This section examines how caseworkers and decision-makers, frequently perceived as passive or neutral, actively co-construct the narratives that support asylum decisions, despite institutional narratives that downplay their influence. Unlike the applicant, who is viewed as almost a full constructor of meaning, the role of caseworkers is 'minimised' (Smith-Khan, 2017b) and they are often seen as merely passive or even as non-participants in the interaction.

Minimal attention, if any, is given to caseworkers' style of communication. Their role as active co-constructors of meaning does not receive attention either. The observations and assessments made by the caseworker and decision-maker are considered objective truths, even though research has shown that external pressures – from political contexts, public opinion and media portrayals of migration issues – significantly influence decision-makers and their work. This influence was particularly evident in Finland after 2015, when there was a notable decrease in the rate of positive asylum decisions (Vanto *et al.*, 2021).

The entextualised pieces of talk are considered 'objective' reflections of what the applicant has said (Stobb, 2009). In its credibility assessment, the INS does not engage with the process of meaning-making that led to the production of the entextualised text. The role of caseworkers is theorised as being almost solely as probers, not as co-constructors of meaning. As such, their personal subjective opinions are not seen to mix with their judicial work. Caseworkers are theorised as being 'capable of objectivity and neutrality when assessing credibility' (Smith-Khan, 2017b: 531) without engaging their 'cultural and social perspectives' (Smith-Khan, 2021: 2). It is undeniable, however, that these perspectives inform their judgement (Nielsen *et al.*, 2023). Their decisions are framed by the discretionary power afforded by the legal frameworks, which allow them broad leeway to influence outcomes based on their interpretations (Vanto *et al.*, 2021).

In the guidelines governing their work when making decisions, decision-makers are not given enough tools or powers in their credibility assessments to take account of any counterarguments of the applicant. The guidelines' lack of emphasis on a 'decision maker's self-reflection, resulting from the hierarchical representation of diversity' can cause 'the social or cultural reasons provided by the applicants to be rejected without explanation' (Smith-Khan, 2017c: 412).

The decision-making and credibility assessment have subjective elements even though the INS overall does try to reduce the impact of the individual influences of caseworkers. How plausibility and coherence indicators are applied during a credibility assessment are 'inevitably shaped by a decision maker's perspective' (Smith-Khan, 2017c: 393). The decision-maker belongs to the INS, so issues of power have a strong bearing on the actions of the different actors within each communicative encounter. These decision-makers do not have to defend their decision as the INS theorises this decision as the actions of somebody who represents normality and objectivity. The personal traits of the decision-maker and the cultural values they represent do not get the attention they deserve. In addition to the influence of ideologies, this probably results from a desire on the part of the INS to have a unified manner of dealing with applications. It seems reasonable to suggest that the INS might be aware of the potential logical deficiencies inherent in such a stance, although it does not openly address these, possibly for pragmatic reasons aligned with enforcing the powers granted by governmental directives (see Chapter 1).

This tendency of the INS to standardise procedures extends to how it theorises applicants' performance and what their narrative of escape should look like. The trouble is that the INS's understanding of what a narrative should look like is, again, derived from its understanding of how it is told. The INS applies criteria to the narrative it deems applicable even though research has shown that the narratives of the applicant are based on understandings potentially far removed from those of the INS. In addition to these factors, the contribution of other interlocutors, namely the caseworker and the interpreter, to sense-making is not taken into consideration as it should be. As I will show in the next chapter, this is a must. The decision-maker is 'presented as a receiver of evidence who must think and make decisions' (Smith-Khan, 2017c: 400). This aligns with the ideology of the INS explained above. Caseworkers and decision-makers are, then, presented as wholly objective – flawless functionaries who impart no influence on the content of a procedure. This is said not to belittle the hard work done by caseworkers and decision-makers in the INS, nor to underplay their critical role in facilitating procedures that in so many cases afford a lifeline to those who need it most: genuine refugees. Rather, the point here is to underscore how the design of asylum procedures erases the subjective elements of these critical workers' day-to-day decisions.

2.6.3 The lawyer: Backgrounded by law

This section addresses the critical, yet often institutionally marginalised, role of lawyers in the asylum process. It highlights their strategic contributions to shaping and defending applicants' narratives against a backdrop of complex legal and procedural requirements.

During asylum hearings (or 'interviews' as they are sometimes called), interaction is 'shaped by the interplay of the interviewers' expectations of certain stories and the divergent texts produced by the asylum seekers' (Kjelsvik, 2014: 110–111). Lawyers have a key role in influencing how asylum-seekers' narratives are constructed and perceived by decision-makers. They work to frame these narratives in ways that comply with legal standards of credibility and plausibility (Campbell, 2020). Hambly (2019) discusses the multifaceted role of lawyers in the asylum process and emphasises their critical functions in preparing clients, navigating complex procedures and mediating cultural and language barriers to support asylum-seekers through the legal and psychological challenges. However, even though the state assigns lawyers to applicants and pays the lawyers' fees, it is striking that lawyers are not mentioned much in the guidelines for caseworkers/decision-makers (Smith-Khan, 2019b). How the institution perceives the impact of the lawyer 'backgrounds the valuable and complex contributions that legal representatives make to applications and appeals, and more specifically the way they shape how claims or responses to adverse information are communicated' (Smith-Khan, 2019b: 414–415). Their guidance and communication with clients are deeply influenced by their knowledge of how credibility evaluations are conducted (Campbell, 2020)

Lawyers' contribution is crucial at all stages of the procedure, from the start to the finish, but especially when they deal with complex applications or applications from applicants from countries that are considered 'safe'. In pre-hearing consultations, lawyers 'meet and interview clients to collect information about their experiences and fears and to advise them about relevant procedures and law' (Smith-Khan, 2021: 3). 'Their support is particularly important during preparatory consultations where they prepare their clients for the interview' (Jacobs & Maryns, 2021: 2). Lawyers explain the asylum procedure and 'provide assistance by means of strategies' (Jacobs & Maryns, 2021: 2). The lawyer and the applicant meet during consultations at the lawyer's office or one of the asylum registration centres. In the initial consultation, the main purpose is to 'prepare the asylum seeker for testifying at the asylum hearing' (Jacobs & Maryns, 2021: 3), for not only may applicants lack legal knowledge but they may have 'experienced some form of trauma' (Fiske & Kenny, 2004: 137).

These initial meetings can be very important as many applicants have only vague knowledge of the 1951 Refugee Convention's definition of international protection and very little about the rules of the PCA regarding international protection (Kynsilehto & Puumala, 2015). The intervention of a lawyer, and before that the Dutch Refugee Council in the case of the Netherlands, can be very important. The Refugee Council and the lawyer explain the rules that govern the asylum procedure to the applicant, who learns the 'requirements of political asylum policies and learn how to shape their stories to emphasise persecution, torture, and violence rather than, for example, poverty' (Bohmer & Shuman, 2018: 161). Lawyers and the members of the Council are acutely aware that the way 'applicants represent themselves matters enormously' (Bohmer & Shuman, 2018: 162).

The national rules on international protection and the application of the 1951 Refugee Convention differ across countries, and while the contribution of lawyers therefore differs, generally their task 'consists of representing their clients in the best possible way' (Jacobs & Maryns, 2021: 4). In Belgium, lawyers are permitted to attend the second hearing but are 'constrained from intervening', as is the case in the Netherlands, and while they are 'physically co-present', they are only 'marginally involved in the interview event' (Jacobs & Maryns, 2021: 6).

In Australia, the lawyer can decide to 'draft a statutory declaration for the client setting out their persecution fears' (Smith-Khan, 2021). They may also decide to 'draft a written submission in which they supplement this narrative with references to third-party sources about the client's country of origin and/or relevant group, explain how the law applies in their case, and address any credibility or other concerns the officer may raise' (Smith-Khan, 2021). They can also choose to 'complete application forms and communicate on behalf of the client with immigration officials' (Smith-Khan, 2021: 3).

The constraints on lawyers during the procedure do not mean that the lawyers' role is necessarily marginal. They contribute to the procedure just by being assigned to an applicant. Applicants feel empowered and, in the Netherlands, the INS has to take applicants seriously partly because they have legal representation. Caseworkers and decision-makers also know the lawyers contribute to the procedure, which is evident from their exchange of information with lawyers.

During pre-hearing consultations and subsequent interviews, lawyers are actively engaged in anticipating how decision-makers might respond to certain aspects of an asylum claim, particularly those related to the claimant's credibility and mental health (Wilson-Shaw *et al.*, 2012). No consultation is the same as another. What is the same, though, is that lawyers can and will engage with the story of the applicant with the assessment criteria in mind. They apply 'similar evaluative processes to those that would be undertaken by decision-makers, albeit more generously' (Smith-Khan, 2020: 121).

The country the applicant comes from and the PCA are often vastly different, and lawyers may find it difficult to bridge that gap. Also, the expectations of the lawyer and client regarding what to expect from the consultation, the responsibilities of both parties during the consultation and what the outcomes of the consultation can clash, causing confusion (Jacobs & Maryns, 2021). However, lawyers are the link between the INS and the applicant, and reformulate 'clients' socially-oriented narratives into legally identifiable categories' (Reynolds, 2020a: 95). They tend to use 'lay discourse strategies to bring the legal world closer to the client's world' using a 'lexis of appreciation and encouragement [...] to put clients at ease ' (Reynolds, 2020a: 95). This has also been seen in this book's case study (Chapter 3).

The role of the lawyers in the procedure is small compared with that of the INS. 'Applicants are required to present their claim in person' and lawyers can only offer 'backstage assistance to their client's future narrative performance during the upcoming asylum hearing, a performance that has to meet institutional requirements of credible narration' (Jacobs & Maryns, 2021: 3).

2.7 Conclusion: Unveiling the Inequities and Ideologies Shaping Asylum Procedures

Building on Chapter 1, this chapter has shown that politics significantly impacts how asylum procedures are designed and that such procedures are not a solely legal matter as authorities like to make others believe. I explained how the authorities design procedures in the Global North and discussed why they do so. I then discussed the core component of such procedures, credibility assessments, and showed how these are built on political and language assumptions which disempower the asylum applicant.

Simply put, the asylum procedure is 'fraught with unexamined assumptions about language, national identity, and communicative competence, leading to egregious violations of the asylum seekers' human rights' (Jacquemet, 2009: 525). What the INS fails to acknowledge is that not all good asylum backstories are genuine, and not all bad stories or badly told stories are fraudulent: 'legitimate asylum seekers are not always able to produce a coherent account of the persecution they experienced, and fraudulent applicants can take advantage of the system by producing exactly the kind of seamless, coherent account that the officials will accept' (Bohmer & Shuman, 2018: 160).

Many of these assumptions can be traced to the use (deliberate or otherwise) of monological language ideologies. Even though the applicant is considered by the INS to be the sole creator of the entextualised talk, it is widely accepted in the literature that the interpreter influences how meaning is negotiated and created during the hearings and indeed the entire procedure. Both of these convictions stem from how language is theorised – the INS generally has a monological view of language, while communication and interpreting scholars view language as interactional. In this latter conception, it is theorised that when the interpreter's translation for the caseworker does not represent an exact copy of what the applicant has just said but is an adaptation. As Chapter 3 will show, the talk of the applicant is internalised by the interpreter and then presented to the caseworker in another language. During that internalisation, the applicant's meanings will be coloured by how the interpreter understood the statements, and by factors connected to the immediacy of the interpreter-mediated interaction, such as memory. What the caseworker gets to hear can be slightly or even hugely different from what the applicant has said, or meant, or both. It is *this* understanding that gets entextualised and sent to the decision-maker (who in turn will internalise it). How many of the understandings used in the credibility assessment reflect a 'true' version of what the applicant wanted to say will be unknown, and this raises the question of how fair the assessment is.

Language ideology plays its hand in the roles assigned to the various interlocutors in an asylum procedure. How the immigration institution assigns roles to applicants and decision-makers/caseworkers is not always logical, but is closely related to power and the underlying political and communicative ideology. The role as theorised and assigned to each participant in the asylum procedure 'reflects a dominant discourse that divides responsibility for text creation unequally across the different participants in ways that have important implications for credibility' (Smith-Khan, 2019b: 412). Naturally, the institution and its representatives are more powerful than the applicant and the lawyer, to say nothing of the interpreter.

3 The Case Study: Lost in Translation – Exploring Sense-Making in Interpreter-Mediated Encounters

3.1 Introduction

This chapter serves as the empirical cornerstone of the book, as a detailed case study of an interpreter-mediated legal consultation involving a Syrian asylum-seeker in the Netherlands. As explained in the preceding chapters, legal consultations are part of the asylum procedure. Through careful examination of this case study, this chapter elucidates the broader communication challenges within asylum procedures and demonstrates how interpreter-mediated exchanges are, in the form seen here, poorly suited to capture the complete spectrum of meaning-making and sense-making, leading to the potential loss of crucial information. The dynamics of the interlocutors render the external (i.e. recorded) dialogues only a partial reflection of their internal dialogues.

I transcribed, translated (for the purposes of publication) and analysed the data collected during the legal consultation. I am proficient in Dutch, Arabic, Kurdish and English; nevertheless, to ensure accuracy, the translations were reviewed by two experienced colleagues. The reflective interviews, discussed in detail in Chapters 4 and 5, were conducted by me mostly in Arabic but also some Dutch with the interpreter, and exclusively in Arabic with the applicant.

The examples chosen for this chapter are derived from a meticulously documented case study to showcase typical issues in asylum procedures (see Mizori, 2017). These examples are not exhaustive but are strategically used to demonstrate the potential gaps in communication through interpreter-mediated encounters. This approach is underpinned by a comprehensive methodological framework (see Section 4.6) which describes the data collection, analysis, categorisation and preparation for further examination through reflective interviews.

This chapter sets the stage for subsequent theoretical discussions that explore what may be lost in the dynamics of the communication. It advocates for systemic changes in interpreting practices within asylum procedures. The integration of dialogist principles into interpreting practices, advocated for by the book's overall narrative, is designed to make the communication process within asylum procedures more transparent and just for all parties.

Chapters 1 and 2 have established the historical and political context of asylum procedures, and have stressed the dual nature of these procedures as both legal and political constructs influenced by governmental attitudes towards communication quality, which can be expected have underlying political motivations. This backdrop highlights the complexity and the often politicised nature of asylum determinations, and sets a foundation for the ensuing detailed empirical exploration and theoretical discussions.

3.1.1 Setting the stage: The challenges of credibility assessment

The *fil rouge* of this book is that assessing credibility in asylum applications is a tricky, complicated and multidimensional matter for the reasons mentioned in Chapters 1 and 2, and that the current approach adopted by institutions processing asylum applications is insufficiently fair and lacks an up-to-date theoretical grounding. The Dutch INS represents but one example of this unfortunate phenomenon. I have argued that political and interrelated language ideologies contribute to this. It is not easy for the applicant to live up to the expectations of the INS because these expectations are high and sometimes unrealistic. In addition to its politicised design, the asylum procedure is a sense-making and meaning-making exercise. Sense-making and meaning-making (the constituents of communication) are complicated matters, and the procedure currently does not accommodate them properly because the language ideology that underlies its communicative dimension, namely monologism, cannot sufficiently account for how these sense-making and meaning-making processes occur. This book is not the first publication to present this claim. It is, however, one of the first which seeks to elucidate the political and societal dimensions behind these shortcomings (see Chapters 1 and 2), and beyond this provides a detailed account of the information that is lost or goes unnoticed, in addition to providing a way to address this (see Chapters 5 and 6).

In this chapter, I concentrate on the communication dimension of the procedure and show that, for the INS to gather the information on which to base its decisions, it has insufficient capacity to capture certain key aspects of the sense-making process, and as such needs to be reassessed and readdressed. In the examples below I show that the record of the substantive interview (see Chapter 2) does not always provide a clear and unambiguous picture about what each interlocutor says and means. The meaning-making and sense-making processes described here do not originate from an INS hearing. Instead, they occur during a legal consultation that involves discussion of processes during previous hearings. Although the interactions in legal consultations may appear to have a quite distinct context, they are comparable to interviews within the asylum application because: (1) the material discussed is derived from the hearings, and (2) the interaction occurs in an institutional setting, which, albeit less daunting than a hearing, can still be intimidating for many asylum applicants. As noted previously, not all applicants know the true difference between the INS and legal representatives.

I discuss these examples to show there is a reason to dig deeper. The ultimate goal of this book is to help improve the quality of the procedure and the associated credibility assessment. The primary means of achieving this is by identifying the deficiencies in the communicative dimension of the procedure and suggesting improvements to enhance the procedure's fairness. The examples in this chapter demonstrate that while many of the interactions in the interpreter-mediated encounter (IME) that forms this case study may seem unimportant at first, upon closer inspection they demonstrate moments when the efficacy of communication, that is, the exchanging of information between the IME participants, may be questioned. The importance and potential impact of these moments is highly significant, as the information that is recorded in IMEs throughout the procedure forms the 'reality' that decision-makers use to make their judgements. In this sense, it might be said it is never the applicants themselves who succeed or fail in an asylum claim – it is the information that is recorded at various stages that is scrutinised. As such, and as the examples in this chapter will illustrate, interactions in IMEs that raise questions are of vital significance to the integrity of an application.

Within this case study, the client in question is an applicant for international protection and the background of their case can be found below. Henceforth, this individual will be referred to as the *applicant*, in light of the terminological considerations outlined in Section 1.2.1. Specifically, this data was generated through: (1) a transcribed recording of the IME; (2) the author's interviews with the applicant and the interpreter after the legal consultation; and (3) corridor conversations and personal exchanges with the participating lawyer and post-IME phone calls.

Given the stated goals of this book, I was particularly interested in how sense-making develops during IMEs (such as those with a lawyer) in an asylum procedure. To frame my enquiry, I asked the following research questions:

(1) How does the interpreter render (in Arabic) the original (Dutch) utterances of the lawyer? The translations of these 'originals' are called 'renditions'.
(2) Does the applicant understand these originals (via the renditions), and what can be learned from the applicant's answers in terms of the sense-making processes and meaning-making processes?
(3) How does the interpreter explain his translation decisions, and what can be learned from his answers in terms of the sense-making and meaning-making?

These research questions progress thematically from examining the interpretation of the lawyer's original statements, to analysing how these interpretations are received, and finally exploring the decision-making process behind the interpretations. The questions are interconnected by their shared objective of understanding how sense-making and meaning-making occurred in the IME. These questions arise from the inability of direct textual analysis to shed light on these aspects of the IME.

Before delving into the case study, it is crucial to outline this book's approach to communication in IMEs. While the influence of culture on communication is widely acknowledged, this book adopts a broader perspective. Instead of focusing narrowly on cultural aspects, it emphasises an open approach towards fieldwork, where participants are free to bring up any topics, avoiding predefined subjects like 'culture'. This is grounded in the theoretical perspectives I apply in this book (Chapter 4). In addition to this broader approach to communication, the study also differs from traditional research in dialogue interpreting (DI). Traditional DI research is often centred on the interpreter and his role (Jacobsen, 2009), whereas this study focuses on the interpreting process. It includes an in-depth examination of the perspectives and experiences of interpreters, considering both detailed and broader aspects of their work. While the role of the interpreter is a significant element, this study does not isolate it as a primary focus. Rather, the interpreter's role is integrated into the larger exploration of the interpreting process. This means acknowledging the varied and evolving opinions on the interpreter's role in IMEs but situating these within a more comprehensive analysis of interpreting as a complex and dynamic activity.

3.2 Introducing the Case Study: Background, Data Collection, Notation

The examples given below (beginning in Section 3.3) illustrate a spectrum of communication issues likely to be missed by the asylum process. They will be examined in full in Chapter 5 (following the presentation of the theoretical basis and methodology of this book in Chapter 4). They are presented in the form of excerpts, preceded and/or followed by brief commentary. They vary in the extent to which they demonstrate shortcomings in the procedure and the degree to which these shortcomings originate from the specific procedures of the INS in conducting credibility assessments. They span the impact of specific INS design decisions to the inherent challenges of interpretation and translation as human activities. First, though, it is pertinent to grasp the background of the case study (Section 3.2.1), the analytical process that was applied (Section 3.2.2) and the notation conventions used in the case notes (Section 3.2.3).

3.2.1 Background: Information on the applicant for international protection, legal consultation, and case study

The applicant had applied for international protection but had been granted only a subsidiary asylum permit. This was also confirmed in the post-IME interview I held with the applicant. The subsidiary asylum permit was essentially a residence permit, which does not offer the same protection as that granted under international protection, whereas the lawyer and the applicant had hoped for international protection – granted when an asylum-seeker has, in the words of the 1951 Refugee Convention, a 'well-founded fear of being persecuted for reasons of race, religion, nationality, membership of a particular social group or political opinion'. The lawyer and the applicant held the legal consultation to discuss the appeal they had lodged and to discuss the backstory of the applicant.

The INS seemed to consider the backstory of the applicant insufficient, or not sufficiently credible, to grant him international protection, as noted by the lawyer. The INS had not provided its reasons for this, according to the lawyer. The applicant, together with the lawyer, had decided to appeal to the court to force the INS either to grant him the residence permit he had been seeking or to provide the reasons why it had decided to deny him one. The applicant had won that appeal before the IME under study was held. The lower court had ordered the INS to reconsider its decision and had given the INS four weeks to lodge a higher appeal. During the IME, it became apparent that the INS had failed to do this. It then had six weeks to make a new decision, starting from the date of the lower court session which had ordered the INS to reconsider its decision. This deadline was a few days after this IME. According to the lawyer, the INS now had two choices: to grant the applicant the residence permit he wanted or to send him a new decision explaining the reasons why it was refusing to grant the asylum residence permit.

During the IME I recorded for this study (for the full transcript see the online Appendix I), the lawyer is preparing himself and the Syrian client for the possibility that the INS may again refuse to grant the applicant international protection. During the recorded encounter, the lawyer performs, among other things, three 'interactional goals' (Drew & Heritage, 1992):

(1) He discusses with the applicant the legal process in which the latter has been involved since submitting his asylum application. He sums up step by step how the procedure has developed from the date of application until the consultation under study. The summary he gives has two functions: to remind the client (and most probably himself) of the procedure to date, and to provide the client with the opportunity to correct any mistakes that might have slipped into the report.

(2) He revisits the backstory of the applicant and reads parts of it out. Here as well, the lawyer not only wants to refresh his and the client's

memory, but also to get the view of the applicant on whether misunderstandings or mistakes have slipped into the report.

(3) He asks the applicant questions related to his backstory. These questions can have multiple functions. Some are used to double-check information in the report that is unclear. Others are used to identify weaknesses in the client's backstory. Lawyers know the credibility criteria and want to address these during their consultation meetings.

Within an academic context like the present study, it is important for me to provide some perspective on myself as a researcher and my professional and academic background. I have extensive experience in translation, interpreting and linguistics, having operated in these areas since 1998. My academic roles have included teaching specialised translation and supervising translation projects at the University of Manchester and the University of Leeds. My editorial work includes contributions to the award-winning *Oxford Arabic Dictionary* at Oxford University Press and the well-received Dutch–Arabic dictionary *Nederlands-Arabisch Woordenboek*. I hold a PhD in Interpreting and Translation Studies from the University of Leeds and have completed numerous specialised programmes and summer schools across Europe.

3.2.2 Data analysis

Coding and thematising

In the empirical component of this study, thematic coding was meticulously applied to systematically analyse the interpreter-mediated encounter (IME). This enabled the identification of recurrent themes that reflect the interaction dynamics, based on a framework adapted from Wadensjö's (1998) model of dialogue interpreting. The identification of these themes was essential for interpreting the complex communication patterns observed and for grounding the observations in a structured analytical framework.

The coding process began with an exploratory phase, in which the recorded IME data were categorised into emergent themes consistent with Wadensjö's taxonomy of interpreting. Each theme was scrutinised to ensure comprehensive coverage. Through this analytical methodology, the study transcends simple observational reporting by situating the analysis within a scholarly framework that emphasises systematic rigour and methodological robustness.

Furthermore, the study is underpinned by a theoretical-methodological perspective that incorporates elements of dialogism, drawing on the work of scholars such as Bakhtin and Linell. This theoretical orientation provides a nuanced understanding of how meanings are co-constructed in IMEs, highlighting the dialogic engagement's transformative potential within legal settings.

By rigorously coding the data and applying Wadensjö's model alongside dialogism, the research not only enriches the analytical depth but also solidifies its academic foundation. This approach ensures that the recurring themes within the interpreter-mediated dialogue are clearly articulated, providing a robust, scholarly narrative that substantiates the complexities and critical significance of communication in asylum procedure. For a detailed explanation, refer to online Appendix II.

Researcher presence during data collection

I was not physically present during the recorded IME, to avoid influencing the participants' behaviour, thereby preserving the interaction's naturalness and authenticity. However, I conducted the subsequent reflective interviews in person to gain deeper insights into the participants' perspectives and their sense-making processes during the IME.

Data collection timeline

Data collection occurred in two phases: the audio-recorded IME; interviews with the applicant two weeks later and the interpreter a week thereafter. This schedule allowed for transcription and preliminary analysis of the recorded data before the reflective interviews were conducted.

Duration of interviews and consultation

The legal consultation (IME) lasted approximately 45 minutes. The subsequent reflective interviews with both the applicant and the interpreter three to four hours each. The extended duration was vital for exploring the participants' perspectives thoroughly and ensuring their comfort and willingness to participate fully. The participants were informed that the interviews would occupy an entire afternoon.

Sources of data

The data for this case study are fully presented and examined in my doctoral thesis (Mizori, 2017), which explores sense-making processes in IMEs within a legal context. It examines how the interpreter translates the lawyer's utterances, how the immigrant interprets these translations, and how the interpreter and immigrant explain their decisions and understandings, utilising dialogism as the theoretical framework.

Case study selection

I leveraged my professional background and networks within the legal and interpreting communities in the Netherlands to access this case. After obtaining ethical approval from relevant institutional review boards (University of Leeds, UK) and securing informed consent from all participants, which included detailed explanations of the research objectives, confidentiality assurances and the voluntary nature of participation, I was able to record and transcribe the IME and conduct the post-IME reflective interviews. The Syrian applicant received reassurances from me and his lawyer regarding the professional handling of data and confidentiality.

Difference between my thesis and the book

This book builds upon the empirical foundations and theoretical insights developed in my doctoral research (Mizori, 2017). While the core empirical case study – a detailed analysis of an interpreter-mediated encounter during a legal consultation in an asylum procedure in the Netherlands – remains central, this monograph extends well beyond the thesis, to situate the findings within a broader historical, legal and sociopolitical context and introduces dialogist interpretation as a practical framework for reform in interpreting and asylum procedures, offering a new paradigm for understanding communication in asylum settings.

Analysis of the data recorded during the legal consultation (the IME)

The primary focus of the initial analysis was on assessing the accuracy and completeness of the interpreter's translations of the lawyer's utterances, and on identifying any modifications therein:

1. Segmentation of utterances

- Transcription segmentation. The recorded interaction was transcribed and segmented into individual utterances.
- Identifying translation units. The translation units within the transcriptions were identified and isolated for detailed analysis.

2. Comparative analysis

- Source versus target comparison. Each utterance by the lawyer was compared with the corresponding translated utterance by the interpreter.
- Accuracy check. The analysis assessed whether the translations conveyed the original meaning of the lawyer's utterances accurately.

3. Analysis of completeness

- Content analysis. The completeness of each translation was examined to ensure all relevant information in the lawyer's utterances was included. Thereafter I analysed the responses of the applicant to see if there was any reason to assume he might not have understood the renditions (for a detailed account see Chapter 4; online Appendix II).

3.2.3 Transcription conventions

The excerpts presented in this chapter to support the arguments and allow the reader to view the data a first-hand are derived from recordings of oral speech. To improve the readability of these transcriptions, specific transcription conventions have been employed.

The signs used to reflect phonetic features of the oral text which are not captured by standard features of writing are as follows:

- The colon [:], whether in Dutch, Arabic or English, represents a lengthening of the sound which precedes it. For example, the colon in [So:] indicates that the word is pronounced with a lengthened vowel. A repeated colon indicates that the vowel is even longer than a standard elongation. For example, [e:::] indicates that [e] here is much longer than the [e] when one or two colons have been used.
- A dot placed between parentheses *(.)* means that there is an interval between the word that precedes it and the one that follows it (shown as asterisks here). It is utilised to indicate a 'very short silence (micro-pause)' (Wadensjö, 1998: xxi). Again, repetition indicates lengthening, and (..) indicates a pause roughly twice the length of (.).
- To indicate that an element has been spoken more quietly than the rest of the passage, [°] is used. For example, in °صح، صح° these two Arabic words have been spoken quietly.
- [.hh] indicates that the speaker is inhaling.
- 'Walla(h)' is an Arabic filler.
- The text between angle brackets, <text>, is spoken more quickly than usual for that speaker.
- [e::] indicates that the speaker is making a hesitation or other filler sound in Dutch (sometimes represented in writing in English as 'errr').
- In the Arabic text, [إي] indicates that the speaker is making a hesitation or another filler sound in Arabic, similar to [e::] for the Dutch.
- .. [*Unintelligible*] indicates that the audio is difficult to understand or totally incomprehensible due to muddled talk, and so on.
- When the speaker stresses a particular syllable or word, this is indicated in bold type. For example, in [**de**gelijk], the first syllable is stressed.
- [,] indicates a questioning intonation.
- [?]is used to show a rising intonation higher than that indicated by the comma sign mentioned in the previous point. It shows that there is a questioning intonation with a rising tone.
- Text placed in square brackets [ ] or parentheses ( ) is not part of the original utterance but put in to make the transcript more readable.
- [.] represents terminating intonation (usually with a falling tone).
- [=]indicates that the utterance which comes next is produced immediately after the first speaker has stopped talking.
- 'yaʕni' is a word that can have different functions in Arabic. Where it is used untranslated, it functions as a filler.
- He::m is also a filler. In the examples presented here, it indicates that the lawyer is about to start his rendition.
- Hehum is a minimal response which may indicate that the speaker wants to show he understood the preceding utterance.

3.3 Applicant Comprehension: Questions Raised

During data collection I did not probe every single utterance and its rendition due to time constraints. Those which appeared unproblematic were not investigated further. The following is an example of an unproblematic utterance:

3 Lawyer: .hh we zijn e:: een aantal weken geleden bij de rechtbank geweest (.) in Den Helder.
Lawyer: .hh we went e:: to court a number of weeks ago (.) in Den Helder.
4 المترجم: قبل إي: عدة أسابي:ع (.) كنا: في محكمة في دن هيلدر.
Interpreter: several wee:ks ago e: (.) we had a court session in Den Helder.
5 اللاجئ: °صح صح°.
Immigrant: °correct correct°
6 Interpreter: klopt
Interpreter: correct

Here it is very probable that the applicant has understood the translated original (the rendition). It is simple, and the applicant had just gone to court, which is the topic of this utterance. We also see the applicant shows that he understood what was said. Further investigation of the interpreting decisions here is unnecessary.

Unlike the example above, the interview observations that follow do require further scrutiny. While the discussion presented in each case will illustrate why, it should noted that each case is not exhaustive, both in and of themselves, and in terms of all aspects of the IME that may be of interest. Rather, they provide a range of exchanges featuring renditions produced by the interpreter,[1] and raise questions regarding them. It should

---

1 The interpreter who participated in the study was a man born in the Middle East who had an extensive professional background in both his home country and the Netherlands. Before moving to the Netherlands, he completed his higher education (in a field unrelated to interpreting or translation), having studied a technical discipline at the university level. For reasons of confidentiality, the exact field of study and nationality are not specified. Upon relocating, he pursued further education through the Dutch vocational education system.

In terms of interpreting-related education, the interpreter attended a well-regarded interpreting program in the Netherlands, followed by several short courses specifically related to interpreting. His knowledge of Syrian Arabic, one of the five dialects he interprets, was acquired through practical experience, television, and social interactions, as there are no formal institutions in the Netherlands that teach Arabic dialects. His proficiency in Dutch was initially developed through language courses provided by volunteers, culminating in passing the State Exam (Staatsexamen), a Dutch language proficiency exam. This educational and professional background highlights his extensive training and experience in both general and specialized interpreting contexts.

In addition to working for lawyers, the interpreter indicated that he also works for the Immigration and Naturalisation Service (INS). In the Netherlands, once you have satisfied the official criteria for working as a sworn interpreter and translator, you can apply to work for the INS. You need to pass a selection procedure, which is mainly related to security concerns.

be noted that some turns feature in part or in full in multiple excerpts. The extraction of excerpts from the full transcript of the IME should by no means be taken as an indication that the utterances are in some way self-contained. While a certain discussion point may be found in each excerpt, as their overlapping nature suggests, communication takes place throughout and across the IME, even when considered only at a textual level.

Across many of the excerpts in this chapter, I argue that it is challenging, and sometimes impossible, to ascertain, without talking to the applicant, whether or not the applicant has understood a given rendition. These interview observations pertain most immediately to my second research question, which probes whether or not the applicant has comprehended the originals (the utterances of the lawyer) through the rendition (the translated utterances) provided by the interpreter. As will be seen below, a solely textual analysis is an inadequate conceptual tool to investigate these renditions, which when assessed from a dialogical basis reveal significant and varied instances of lost information. This lost information is, this book argues, an element of IMEs missed by monologist conceptions of communication, which if routinely (re)captured in asylum procedures provides an avenue for significant improvements in terms of efficacy and fairness (see Chapter 6).

Excerpt 1: Difficulty to verify applicant comprehension

During the IME, in turn 30 below, which is part of the first interactional goal of the lawyer (discussing with the applicant the legal process in which the latter has been involved since the date of submission of his asylum application), the lawyer indicates that it seems that the INS has not considered the applicant's backstory 'sufficient' for him to be granted an asylum residence permit (international protection). He mentions then that the problem is that he and the applicant do not know why the INS thinks this. The lawyer argues that the INS must explain its original decision not to grant an asylum permit, which it has not done. If this happens, the lawyer will be able to provide counterarguments to the decision, to help the applicant receive an asylum residence permit. He goes on to mention that the lack of an asylum permit will have serious consequences for the applicant's residence position in the future. The applicant says 'correct':

Excerpt 1

27 المترجم: إيه يعني (.) هو قال (غير واضح) إذا إنتو (.) إي عيّنتو إي تاريخ بداية الإقامى (.) تاريخ مختلف (.) فَلازم
ت تقولّولنة (.) توضّحوننة السبب (.) لَشو ما: أخدتو بتاريخ الفين وتسعة=الفين وتسعة،
Interpreter: e: yaʕni (.) he said [*unintelligible*] if you (.) e set e the start date of the residence (permit) (.) a different date (.) then you need to to say to us (.) explain to us the reason (.) for what reason you did no:t pick two thousand and nine=two thousand and nine,

28 اللاجئ: صح

Immigrant: correct

29 Intepreter: =klopt

Interpreter: correct

30 Lawyer: want mijn standpunt e: (.) is dat bekent dus **ei**genlijk als als ss je zo een beslissing neemt (.) dat ze jouw asielverhaal (.) e on voldoende vonden= wat je hebt verteld .h= maar wij weten niet waar**om** en dan moeten nog op kunnen reage:ren .h = omdat het grote gevolgen heeft voor jouw e::: verblijfspositie in Nederland.

Lawyer: for my point of view e: (.) is that means thus **ac**tually if if ss you take such a decision (.) that they consider your backstory (.) e insufficient= what you said .h= but we do not know **wh**y and we must then be enabled to res:pond to it [the decision] .h = because it has big consequences for your e::: residence position in the Netherlands.

31 المترجم: يعني هوّى (.) وجهة نظروو (.) إنّوو (.) هنّى (.) في هالحالى (.) قرّروا بانّو قصّة اللجوء تَبعك مَنّا كافية (.) وفي هالحالى (.) بدّون يقولولْنا لَشو (.) شو السبب مشان نقدر كمان نقدم بِردّ على (.) هالموضوع= لأنّو هالشي ممكن يكون إلْه (.) عواقب (.) او تأثي:ر (.) على (.) إقامتك في هولندا.

Interpreter: yaʕni he (.) from his point of view (.) that (.) they (.) in that case (.) decided that your backstory isn't sufficient (.) **and in such a case** (.) they must say to us **for what** (.) **what is the reason** so that we can also submit a response (.) regarding this subject=for this thing can have (.) consequences (.) or influen:ce (.) on (.) your residence in the Netherlands [*Interrupted by immigrant*].

32 اللاجئ: صح

Immigrant: correct

33 Lawyer: .hh em: (.) want op het moment dat wij gelijk krijgen (.) en dat je **toch** een verblijfvergunning krijgt (.) met datum ingang e: jouw asielaanvraag (.) dat betekent dat je komende **juni** (.) al asiel onbepaalde tijd kan aanvragen en ook je Nederlandse paspoort kan krijgen.

Lawyer: .hh em: (.) for the moment that we are said to be right [by the court] (.) and that you nonetheless receive a residence permit (.) with a start date e: [which is] your asylum application [date] (.) this means that you coming June (.) already can apply for a permanent asylum [residence permit] and you can also get your Dutch passport.

34 المترجم: لأنّو إذا (.) إحنة (.) إي أخذنه (.) اللي بَدنا إيّاه (.) وَ وَ إعترفوا بأنّو (.) تاريخ الإقامى تبَعك (.) هو نفس (.) تاريخ (.) طلب اللجوء (.) ففي=هالشي معناه إنّو في شهر ستّى الجاي، من حقّك انه تقدم بطلب للحصول على إقامى مفتوحة، (.) وَفينك انّو تقدم على إي (.)البَسبور= على الجنسية.

Interpreter: Because if (.) we (.) e took (.) what we want (.) and and they admitted that (.) your residence [permit] date (.) is the same as (.) the date of (.) the asylum [application] date (.) in this=this thing means that in month six which is coming you have the right to apply for an open-ended residence [permit] (.) and you can apply for a e (.) the passport=for the nationality.

35 اللاجئ: صح

Immigrant: correct

36 Interpreter: klopt

Interpreter: correct

37 Lawyer: .hhh nou die beslissing van de rechtbank was op 15 oktober (.) en de IND had vier weken de tijd om daar tegen in hoger beroep te gaan.

Lawyer: .hhh well that decision of the court was on October 15 (.) and the INS had four weeks to lodge a higher appeal against it.

38 المترجم: قرار المحكمى كان صادر في 15 عشرة (.) ودائرة الهجرة والتجنيس كان الا (.) اربع اسابيع من الوقت (.) مشان تتقدم بإستئناف في المحكمة العليا.

Interpreter: the decision of the court was issued on October 15 (.) and the Immigration and Naturalisation Service had (.) four weeks of time (.) in order to lodge an appeal at the Higher Court.

39 Lawyer: nou die zijn voorbij, (.) en ik heb niks gehoord (.) dus ze zijn niet in hoger beroep (.) gegaan.

Lawyer: these have passed (.) and I have heard nothing (.) so they have not lodged an appeal (.)

40 المترجم: الأربعة أسابيع (.) مرّوا (.) وخلصوا (.) وهو ما سم. شي فمشان هيك (.) دائرة الهجرة والتجنيس ما قدمت إستئناف في المحكمة العليا.

Interpreter: The four weeks (.) have pass.. (.) and come to an end (.) and he has not (heard?) anything and this is why (.) the Immigration and Naturalisation Service has not lodged an appeal at the High Court.

41 Lawyer: de rechtbank heeft ook gezegd dat ze binnen zes weken nieuwe besluit moeten nemen en **dat is** komende disnsdag.

Lawyer: the court said also that they have to take a new decision within six weeks and **that is** next Tuesday.

42 المترجم: والمحكمة .. (غير واضح) خلال ست أسابيع بدّون يتّخذو قرار جديد (.) وهَدول بيخلصو (.) يوم التلاتاء (.) الجاي.

Interpreter: and the court .. [*unintelligible*] within six weeks they need to have taken a new decision (.) and those will end (.) coming (.) Tuesday.

43 اللاجئ: الجاي .. (غير واضح)

Immigrant: the coming .. [*rest unintelligible*]

44 Lawyer: .hh dus ik ben heel benieuwd (.) [1] of het gaat gebeuren.

Lawyer: .hh thus I am very curious (.) whether it is going to happen.

45 المترجم: فهو متشوق متشوق كتي::ر (.) شو بدو يصير.

Interpreter: so he is longing really longing (.) [to know] what is going to happen.

46 اللاجئ: والله شكرا شكرا يعني هو عمل اللي عليه.

Immigrant: well thanks, thanks, he did what he had to do.

Because legal talk like this can be challenging for lay people (including many applicants) the word 'correct' should not automatically be considered to indicate understanding. It could just be a back-channelling device to show that the listener is indeed listening (O'Connell *et al.*, 1990). Further, looking at the text produced in Arabic, we can see that its structure could also be considered challenging. The interpreter begins with the pronoun 'he', referring to the lawyer, but then uses the pronoun 'they' in the same clause. After that, the interpreter uses the phrase 'this matter' which is not very tangible. He then uses a subject phrase 'this thing' without indicating what this refers to. The legal language and the difficult phrasing make it open to doubt whether the applicant has understood the original. The 'Correct' of the applicant at the end of the exchange (turn 32) cannot be seen as evidence either that he understood or of what he understood.

In Chapter 5, where I discuss the findings in detail, among them this instance, I conclude that the applicant in this example had probably understood this original when he said 'Correct' (turn 32). With this, I mean that when the applicant said 'Correct' in turn 32, he had probably understood what the lawyer was talking about at this point of the consultation. As we will see in other examples, however, 'Correct' does not always indicate the applicant understood. I came to this conclusion during a post-IME interview with the applicant. For more details, see Chapter 5.

1 Interpreter interrupts here and starts producing his rendition (turn 45).

The excerpt below (which is still a part of the first interactional goal of the lawyer) provides a further example of how challenging it can be to determine whether or not a rendition has been understood. The lawyer is discussing the legal procedure. He explains to the applicant the benefits of getting an asylum residence permit (i.e. one that is based on his own personal backstory, unlike the one he has now, which is based on the general situation of Syria); see turn 33 above. Then, he explains that the applicant has apparently won the appeal the lawyer had lodged, because the deadline imposed by the court on the INS for lodging a higher appeal has expired (turn 39). After that, the lawyer explains to the applicant that the INS is expected now (as ordered by the court) to make a new decision within a few days on whether or not it will grant the applicant the residence permit he wants (turn 41). In turn 44, he tells the applicant that he is very curious what this decision will be. In turn 45, the interpreter produces a substituted rendition of this last original of the lawyer: the lawyer says: '.hh thus I am very curious (.) whether it is going to happen', while the interpreter, interrupting the lawyer at the word 'whether', produces the following rendition: 'so he is longing really longing (.) [to know] what is going to happen'. The lawyer is showing that he is curious about what the INS is going to do, while the translation suggests more that the lawyer is feeling excited about the possible outcome of the expected decision on the part of the INS. The applicant shows his appreciation for the lawyer and says that the lawyer has done everything that he could (turn 46). One can sense a possible 'trouble source' for understanding here; it is not clear whether or not the applicant really understood what the lawyer had just said. In addition to the fact that the interpreter produced a substitution ('curious' is substituted with 'longing'), it is noticeable that the applicant did not provide a (verbal) response when the lawyer was talking earlier about technical issues related to the legal procedure, while trying to make a point to the applicant about that procedure (turns 37 and 39). The applicant also produced a minimal response when the following rendition was made, which noticeably was not translated by the interpreter (turn 43). Based on the 'material' considered above, it is unclear whether the applicant has understood the lawyer's message or not. While it can be doubted that he understood, no real evidence is apparent in the textual material either way.

Chapter 5 considers what the applicant said when I raised this point with him during the reflective interview. Briefly, it turns out that the applicant had miscommunicated the original, in which the lawyer showed that he was curious about the decision of the INS. The applicant indicated that he thought the related rendition meant that the lawyer was *optimistic* about his legal procedure, not *curious*. It made the applicant think, according to the applicant, that the lawyer was eager, in the sense that he was optimistic. In Chapter 5 I will discuss this example in full, exploring how the complexity of legal language can cause the applicant to 'miscommunicate' renditions (see Section 5.3.1).

Excerpt 2: Interpretation inadequacies

A few turns later, as depicted in Excerpt 2, after reminding the applicant about how the debate between him and the representative of the INS in front of the judge had developed, which constituted the first interactional goal of the lawyer during the IME, the lawyer then revisited the backstory of the applicant, which was his second interactional goal (see Section 3.2.1). In the first turn below (turn 51), the lawyer mentions, among other things, that, according to the INS report he is citing, the applicant came to the Netherlands together with his cousin because they got into trouble together, meaning they got into the same problem, that is, they did not both leave Syria due to different issues. Examining the rendition, it is clear that the interpreter reduced ‘together’. The applicant says ‘correct’ and does not say anything about the reduction. The reduction of ‘together’ in turn 52 may seem like a small detail, but in the context of an asylum application, such reductions are important. The asylum process relies on the consistency of applicants’ stories, particularly when narratives are compared between individuals with shared experiences. Even minor discrepancies can raise concerns about credibility, which, as discussed in Chapter 2, is critical to a successful application. The omission of ‘together’ introduces a potential inconsistency that merits further investigation, given its possible implications for the applicant’s case. The applicant will have known this, as he must have been told it in the past by the lawyer and/ or organisations like the Dutch Council for Refugees (DCR). So why did he not intervene here?

Excerpt 2

51 Lawyer: goe:d e::: ok e: nou je hebt in jouw interview e: verteld (.) dat (.) jij samen (.) met jouw neef die hier nu even niet is maar wie ik nog een gesprek ga hebben (.) dat jullie samen naar Nederland zijn vertrokken= omdat jullie samen problemen hebben gekregen in Syria.
Lawyer: goo:d e::: ok e: well you said in your e: interview (.) that (.) you together (.) with your cousin who is not here right now but with whom I will have a conversation (.) that you together departed to the Netherlands=because you together got into troubles in Syria.

52 المترجم: انت (.) حكيت في المقابلى (.) انّو انتى إي في وقتا غادرت إي البلد (.) مع ابن عمك أو ابن اخوك (.) الي اليوم مو معانا [1] ابن عمك إي: غادرتو إلى هولندا=لأنو انتو الإثنين تعرّضتو إلى: مشاكل.
Interpreter: you (.) said in the interview (.) that you e at the time left e [your] country (.) with your cousin or your nephew (.) who is today not with us[2] your cousin e: you left to the Netherlands=because both of you got into: troubles.

53 اللاجئ: °صح°
Immigrant: °correct°

54 Interpreter: klopt
Interpreter: correct

55 Lawyer: e:m ik heb begrepen dat e: tus ik heb het verhaal zo begrepen= jouw vriendin

1 Here the immigrant interjects ‘my cousin’.
2 Here the immigrant interjects ‘my cousin’.

(.) of nee jouw jouw neef had een vriendin e: een meisje leren kennen .hh waarmee e: ja die wat aanrommelde [*Laughs nasally*] om het zo maar te zeggen .hh (.) en (.) en op een gegeven moment heeft **jou** neef aan jou gevraagd om mee te gaan= zodat het meisje **ook** een vriendin mee zou nemen (.) en dan zou het allemaal wat minder (..) opvallen.

Lawyer: e:m I have understood that e: tog. I have understood the story in such a way=your **girl**friend (.) or no your your cousin had a girlfriend e: had met a girl .hh with whom e: yeah he used to mess around a little bit (*chuckles*) to put it this way .hh (.) and (.) and at a given moment **your** cousin asked you to accompany [them]=so that the girl **too** would take along a [girl] friend (.) and then things would be less (..) noticeable.

56 المترجم: يعني: (.) حسب ما هوى (.) فهم انّو ابن عمك (.) كان عندو رفيقة: (.) وعمل معا شغلا:ت، (.) وقال لك قال لك انّو تجي معو مشان هي كمان تجيب رفيقتها معا= مشان تغطو على هالموضوع.

Interpreter: yaʕni: (.) according to how he (.) has understood your cousin had a girl:friend (.) and he did things to her (.) and he said he said to you to come with him so that she too brings her [girl] friend with her=so you cover up this thing.

57 اللاجئ: أختا أختا.

Immigrant: her sister her sister

Looking at the text as it is, it is very difficult, if not impossible, to conclude how the applicant understood the original. Was the applicant aware of the reduction when he said 'correct' in turn 53? If so, what made him accept the rendition as it is? Could it be that he decided at that point to include the reduced item in the evaluation in his internal dialogue, even though he was aware the item was not there? Or is it possible that he felt he knew enough and that he did not think the reduction was a problem? Or might it be that he was not aware of the reduction?

It is also possible that, during the IME, he felt that there was something missing but might have felt that this was acceptable when the rendition in turn 56 was produced, where it becomes more or less clear that the applicant and his cousin had the same problem. Probably, he just felt that the rendition in turn 51 above was acceptable for 'current practical purposes' and there was no need to correct it, especially given that this was not the first time that he had had a meeting of this kind with the lawyer. That said, if we examine how the renditions developed afterwards, we will see that the applicant is not always tolerant of divergent renditions.

The next rendition (turn 57) shows that when the interpreter produces a substituted rendition, the applicant intervenes and corrects the interpreter: the person concerned is the sister of his cousin's girlfriend, not her friend. This might arguably mean that when an integral part of the rendition is not right, the applicant does in fact intervene to correct the interpreter. The question remains, however – was the reduction mentioned above (turn 52) not important and did it not deserve to be corrected? I claim it was. We just do not know what happened at that point. The significance of this reduction should not be understated. In terms of lay conversation this may seem like an inconsequential detail, but in the context of an asylum application it bears considerable significance to the outcome of the process. This is to say, two individuals fled their homeland and sought asylum in the Netherlands due to a shared predicament. The INS scrutinises both individuals' narratives, comparing them, to identify any contradictions or falsehoods. If the INS perceives any discrepancies in their accounts – whether one significant discrepancy or multiple smaller ones – this could adversely affect the assessment of their stories' credibility. Credibility, as explored in Chapter 2, is a cornerstone of successful application.

As will be seen in Chapter 5, when I raised this point with this applicant in a post-IME reflective interview, it became clear that the applicant understood the rendition under discussion (turn 51 in the excerpt above) in a way that does not reflect how the rendition was produced but rather how the *original* (lawyer's utterance) was produced. What the textual analysis here cannot reveal, is that the applicant engaged with information in his sense-making not only from originals within the IME, but also from other streams of information, outside it. For a full discussion of this see Section 5.2.

Excerpt 3: A triangle of miscommunication

A few turns later, in Excerpt 3, the lawyer continues revisiting the applicant's backstory, which is his second interactional goal during the IME. In turn 68, he asks if the girl the applicant had a relationship with was 'nice'. The Dutch word 'leuk' (in "t was een leuk meisje') broadly translates to 'nice', 'pleasant' or 'fun', referring to social qualities like being likable or charming rather than purely physical attractiveness.

However, the interpreter substitutes 'nice' with 'beautiful' (turn 69), using the Arabic word حلوة ('hilwa'), which specifically means 'beautiful' or 'pretty' and refers to physical appearance. This substitution shifts the meaning from social traits to a more appearance-focused term, altering the intent of the lawyer's original question. The substitution was avoidable, as a closer Arabic equivalent, such as لطيفة ('lateefa'), meaning 'nice' or 'pleasant', could have preserved the broader, socially oriented meaning of 'leuk'.

The applicant responds with '[she] was beautiful yes' (turn 70), aligning with the interpreter's rendition rather than the lawyer's original question. This response reflects the interpreter rendition's focus on physical beauty, prompting the applicant to respond accordingly. It remains unclear whether the applicant recognised the shift in meaning or simply responded to the interpreted version. Based on the textual evidence, we cannot definitively conclude whether the applicant was aware of the divergence or understood the lawyer's intended question.

Moreover, it is unknown whether the applicant was aware that the interpreter's subsequent Dutch rendition (turn 72) reverted to the original phrasing, 'nice', corresponding to the lawyer's initial question. This raises questions about why the interpreter chose 'hilwa' in Arabic in turn 69, only to revert to the Dutch 'leuk' later.

Excerpt 3

68 Lawyer: 't was een leuk meisje.
Lawyer: she was a nice girl.

69 المترجم: كانت إي: صبية: حلوى:؟
Interpreter: she was e: a beautiful gi:rl?

70 اللاجئ: كا:نت حلوة نعم .
Immigrant: Was beautiful yes.

71 Lawyer: [*Chuckles*]
Lawyer: [*Chuckles*]

72 Interpreter: 't was een leuk meisje.
Interpreter: she was a nice girl.

As previously noted, the interpreter rendered the applicant's confirmatory response (turn 72) in a way that aligned with the lawyer's original statement. Instead of closely translating the applicant's response, the interpreter substituted it with 'nice', matching the lawyer's original phrasing. This suggests that the interpreter was aware that his earlier rendition, in turn 69, using 'beautiful' ('hilwa'), did not accurately reflect the lawyer's question. The applicant's lack of correction raises several possibilities. He may have trusted the interpreter's rendition, been unaware of the shift in meaning, or perhaps understood the lawyer's original Dutch but chose not to intervene.

In Chapter 5, I discuss the findings from a reflective interview with the applicant. In this case, the applicant indicated that he understood the lawyer's original Dutch directly and agreed with the original statement, rather than the interpreter's rendition. This suggests that the applicant may have relied on his understanding of Dutch, making it unnecessary to correct the interpreter's substitution. In this and several other examples, as will be seen in Chapter 5, the analysis shows that the applicant does not solely depend on sense-making material provided by the other interlocutors in the moment. He also relied heavily on pre-encounter knowledge.

3.4 Translation Decisions: The Unknown Process

Building on the discussion in Chapter 2, which highlighted the limitations of monological theorisation in addressing questions about the asylum applicant's understanding in the studied case, this section turns to similar shortcomings evident in the interpreter's renditions. By examining representative examples from the data, this section critiques the textual approach frequently used to assess the efficacy of renditions in IMEs, drawing attention to its failure to capture the co-constructed nature of sense-making and meaning-making. Numerous nuances remain unexplored when viewed through monological frameworks.

The examples are presented in the chronological progression of the IME recorded for this study. This approach enables a nuanced exploration of recurring communication challenges, paving the way for a shift towards dialogical theorisation and methodology. This section bridges the empirical findings of this case study with the theoretical and practical advancements elaborated in Chapter 4, where dialogist interpretation is conceptualised, and Chapter 5, where its application is demonstrated through evidence and recommendations.

Ultimately, this section highlights the need for systemic change in interpreting practices, aligning with the book's central argument: that a dialogist interpretation is essential to addressing the complexities and inequities in interpreter-mediated communication within asylum procedures.

Excerpt 4: 'because it is not in your interest'

In turn 10 below, the lawyer revisits the legal procedure involving the applicant and begins to introduce the perspective of the INS. He tells the applicant that, during the court session that considered the appeal against the earlier INS decision, the INS made it clear that the applicant had no interest in submitting an appeal, as he had already been granted a residence permit.

The interpreter produces a rendition where he makes a substitution. It concerns the clause 'omdat je geen belang had' ('because you had no interest'), which was translated as لأنو ما من مصلحتك (Ii anno ma min maslahtak; 'because it is **not** in your interest'), which in this case, at least in Arabic, could carry the pragmatic meaning that this course of action may turn out bad for you. This is clearly not what the lawyer wanted to convey to the applicant. Leaving aside whether or not, or how, the applicant understood the translation, it is not clear why the interpreter made the decision and whether or not he made this choice consciously. Was there a strategy behind this?

In turn 12, the lawyer reintroduces the same phrase. It is noticeable that the interpreter produces a closer rendition this time (turn 13). This might be an indication that he had considered his previous translation and thought of a closer rendition than the one produced in turn 11, and that he might have decided that the substitution made the first time was not a good choice. It seems that in the time interval between this latter rendition (turn 13) and the first version of it (turn 11), the interpreter found enough time to re-evaluate his translation and produce a rendition he might have thought was a better reflection of the original. However, we need more evidence than the transcription alone can provide to determine what truly happened here regarding the interpreter's choices.

Chapter 5 discusses the interpreter's insights into these questions. The interpreter mentioned during the post-IME interview that this translation was what he was 'able to think of at that moment' and admitted that this element should have been translated differently.

The interpreter's statement about what he was 'able to think of at that moment' shows the challenges faced by interpreters during real-time translation. I wished to know how the need to produce spontaneous renditions influences the interpreter's decisions. Here, the interpreter admitted that the substitution he made was what he could think of in that moment, and he acknowledged that it might not have been the best translation and that he was constrained by the immediacy of the event. This phenomenon was noted several times within my data, indicating a recurring challenge in dialogue interpreting, where the interpreter must balance accuracy with the need to provide immediate translation. Many more examples can be found in the thesis dataset from which this case study is derived (see online Appendix II). It is worth mentioning here that the interpreter came over as a confident professional, and such moments represent an inherent challenge in interpreting. Chapter 5 examines the use of translation strategies, including substitutions, in further detail.

Excerpt 4

1 Lawyer: goed (....) .hhhh (.) ja we zijn al la:ng bezig met jouw:: asielprocedure.
Lawyer: good (....) .hhhh (.) yeah we have been busy with you::r asylum procedure for a lo:ng time.

2 المترجم: إحنا صارنّا فترة (.) عَم نشتغل مشغولين ب: (.) إجراءات لجو:ئك.
Interpreter: we have been working on been busy with: (.) your asylum proce:dure (.) for some time.

3 Lawyer: .hh we zijn e:: een aantal weken geleden bij de rechtbank geweest (.) in Den Helder.
Lawyer: .hh we went e:: to court a number of weeks ago (.) in Den Helder.

4 المترجم: قبل إي: عدة أسابي:ع (.) كنا: في محكمة في دن هيلدر.
Interpreter: several wee:ks ago e: (.) we had a court session in Den Helder.

5 اللاجئ: °صح صح°.
Immigrant: °correct correct°

6 Interpreter: klopt
Interpreter: correct

7 Lawyer: he:m dat was (.) e: een beetje bijzondere procedu:re (.) want ik ben in beroep gegaan tegen een beslissing van de IND (.) ter**wi**jl je een verblijfsvergunning had.
Lawyer: he:m it was (.) e: a unusual procedu:re a little bit (.) for I lodged an appeal against a decision of the INS (.) at a **time** when you [already] had a residence permit.

8 المترجم: هذه الإجراءات كانت إيه استثنائية بعض الشيء لأنو هوىَ (.) عمل (.) إستئناف (.) ضد (.) قرا:ر (.) دائرة الهجرة والتجنيس في حين إنّو القرار كان إقامة،
Interpreter: this procedure was e somewhat exceptional for he (.) made [*sic*] (.) an appeal (.) against (.) the deci:sion of (.) the Immigration and Naturalisation Bureau when the decision [already taken by the INS] was a residence permit,

9 اللاجئ: صح (.) شكرا.
Immigrant: correct (.) thanks

10 Lawyer: en e: (.) de IND (.) heeft (.) daar op zitting ook gezegd dat ze vonden dat we eigenlijk=dat je helemaal geen recht had om in (.) beroep te gaan (.) omdat je geen belang had=want je hebt nu verblijfsvergunning .h dus dan kun je niet in beroep e e tegen een asielbesluit.
Lawyer: and e: (.) the INS (.) said (.) there during the [court] session indeed that they were of the opinion that we actually=that you had no right whatsoever to (.) lodge an

appeal (.) because you had no interest=for you have now a residence permit .h so you cannot lodge an appeal e e against an asylum decision.

11 المترجم: وأث (.) وأثناء الجلسى (.) دائرة الهجرة والتجني:س قا:لت أنّو هنّى (.) إي بيشو إي يعني من رَأيُن إي أنوّ إنت إي ما من حقك أنو تتقدم ب: (..) طَلب إي إي ب: إستئناف ضد القرارْ لأنو ما من مصلحتك لأنّو أنتى حصّلت (.) على الإقامة.

Interpreter: and du (.) and during the [court] session (.) the Immigration and Naturalisation Servi:ce sai:d that they (.) e: think e: yaʕni [1] they are of the opinion e: that you e: have no right to lodge (..) e: e: an appeal against °the decision° because it is **not** in your interest because you [already] have (.) received the [residence] permit.

12 Lawyer: e: en ik heb toen uitgelegd (.) **bij** de rechtbank (.) dat ik vind dat er wel **de**gelijk belang is omdat jij .hh e een verblijfsvergunning heb gekregen vanwege de de algeme slechte siuatie in Syria (.) op dit momen.

Lawyer: e: and I explained then (.) **in** court (.) that I believe that there is **cer**tainly interest because you .hh e received a residence permit due to the the general bad situation in Syria (.) at this moment.

13 المترجم: وهو إي وضّح (.) مَعُن عند المحكمة (.) إنّهو (.) أنتى فعلا (.) في إلَك مصلحة (.) في الإستئناف (.) لأنّو إنتى حصلت على الإقامة (.) على ضوء (.) الوضع (.) إي: السيئ (.) حاليا (.) في (.) سوريا؟[2]

Interpreter: And he e explained (.) with [*sic*] them at [*sic*] the court (.) that (.) you do indeed (.) have an interest (.) in [lodging] an appeal (.) because you have received the residence [permit] (.) in view of the (.) bad (.) e: situation (.) at present (.) in (.) Syria?

14 اللاجئ: صح

Immigrant: correct

15 Lawyer: en e: (....) toen is jou (.) een (..) verblijfsvergunning verleend (..) **met** (.) **ingang** (..) **van?** .hh even **kijk**:en (....) mart twee ja maart of juni tweede duizend (...) **elf** Geloof ik **he**?

Lawyer: and e: (....) back then you (.) were granted a residence permit (..) **with** (.) start **date** (..) **of?** .hh let's **see**: (....) March two yeah March or June two thousand (...) **eleven** I think **heh**?

Excerpt 5: 'and at a given moment your cousin asked you to accompany [them]'

Excerpt 5 revisits several turns found in Excerpt 2, but with a new analytical focus. To reiterate, here the lawyer is engaging with the backstory of the applicant (his second interactional goal). He is trying to ascertain whether his understanding of a certain part of the backstory is correct. In the context of the IME, the applicant is expected to indicate whether the understanding of the lawyer is correct or not. If not, the applicant is supposed to provide a correction.

After the lawyer produces his original, the interpreter starts producing his rendition. The rendition may be categorised as reduced+substituted, which means there is at least one item which is 'reduced' and one item which is 'substituted' (see online Appendix II). One of the reductions the interpreter made concerns the adverbial 'op een geven moment' ('at a given moment'). Linguistically, 'op een gegeven moment' functions as an adverbial phrase that acts as a temporal marker, indicating when an event

1 This is a filler probably used here by the interpreter to give himself time to think/ reformulate.

2 While producing this rendition, the interpreter sounds as if he is thinking.

occurs and helping to establish the sequence and flow of the narrative. This marker contributes to the coherence of the story by linking events and signalling important transitions. It also provides contextual information, framing the action as occurring at a specific, meaningful time, even though the phrase itself remains flexible and vague in terms of precision. When omitted, as in the interpreter's reduction, this temporal marker's absence can lead to ambiguity, affecting the clarity and perception of the narrative's timing and significance. In legal contexts, where consistency and precision are key, such omissions can impact how events are understood and evaluated.

In the narrative explored in this part of the IME, the cousin of the applicant, 'at a given moment', after he had known the girlfriend for some time, came up with a suggestion: that the applicant and his girlfriend should accompany the cousin and his own girlfriend somewhere, for security reasons. The phrase 'at a given moment' was reduced by the interpreter. The excerpt does not give any clue as to why the applicant does not say anything about this reduction. The interlocutors proceed and nothing is said about the adverbial phrase. There are no textual or activity clues as to what made the interpreter adopt this apparent strategy, or even whether it was deliberate.

Excerpt 5

55 Lawyer: e:m ik heb begrepen dat e: tus ik heb het verhaal zo begrepen= jouw vriend**in** (.) of nee jouw jouw neef had een vriendin e: een meisje leren kennen .hh waarmee e: ja die wat aanrommelde [*Laughs nasally*] om het zo maar te zeggen .hh (.) en (.) en op een gegeven moment heeft **jou** neef aan jou gevraagd om mee te gaan= zodat het meisje **ook** een vriendin mee zou nemen (.) en dan zou het allemaal wat minder (..) opvallen.
Lawyer: e:m I have understood that e: tog. I have understood the story in such a way=your **gir**lfriend (.) or no your your cousin had a girlfriend e: had met a girl .hh with whom e: yeah he used to mess around a little bit (*chuckles*) to put it this way .hh (.) and (.) and at a given moment **your** cousin asked you to accompany [them]=so that the girl **too** would take along a [girl] friend (.) and then things would be less (..) noticeable.

56 المترجم: يعني: (.) حسب ما هوى (.) فهم انّو ابن عمك (.) كان عندو رفيقة: (.) وعمل معا شغلا:ت، (.) وقال لك
قال لك انّو تجي معو مشان هي كمان تجيب رفيقتها معا= مشان تغطو على هالموضوع.
Interpreter: yaʕni: (.) according to how he (.) has understood your cousin had a girl:friend (.) and he did things to her (.) and he said he said to you to come with him so that she too brings her [girl] friend with her=so you cover up this thing.

57 اللاجئ: أختا أختا.
Immigrant: her sister her sister

58 Interpreter: nee? Ze zou haar zus meenemen.
Interpreter: no? She would take her sister with her.

59 Lawyer: haar **zus** is het, .hh **Ok** = ik heb hier een vriendin staan, een vriendin van een vriendin=maar het gaat om de zus.
Lawyer: it is her **sister, .hh OK** (.) I have girlfriend noted here, a girlfriend of a girlfriend=but it is a sister.

60 [*the interpreter interrupts the lawyer and addresses the immigrant*:]

61 المترجم: هون المكتوب رفيقة رفيقتا.
Interpreter: here the text says a friend her friend.

62 اللاجي: (غير واضح).
Immigrant: [*unintelligible*]
63 Interpreter: = haar zus.
Interpreter: her sister.
64 Lawyer: °ok° .hh en e: jullie zijn ee met z'n vieren weg- geweest en d'rna ben je die zus vaker gaan ontmoeten.
Lawyer: °ok° .hh and e: you went out the four of you and then you started to meet her sister more often.

Without engaging with the perspective of the interpreter, as Chapter 5 will show, the decision for this reduction (concerning the adverbial phrase في لحظة معينة ('fi lahtha muayana'; 'at a given moment') is not apparent. While the prospect of negative consequences from this exact reduction was minimal, the same ad hoc judgement and resultant translation strategy (demonstrative of the active role of an interpreter) could in other cases result in a significant shaping of the sense-making experience for the applicant. Chapter 5 provides an in-depth rationale for this claim. In short, interlocutors depend on each other for sense-making and meaning-making. Every piece of information, whether added, removed or forgotten, can influence how the interaction develops further. Miscommunications in the interaction can lead to inconsistencies or contradictions, which can leave an asylum application in jeopardy (see Chapter 2). While Excerpt 5 does not show a critically important reduction, it draws attention to two points: (1) there is no capacity in the current asylum procedure to investigate the rationale behind reductions; and (2) what is said in an IME is by no means guaranteed to make it through the entextualisation process such that it can be of use to decision-makers. As Chapters 4 and 5 will explore further, this raises questions about the capacity of asylum procedures to record information accurately, and hence its utility.

Excerpt 6: 'one of them (.) of these policemen hit you?'

In Excerpt 6 (turn 95), the lawyer continues revisiting the applicant's backstory. The interpreter produces a substituted rendition and the applicant agrees with it, even though it arguably does not reflect the original exactly. 'Klap krijgen' (to get hit or get a slap) was rendered as ضربك ('darabak'; 'beat you'). It is unclear why the interpreter made this substitution or whether he was aware of the difference in meaning. 'Klap krijgen' specifically refers to receiving a slap or smack, typically a single quick blow with the hand, most often to the face or body, and carries a precise meaning, whether literal or figurative. It does not usually imply prolonged or repeated violence; for more sustained or severe physical assault, Dutch would typically use expressions such as 'elkaar geslagen worden' ('to be beaten up'). In contrast, the Arabic ضربك is a more general term for 'beating' or 'hitting' which can refer to various types of physical contact, such as punching, slapping, or other forms of assault, without specifying the method or intensity. This broader interpretation in Arabic could lead to a loss of nuance compared with the Dutch original. If the interpreter was aware of this distinction, it raises the question of why he chose not to use a closer rendition.

Excerpt 6

94 Lawyer: en jij krijgt toen een klap (.) van een van de agenten.
Lawyer: and then you received a blow (.) from one of the policemen.

95 المترجم: واحد منّون (.) من هدول الشرطة ضربك؟
Interpreter: one of them (.) of these policemen hit you?

96 اللاجئ: صح
Immigrant: correct

Section 5.4.5 gives the perspective of the interpreter on this interaction. Briefly, he mentioned, among other things, that a close translation would be وجهلك ضربة ('wajjahlak darba'; 'to deal you a blow') but this is not used in Syrian colloquial Arabic, where one would say ضربك ('darabak'; 'beat you]'). When I referred to other possible translations, he said '[my translation] gives the intended meaning; it suffices'. When asked if there were any other possible reasons, he responded 'e::, because both [the applicant and the lawyer] are talking about something they already know, they understand it and I thought the word ضربك is sufficient and the meaning is clear to both parties already'.

Divergent renditions, as seen here, can influence an interaction's flow. They may cause an interaction to proceed differently from what an interlocutor intended. In the studied context, this can sometimes lead to the applicant's story being compromised. Additionally, in such instances, the INS would likely blame the applicant for any inconsistencies or contradictions that might slip into the report due to translation decisions like these (Chapter 2). The assumption of comprehension on part of the interpreter, as his justification implies, is a particularly elusive area of sense-making when an IME is analysed without dialogism. While such assumptions are necessary and inevitable to some degree, when coupled with a divergent rendition there is always the risk that a misunderstood or partially misunderstood element of a narrative will be built on and elaborated by an interlocular, without their knowing that another interlocutor has developed a different understanding (see Chapter 5). In Chapter 6, I recommend that interpreters be taught the essentials of dialogism theory to provide them with the conceptual tools needed to mitigate this problem.

Excerpt 7: 'he corrected this matter'

In Excerpt 7, the lawyer revisits the backstory of the applicant. In a previous turn (turn 57, in Excerpt 5), the applicant corrected a piece of information for the lawyer: the girl he pursued a relationship with was the sister of the girlfriend of his cousin, not her friend. In turn turn 119 below, while reading the backstory of the applicant, the lawyer notices in his older notes that the information corrected in turn 57 had already been corrected by the applicant in a previous IME between him and the applicant. He declares this to the applicant. The interpreter makes a 'reduced' rendition of this original. He reduces 'goed' ('good') and 'trouwens' ('by the way'). Generally, dropping discourse markers like these in translation can lead to a loss of important discourse structure and subtle social cues. This might make the talk appear more abrupt, alter the perceived tone and affect the flow of ideas. These markers also help regulate politeness and engagement, so their omission could make the speaker seem less responsive or overly direct. As a result, the hearer may misunderstand the speaker's intent, miss key transitions or perceive the talk as more formal or rigid than intended, and lose some of the pragmatic nuances that guide interpretation.

What makes the interpreter reduce these utterances? The recorded and transcribed text does not provide us with direct clues. It is impossible to determine purely from the textual material what led the interpreter to make these reductions. Several factors related to the inherent nature of interpreting could have influenced this decision, such as the immediate and real-time nature of interpreting, the unfolding and dynamic nature of discourse, or memory limitations. Perhaps a combination of these, or other contextual factors, like cognitive load, time pressure or an attempt to streamline communication, led to these reductions.

While these reductions may seem minor or inconsequential at first glance, they carry the potential for deeper misunderstandings. As detailed above and in Chapter 2, these discrepancies – however minor – can inadvertently lead to a skewed representation of the original message, which may serve as grounds for the rejection of an application. Therefore, it is essential to consider not just the content of what is said but also how the delivery, including discourse markers and nuances, can affect the outcome.

Excerpt 7

119 Lawyer: ok (…) °goed° Jah ik zie trouwens dat ik in de correcties en aanvullingen had ik dat al gecorrigeerd (.) dat het niet om de vriendin ging (.) maar om de zus.
Lawyer: Ok (…) °good° yeah by the way I see in the Corrections and Additions that I already had corrected that (.) that it was not about a girlfriend (.) but about her sister.

120 المترجم: هو (.) شايف هون (.) في التصحيحات والإضافات (.) انّو صلّح هالموضوع (.) انّو مو رفيقتا (.) وانّما اختا.
Interpreter: He (.) sees here (.) in the Corrections and Additions (.) that he corrected this matter (.) that it's not her girlfriend (.) but her sister.

121 اللاجى: اختا صح
Immigrant: her sister correct

When I asked about the translation choice in the reflective interview shown in Excerpt 7, the interpreter did indicate that, with specific reference to these examples (at the time of the post-IME interview), he was not certain anymore as to why he made the reduction. He thought that, at that point, he must have thought that they could be 'neglected' because they were considered not important in the utterance. He went on, however, to remark on his practice in general of adapting his interpretation approach to certain settings (see Section 5.5.4). As Chapter 4 will show, however, in dialogism nothing is unimportant during sense-making. Every piece of information influences how sense-making and meaning-making are shaped, as the interpreter himself said.

Excerpt 8: 'several weeks after this thing (.) there was no contact'

In Excerpt 8, the lawyer is still recounting the backstory according to the information he has in his files, which again is his second interactional goal during the IME (see Section 3.2.1). As mentioned in Section 3.1.1, the lawyer expects the applicant to either confirm this information or to correct and/or complement it. In the rendition in this excerpt the interpreter produces an expansion with the adverbial بعد هالموضوع (ba ad hal mawdo; '*after* this thing'). Generally, an adverbial phrase like this serves an important linguistic function as a temporal marker. It provides context by explicitly indicating the timing of events in relation to one another, helping the listener understand that the action mentioned occurred after a specific incident. Such markers are often used to clarify the sequence of events. It is not clear why the interpreter did this. Was this marker a translation of the adverbial 'eventually'? Or was it introduced to give himself more time to think?

From a textual basis, the intervention here may seem granular, if not banal. However, the monological perspective that dominates the asylum procedure provides little to no capacity to investigate, record, or otherwise account for this (or any other) intervention by the interpreter. While such a strictly monological textual approach may register the erroneous alteration of words – depending on how much talk is recorded verbatim – a dialogical examination affords the capacity to understand what occurred here (see Chapter 5). The interpreter is not a verbal poltergeist, moving words for no apparent reason; he is an engaged and competent professional making strategic decisions, albeit under pressure. Although such interventions may appear minor or even inconsequential, their significance should not be underestimated. Even small interpreter interventions can influence legal outcomes, particularly with respect to the applicant's perceived credibility, internal consistency, and the plausibility of the account. Nevertheless, the procedural framework underpinning the asylum process largely operates as though such interventions do not exist, sustaining the fiction of interpreter neutrality that underpins decision-making practices. Where monological and textual approaches must shrug and move on, dialogical approaches can analyse and interpret the sense-making experience.

Excerpt 8

123 Lawyer: ok (..) e:mm (..) nou uiteindelijk hebben ze jullie laten gaan met een waarschuwing en heb je ook aantal weken geen contact met haar gezocht.
Lawyer: ok (..) e:mm (..) well eventually they let you go with a warning and you too did not seek to contact her for a number of weeks.

124 المترجم: وفي النِهاية أعطوكو تحذير و و و إي إي خلّوكن (.) تمشو (.) وانت لمدّة (.) عدّة أسابيع بعد ما كان في هالموضوع (.) اتصال بينك وبينا.
Interpreter: and in the end they gave you a warning and and and e e they let you (.) go away (.) and you for (.) several weeks after this thing (.) there was no contact between you and her.

125 اللاجئ: لا (.) إي ما فهمت عليك السؤال.
Immigrant: no (.) e I didn't understand you the question.

126 Interpreter: Ik zal het herhalen meneer heeft het niet begrepen.
Interpreter: I will repeat the gentleman did not understand it.

127 Lawyer: ja
Lawyer: yes

128 المترجم: بعد ما أعطوكن تحذير (.) تركوكن.
Interpreter: after they gave you a warning (.) they let you go.

129 اللاجئ: مين أعطانا تحذير؟ (..) الشرطة يعني؟
Immigrant: who gave us a warning? (..) You mean the police?

130 المترجم: إيه
Interpreter: yeah

131 اللاجئ : إيه إيه
Immigrant: yeah yeah

132 المترجم: =وبعدا (.) عدة اسابيع بعد هالحادثة (.) ما كان ما كان في إتصال.
Interpreter: = and after that (.) a number of weeks after this incident (.) there was no there was no contact.

133 اللاجئ: صح.
Immigrant: that is right.

134 Lawyer: en toen heeft ze jou opgebeld (.) en gevraagd waarom je haar niet meer wilde zien.
Lawyer: and then she phoned you up (.) and asked why you no longer wanted to see her.

135 المترجم: وبعدا هي تلفنت لك وقالت لك ليه ليه ما بدك (.) تشوفا.
Interpreter: and after that she phoned you up and said to you why why you do not want (.) to see her.

136 اللاجئ: صح.
Immigrant: correct.

Here, as in the other excerpts, it is not possible on the basis of the text alone to infer whether these expansions involved a strategy or not, or what led the interpreter make those decisions. In Section 5.2.1, we see that when requested to explain his expansion of the rendition with the adverbial بعد هالموضوع ('ba ad hal mawdo'; 'after this thing'), the interpreter indicated that he did so 'in order to make things clear for the applicant, in order to avoid questions like "when?" being asked'. The interpreter, therefore, seems to have provided context in order to empower the applicant to understand the rendition. Further analysis of the impact of this strategy on sense-making is given in Section 5.2.1, which also addresses other, similar strategies used by the interpreter. Chapter 5 explores these strategies in detail through the lens of dialogism, highlighting the interpreter's reasoning and theorisation, which provide interesting insights into the decision-making process.

Excerpt 9: 'you said people, Sir?'

In Excerpt 9, the lawyer is still revisiting the backstory of the applicant (turn 244). The interpreter does not start translating immediately. He engages in a side sequence with the lawyer. He wants to obtain information about something mentioned by the lawyer before he produces his rendition. When he gets the answer from the lawyer, without back-channelling with the applicant, the interpreter produces a rendition where the last sentence of the first original is reduced (turn 248). We cannot know exactly what happened at that point from the text alone, but it is probable that the side sequence caused the interpreter to forget the detailed structure of the lawyer's original. What would the interpreter think of this if he were told about it? When asked why he decided to take this decision (see Section 5.3.2), the interpreter claimed it يفي بالغرض ('yafi bil gharad'; 'suffices for the purpose'). This example highlights once again the formative role an interpreter can play in sense-making during an IME. The selection of translation strategies not only follows linguistic reasoning; it is shaped also by an interpreter's perceptions of both other interloculars' understanding and comprehension, and the communicative tasks at hand. This in turn explains why I call for a dialogist approach to interpreting (see Chapter 6). For, as Chapter 4 will show, all interlocutors impact and condition the processes of sense-making and meaning-making.

Excerpt 9

244 Lawyer: en mense mensen zeiden hoe (.) haal het je in je hoofd om met **die** familie e problemen te maken. De familie van (.) jouw vriendin bedoelde ze.
Lawyer: and people people said how (.) did you get it into your head to make e problems with **that** e family. <u>They meant the family (.) of your girlfriend</u>.

245 Interpreter: mensen zei u?
Interpreter: you said people, Sir?

246 Lawyer: ja de politieagenten
Lawyer: yes the police officers

247 Interpreter: o de politie.
Interpreter: oh the police.

248 المترجم: وقلّك (.) الشرطة قلّك شو: (.) كي:ف خطر ببالك انّو تعمل (.) مشكل مع هيك (.) عائلة (.) مع هدولى الناس.
Interpreter: and (.) the police said what the hell (.) how did you get it into your head to make (.) problems with such (.) a family (.) with those people.

249 اللاجئ: صح
Immigrant: correct

Excerpt 10: 'Why are you afraid of the authorities, or the regime,'

Excerpt 10, where the lawyer is busy with his third interactional goal (asking the applicant questions related to his backstory), he asks the applicant a question that is designed to elicit useful information. The interpreter produces an expanded rendition, expanding 'authorities' with 'regime' (turn 365).

However, earlier, at turn 361, the interpreter produced a substitution ('regime' is used instead of 'authorities'). This could mean that expanding 'authorities' in turn 365 with 'regime' was not a considered choice. But why would an interpreter do this? Why not just produce a close rendition? Is there a thinking process behind this? Could the interpreter have made this expansion because he perceived 'regime' as more fitting in the context, or perhaps to emphasise a political nuance he thought was important? Might the interpreter have intended to clarify or strengthen the applicant's case, even if it altered the original tone or meaning? These questions highlight the need to understand the reasoning behind such linguistic choices. The text alone does not reveal anything.

Excerpt 10

360 Lawyer: waar ben je het meeste bang voor, voor de authoriteiten,je vader of voor de familie (.) Hussein,
Lawyer: what are you afraid of the most, of the authorities, your father or of the Hussein (.) family,

361 المترجم: مين أكتر (.) ناس او جهة بتخاف عل حياتك منا؟ (.) بيَّك؟ النظام، ولا عائلة الحسين؟
Interpreter: which (.) people or party are you afraid the most of for your life? (.) your father? the regime, or the Hussein family?

362 اللاجئ: (بنبرة فاترة حزينة) والله الكلّ.
Immigrant: [*In a flat, sad tone*] Actually all of them.

363 ...

364 Lawyer: waarom ben je bang voor de authoriteiten,
Lawyer: why are you afraid of the authorities,

365 المترجم: لشو انتى خايف من السلطات، او النظام،
Interpreter: why are you afraid of the authorities, or the regime,

During the post-IME interview, the interpreter mentioned that he wanted to help the applicant understand what 'authorities' meant; he was concerned that the applicant would not understand the original term, because Syrians, according to the interpreter, generally use the word نظام ('nidham'; 'regime') instead of سلطات ('sulutaat'; 'authorities') in such contexts. Section 5.3.2, where similar examples are explored, offers intriguing insights into how the interpreter theorises and reasons through his translation choices.

Excerpt 11: 'this way they will get into trouble themselves too'

In Excerpt 11, the lawyer discusses a weak point (from his perspective) in the applicant's backstory, which, according to the lawyer, could be used by the INS against the applicant. The lawyer tries to get information from the applicant that might be used, if needed, to counter-argue claims that might be made by the INS. This represents part of the third interactional goal of the lawyer. In the excerpt, the interpreter reduces an important part of the original in which the lawyer explains why the INS might have a strong point (see the underlined part of turn 373).

Excerpt 11

373 Lawyer: .hh dat is al een belangrijk punt in je verhaal= waar de waar de IND ook op gaat **zitten** (.) van **waarom waarom** hebben die politieagenten dit gedaan, ik bedoel= ze kregen de opdrach om jou (.) **op** te pakken =want ze wisten waar je was (.) en ze laten je gewoon (.) lopen= <u>zo zullen ze **zelf** ook in problemen komen.</u>
Lawyer: .hh this is already an important point in your backstory= which which the INS will **scrutinise** (.) in the sense **why why** did those police agents did this, I mean=they were assigned to (.) arrest you=for they knew where you were (.) and they just let you (.) go=<u>this way they will get into trouble **themselves** too.</u>

374 المترجم: يعني هاي النقطة بَدها تركز عليها دائرة الهجرة والتجنيس إي الشرطة لشو عملو هوك هيك هنّى إي كانو عرفانين انت وين وجايين لعندك ومسكوك (صوت اللاجئ يُسمع قائلا «صحيح») ولو كان بدّون ايّاك كانوا أخذوك هيك ما كانوا خلّوك هيك تهرب!
Interpreter: yaʕni this point the Immigration and Naturalisation Service will concentrate on e: the police why did they do this they e knew where you were and they came to you and caught you [*Immigrant interjects: 'correct'*] and if they had wanted you they would've taken you just like that they wouldn't have let you escape so easily!

375 اللاجئ: والله .. (غير واضح) تنزل تحت تس تسمع ضرب رصاص .. (غير واضح) نقوس تهرب انت (.) ابوك عَدنا ترجع تسلم حالك.
Immigrant: well [*unintelligible*] you go down when you hear hear shots [*unintelligible*] we shoot you run away (.) we have your father later you give yourself up again.

376–377
Interpreter: Dat weet ik niet .. [*unintelligible: muddled talk.*] je gaat naar buit= je gaat naar beneden (.) en als je beschietingen hoort [*last four words are pronounced in a nonchalant manner unlike how the immigrant had talked*] dan moet je vluchten en daarna weer melden want (.) wij hebben jouw vader (.) toen ik waarom (.) naar rede vroeg e e zeiden ze e e dat ik m'n mond maar moest doen [*especially the last seven words pronounced in a flat and thinking manner*].
Interpreter: I don't know .. [*unintelligible: muddled talk.*] you go outsi= you go down (.) and if you hear shellings [*sic*] [*last four words are pronounced in a nonchalant manner unlike how the immigrant had talked*] then you must run away and then report again for (.) we have your father (.) when I why (.) informed about the reason e e they said e e that I had to shut up [*especially the last seven words pronounced in a flat and thinking manner*].

I want to know why the interpreter made this reduction and whether this was a conscious strategy on his part. There appears to be no indication in the transcribed text of the IME (see online Appendix I) that this piece of information had been mentioned earlier, which could have been why the interpreter might have felt that it was not necessary to mention it here. Looking at the structure of the utterance, however, it is possible that the complex linguistic nature of the original could have prevented the interpreter from being able to retain the reduced part. The original starts with a statement by the lawyer. Using the second person pronoun, the lawyer directs his utterance towards the applicant. He provides an evaluation of what he will say next: 'hh this is already an important point in your backstory'. Then, he changes footing and talks from the perspective of the INS.

Erving Goffman's (1981) concept of footing is important in interpreting and sociolinguistics. It highlights the dynamic roles of speakers, listeners and interpreters in communication. This framework is pertinent in asylum procedures, where these roles impact the outcomes of high-stakes encounters. Goffman delineates three primary roles:

(1) *animator* – the individual who physically articulates the words;
(2) *author* – the individual who selects or composes the words spoken;
(3) *principal* – the individual or entity whose position or beliefs are represented by the utterance.

In asylum contexts, interpreters are typically expected to function solely as animators, according to the monologic interpretation of language used by the INS. Additionally, the manner in which information is conveyed during asylum interviews – whether assertively, informatively or empathetically – can affect both the clarity of communication and the asylum-seeker's credibility. Footing also encompasses how speakers and interpreters align themselves with the dialogue's content and participants, influencing legal outcomes by affecting how statements are perceived and judged. These facets of footing illuminate the complex interplay of communication roles within asylum procedures, and emphasise the need for a nuanced understanding of these dynamics. Dialogism, the theoretical underpinning of this study, critiques this perspective and argues that all participants contribute uniquely to the interaction's dynamics and outcomes, collectively shaping the shared meaning. During each meaning-making activity, whether at the level of the utterance or of the interaction, all interlocutors shape the meaning-making, albeit in different capacities and to varying degrees.

In Excerpt 11, the interpreter changes footing by predicting that the INS will come up with a stance, which he introduces from the perspective of the INS: 'which which the INS will **scrutinise**'. Note the stressed lexical item '**scrutinise**'; arguably the accent placed on this, together with the accent placed on the lexical items '**why why**' ('**why why** did those police agents did this'), shows that he is presenting the point of view of the INS from the perspective of the INS itself. Then, the lawyer again changes footing and introduces his own point of view by saying 'I mean=....'.

Looking at the rendition, it seems that the interpreter manages to match these changes of footing. This does not mean, however, that this happened at no cost. Possibly, the change of footing required more attention from him than would have been the case if the original had been made without a change of footing. The task of the interpreter might have been made even more challenging when the applicant came in with the interjection 'right' relatively close to where the reduced part would have come. It is thus possible that the interpreter's chain of thought was interrupted with this interjection (turn 374).

The effects of this choice run into the following turns, where they seem to compound with further reductions. When the applicant takes his turn (turn 375), no trace is found of the missing part (the reduced part), which could mean that the reduction on the part of the interpreter caused him to miss that part. It is interesting to observe that when the interpreter takes a further turn, translating the response of the applicant (turn 376), he produces an expanded rendition in which he appears to add information not said by the applicant (he added 'I don't know'), but sought by the lawyer, which is the explanation the lawyer was searching for in his original (see turn 373) posed by the question: '[...] **why why** did those police agents did this [...]'. Recall (turns 375–377) that the lawyer is presenting the view of the INS and hopes to take the perspective of the applicant in the form of an explanation.

It is not entirely clear whether the interpreter made this expanded rendition because he found it difficult to produce a close rendition for linguistic reasons, or because he realised that the lawyer wanted an answer to the missing part that he by then had realised he had reduced in the previous rendition. It is not unthinkable that the interpreter at that point realised that the lawyer's question had been left unanswered, and he might have felt during the interaction that he had to compensate for the reduced part, because that would align with the 'role expectation' on the part of the lawyer. It is impossible to know from the text alone whether, during the interaction, he was aware that he made a reduced rendition; but it is possible that he later became aware that the answer sought by the lawyer had not been given yet. It is also interesting to see that the expansion he produced was made in a way that could be understood to be the answer to the question of the lawyer. This part was articulated in a vague way, possibly to prevent the applicant from knowing he was making a divergent rendition of his original as he might have thought that the applicant knew this would be in conflict with his role, in case the applicant was able understand his rendition towards the lawyer. It was possibly produced to satisfy the lawyer's need for an answer. No clear-cut reference to the lawyer's question was made. The lawyer then proceeded to another point. In terms of what the text indicates, these are all possibilities.

3.5 Conclusion

The asylum procedure is partly a process of sense-making and meaning-making. This chapter introduces examples of these processes in action during an asylum procedure, drawn from the case study that serves as the empirical element of this book and the foundation for the recommendations that follow (Chapter 6).

The excerpts from the transcript of a meeting between the asylum applicant and his legal representative, an IME, illustrate the complexities in comprehending the interpreters' translation decisions. It also examines to what extent we can observe in the transcription alone whether or not the client has understood what has been said correctly. The topics raised in this chapter are explored further in Chapter 5. Overall, I contend that the communication process during the procedure is not what it should be. Many elements of sense-making and meaning-making can remain unclear, and this raises questions about what happened during the procedure from a communication perspective. These issues necessitate re-engagement to understand what occurred during the IME. This is particularly regrettable given the vital importance of communication in assessing the credibility of the applicant's story. My analysis suggests that, in terms of the communication observed in the studied IME – namely, a source of information that forms part of the basis for the decision-making process of the INS – the asylum procedure exhibits shortcomings in its ability to record a detailed account of the talk produced and provides little to no means of investigating why the talk is produced in the manner it is.

This chapter emphasises the complexity of information exchange during these procedures, including legal consultations. It advocates for carefully handling of the communication material collected during hearings and consultations. Later in the book, I propose the introduction of reflective interviews with participants, the significance of which I will demonstrate in Chapter 5. Chapter 6 will present recommendations based on my findings, addressing all parties involved in the asylum procedure.

First, Chapter 4 will explore the theoretical underpinnings of the improved approach I propose in this book in terms of general communication patterns and their application in IMEs. I will then critique and suggest additions to Cecilia Wadensjö's influential dialogic approach, which has significantly impacted the study of IMEs.

4 Theoretical Foundations: Enhancing Understanding of Communication Practices in the Asylum Procedure

This chapter introduces advanced theoretical frameworks to address the key research questions and expand the scope of communication analysis within asylum procedures in this book. My objective is to deepen the understanding of communication dynamics in this context and to lay the groundwork for the recommendations in Chapter 6 that aim to enhance the equity of these procedures.

This chapter will introduce the innovative methodological approach used in the case study around which this book is formed. This approach extends traditional techniques by incorporating reflective interviews and other qualitative methods chosen to uncover the nuanced and often overlooked layers of meaning produced in the interactions of asylum-seekers, interpreters, legal representatives and decision-makers. By refining the analytical tools used for exploring interpreter-mediated encounters (IMEs), I aim to enhance the robustness and the reliability of both the case study's findings and the recommendations. The resulting theoretical insights can refine interpreting practices and influence policy. In particular, this chapter prepares the ground for Chapters 5 and 6, which discuss how reflective interviews can improve the fairness of asylum procedures.

4.1 Introduction: Establishing Theoretical Foundations for Interpreting in Asylum Procedures: From Contextual Insights to Practical Applications

In this chapter, I propose a comprehensive analytical framework that integrates a contemporary version of dialogism with Cecilia Wadensjö's interpreting model. The practical utility of this framework is enhanced by reflective interviews, which are considered crucial for addressing ambiguities during legal consultations and hearings in asylum procedures. The overall approach, referred to as dialogist interpreting, is built upon the theoretical insights found in this chapter as much as it is on the empirical evidence of the case study and my own professional experiences.

Section 4.2 gives an overview of advances in communication theory, centred on the contemporary critique of monologism. Accordingly, a detailed examination of dialogism, and its principles, follows in Section 4.3. Dialogism has been applied in a broad range of academic study, and so Section 4.4 focuses on the influence of dialogical approaches in interpreting studies and what they indicate about contemporary interpreting practices. Section 4.5 then amalgamates these theoretical insights, to present the framework used both to analyse the case study in Chapter 5 and to provide recommendations in Chapter 6. Section 4.6 presents the methodological considerations that shaped the case study design, and Section 4.7 concludes.

As such, this chapter not only establishes the theoretical groundwork but also acts as a bridge to practical applications, ensuring thorough and substantiated discussions on communication dynamics in asylum procedures. Indeed, the framework is essential for advocating reforms in asylum procedures, as it aligns with the central thesis that enhancing fairness and effectiveness requires a comprehensive re-evaluation of communication practices. More pointedly, the information in this chapter serves as the bedrock for the practical recommendations for procedural reform this book makes: the introduction of a reformed mindset to interpretation and communication in asylum procedures – dialogist interpretation – and advocacy for the introduction of reflective interviews as the key tool to cultivate and capitalise on this change.

4.2 Evolving Perspectives in Communication: From Monological Models to Dialogical Interaction

Until the 1990s, interpreting had been conceptualised as a 'transfer' of messages from one language to another, and interpreters as 'voiceboxes' (Davidson, 2002: 1273) or 'as "channels", which are temporarily hosting primary speakers' messages in their brains' – an approach which represents a '*monological* model of language and mind' (original emphasis) (Wadensjö, 1998: 275). In this monological approach, 'words and expressions are understood as entities with a fixed meaning' (Bot & Verrept, 2013: 119). This theorisation finds its origin in the theoretical stance towards the minds of the interlocutors as being the source where reality originates, without the other interlocutors having any share in the development of that reality. The dialogical theorisation of interpreting, represented by Wadensjö's model, by contrast, argues that the interpreter is an active participant in the interaction. Adopting this theorisation would imply accepting that the interpreter is an essential source of meaning-making and thus a full participant in the interaction. Thus, it is not surprising that Wadensjö (1998: 275) theorises interpreting as an 'interaction between participants in a social event'. By doing so, she theorises reality as a co-construction between the mind of the individual and the 'outer world'.

This is why the unit of analysis is not interpreting or the interpreter themselves, as would be the case if a monologic theorisation was adopted: it is the IME in its entirety. By adopting this approach, Wadensjö emphasises not only the relevance of the individuals participating in the interaction in meaning-making but also the importance of the context in which the interaction takes place.

As innovative and influential as it has been, however, Wadensjö's framework is not without its areas of weakness. Notably, within her theorisation, less attention is given to incorporating pre-encounter knowledge. This is probably because her primary interest is in how meaning is made during the interaction at a turn-by-turn level and on the level of the interaction as a whole. Among other things, she aims in her work to show that the interpreter is an active member of the encounter, which challenges earlier theorisations. I argue that this also explains why other important dialogical notions such as intersubjectivity and alterity (discussed in Section 4.3.2.2) have not featured prominently in her work.

The fact that Wadensjö did not put emphasis on problematising communicative capabilities and the interrelated knowledge of the non-Swedish-speaking participants in her study, as this was not one of her primary research aims, is one reason why she might have chosen not to engage prominently with the concept of alterity. In this book, the notions of alterity and intersubjectivity are foregrounded because I want to problematise the communicative skills and the interrelated knowledge of the asylum applicant and to show their influence on sense-making during the IME, on the part of both the applicant and the interpreter. Wadensjö's work was instrumental to the development of this case study and the conclusions that will be drawn from it in Chapter 6. Both Wadensjö's framework and the theoretical approach I have developed from it require a thorough theoretical underpinning, which is the topic of the following section. Therein, dialogism, a core component of Wadensjö's model, will be explored in depth through an analysis of its constituent sub-concepts.

4.3 Introducing Dialogism: A Foundational Framework for Understanding Interaction in Asylum Procedures

This section introduces key concepts from the theory of dialogism. Where possible, I will connect this theory to the case study.

Per Linell, whose works significantly influence this book, defines dialogism as a foundational theoretical approach that highlights the inherently dialogical nature of human sense-making. According to Linell, understanding, miscommunication, communication and cognition are fundamentally social and interactive, characterised by continuous, dynamic exchanges between individuals and their sociocultural environments (Linell, 2009: 13–15). This perspective serves as a counterpoint to traditional monological frameworks that largely view thought and language as isolated individual activities. In Chapters 1, 2 and 3, I discussed how monologism predominates in asylum procedures, explored the reasons for its prevalence and identified its associated flaws.

Dialogism emphasises the importance of interaction and the presence of 'the other' in all communicative and cognitive processes (Linell, 2009: 13–15). It underscores the role of semiotic mediation, positing that meaning-making occurs through symbols and signs embedded within cultural and social contexts. This approach considers human cognition to be deeply intertwined with, and influenced by, the environment and social interactions, thereby positioning it as action-based and context-dependent, rather than purely an internal, individual function.

This expansive and integrative view of human cognitive and communicative activities aligns with the work of Mikhail Bakhtin and other scholars that promotes the concept of language and thought as socially constructed entities (Linell, 2009: 13–16). Linell extends these ideas by suggesting that dialogism provides a crucial foundation for addressing various domains of human activity, including linguistics, psychology and social interactions. He advocates for a perspective that views meaning as co-constructed within communicative contexts (Linell, 2009). His works aligns also with how meaning and sense are made during the asylum procedure.

Dialogism is 'not one coherent school, or theory' (Linell, 2003: 2). Scholars from different disciplines and research traditions have contributed to it. I have chosen Linell's (2009) representation of dialogism for this study because of its comprehensiveness and its utility in understanding how sense-making and meaning-making occur during the asylum procedure. Linell brings together many understandings of how dialogism works. His approach also has practical benefits, as it provides the tools necessary to collect and analyse the data needed to address research questions like those of the present study.

In their review of Linell's 2009 *Rethinking Language, Mind, and World Dialogically*, Lourenço *et al.* (2013: 421) argue that it contributes to the 'unification of an entanglement of different dialogical theories and perspectives, crafting a solid meta-theory', which offers 'an integrated view upon the many strands of dialogism, establishing itself as an essential reference to the field'. Gillespie (2010: 463) even thinks that Linell's book 'consolidates dialogism as a distinctive, synthetic, and fruitful paradigm'. Linell (2009: xvii) adopts a more modest tone and simply states that his book is 'a general overview of dialogical theories of human sense-making'. In his Series Editor's Introduction to Linell's book, Jaan Valsiner says that it is important 'because it leads to generalized knowledge about ways the dialogical ways of thinking are organized. From that general perspective, various constructions of usable knowledge in different contexts can be derived by the readers' (Linell, 2009: xxii). Despite this acclaim in the field, adopting the work of Linell as a theoretical basis brings challenges as well as opportunities. On the one hand, Linell brings different views on dialogism together, which is helpful for researchers. On the other hand, it is difficult to trace the development of thinking about the concepts and notions the theory involves. As Linel deals with a significant number of concepts that apply to this study, I will only briefly review the relevant aspects of each. To understand dialogism, Linell compares it to monologism, the theory utilised by the Dutch Immigration and Naturalisation Service (INS) (see Chapter 2).

4.3.1 Dialogism as a counter-theory to monologism

In his endeavour to theorise sense-making according to the dialogical perspective, Linell (2009) contrasts dialogism to monologism. According to Linell, the constituent theories of monologism are:

> [...] the information processing model of cognition, the transfer model of communication (communication is a transfer of messages from senders to recipients), and the code model of language (language consists of static signs, i.e., stable combinations of expressions and fixed meanings). We might add to this a theory of contexts as external to language, language use, thinking and communication. (Linell, 2009: 36)

Dialogism is considered a counter-theory of monologism, monologism being part of a 'written language bias' (Linell, 1982: 1). Linell provides a view that other scholars accept. For example, in their review of Linell's book, Lourenço *et al.* (2013) do not propose a different understanding of monologism. They also agree with Linell's dialogical definition of meaning-making as being 'constructed in the dynamics of interaction and properly accounting for its contextuality and historicity' (Lourenço *et al.*, 2013: 424). Meaning-making is part of sense-making, and 'sense-making' is the *overall* concept within dialogism. Human beings seek to make sense of the world, and during the process of sense-making they engage in meaning-making, during which interlocutors can understand each other or miscommunicate. According to Lourenço *et al.* (2013: 424), in monologism, meaning-making is viewed as a 'process that takes place in the encapsulated mind of the individual, not accounting [for] the variables mentioned before like time and context'. The views of Linell and Lourenço *et al.* converge in this respect.

The difference between monologism and dialogism is significant both on ontological and epistemological levels. From the ontological point of view, monologism views reality as perceived by individuals as something that is created in the individual's mind by the individual himself/herself. It is born in the mind and already been formed by the individual concerned when expressed. The world outside this individual's mind (including other individuals) does not play a role in creating this reality beyond providing the material, as it were, for this act of perception to take place. This is also how the INS theorises the utterances of asylum-seekers, or at least how their utterances are treated. The asylum-seekers alone are responsible for the text that is entextualised during the asylum application procedure.

In contrast, dialogists theorise (and thus conceive) reality as an entity that does not exist prior to the sense-making process. It develops in the individual's mind during this process. Put alternatively, 'monologism relies on two absolutely sovereign authorities when it comes to determining the nature of the world, the individual perceiver/thinker and the collective norm of understanding. As such there is no place for the "other" that is so central for dialogists' (Linell, personal communication 2019). The constituents of dialogism which contribute to meaning-making during the process of sense-making are the internal dialogues in the minds of the interacting individuals (cognition or thinking) and the 'outer world', encompassing the communication in which the individuals engage during their situated interaction and *situation-transcending knowledge/resources* (STK/Rs). In the context of the present study, this made it crucial for me to ask the interlocutors not only about their interactions with the 'outer world' – that is, the individuals they were conversing with – but also about their thoughts during the recorded IME. They were able to incorporate their STK/Rs into their answers. I will henceforth use the more readily understood term *pre-encounter knowledge* rather than STK/Rs.

Internal dialogue is understood as taking place in the individual's mind. Linell (2009: 119) elaborates: '[a] person's thinking is largely *internal* dialogue, and can often be thought of as arguing with oneself [...]. The existence of internal dialogues is dependent on prior experiences of interpersonal ("external") dialogues'. In this study, I engage with the internal dialogue of both the applicant and the interpreter. During the reflective interviews, I posed questions that prompted them to reflect on how they understood each utterance during the recorded IME (in the case of the applicant) and to consider why they made specific translation decisions (in the case of the interpreter). For a comprehensive understanding of dialogism, it is essential to grasp what Linell refers to as its 'assumptions' and what Lourenço and his co-authors describe as its theoretical 'principles'.

4.3.2 Dialogism: Core concepts and practical applications

In this section and its subsections, I explore the core concepts of dialogism, which are pivotal for understanding how interlocutors communicate during the legal consultations that underpin this study, as well as how asylum-seekers communicate throughout the asylum process. Dialogism provides insights into the processes of sense-making and meaning-making, relevant not only to asylum procedures but to all human interactions.

A key application of dialogism in this study is the use of reflective interviews. I will discuss how these interviews should be conducted to maximise understanding and effectiveness.

In their review of Linell's work (2009), Lourenço *et al.* (2013: 422) state that the meta-theory of dialogism implies 'a perception of reality as built by the relation between the human being and the world that surrounds it', and so dialogism 'stands out by looking at reality as neither being something enclosured in the human mind (as centred on the ego) or something that exists exclusively on the outer world (as diluted in the context)'.

Here as well, Lourenço *et al.* (2013) agree with Linell's (2009) theorisation of dialogism. Moreover Lourenço *et al.* mention that to understand dialogism, its basic assumptions/principles must be understood. These theoretical and epistemological assumptions/principles, which together constitute dialogism according to Linell (2009: 11), concern 'human action, communication and cognition' and also 'language and languaging, knowledge about the world, interventions into the apprehended world, and in general: human sense-making'. When dialogism is adopted, these assumptions/principles are applied for the 'explanation of human action and language use in real mundane life' and for underpinning the empirical description of them (Linell, 2009: 11). One of the assumptions of dialogism is that the human mind is a sense-making system.

4.3.2.1 The social mind in dialogism: Interaction, context and collective sense-making

According to Linell (2009), dialogism theorises the human mind from the perspective of 'action' (followed by 'interaction'); that is the mind is not viewed as a sort of 'machine' responsible for sense-making – a criticism which has been levelled against monologism by a number of scholars (including, for example, Bakhtin and his 'circle'). In the case study, sense-making and/or meaning-making are not simply completed when, for instance, the interpreter has made a translation (action). The other interlocutor (such as the applicant) must engage with it (interaction) before meaning is fully established. In other words, the lawyer and his interlocutors do not create meaning in isolation from each other.

Dialogism theorises that meaning is created through the process of interaction between the individual, others and the world (Linell, 2009: 12). In the present study, the 'world' encompasses the context of the legal consultation and every other aspect of the asylum procedure. The parties to this interaction do not operate in isolation. The INS, the procedural framework and other aspects of their lives, both past and present, play a significant role. As such, sense is conceived to be profoundly interactive and contextual (Linell, 2009: 12). While sense-making involves an action taking place in the mind of an individual (for instance the lawyer), the mind is just one part of the sense-making system, with 'others' (the interlocutors present) and the world being the other parts. It is worth mentioning that 'others' (also called *Alter*) do not have to be other human beings but can be anything with which the mind interacts within a certain context. In the case study, 'the other' could even be the recording device placed on the table during the consultation (in which I was not present). It is possible that the interlocutors 'interacted' with the device, insofar as it could have influenced how they made sense of the utterances during the consultation (see Section 4.6). These concepts of interactionism and contextualism are other assumptions which I will deal with below. To summarise, then, by *other* I mean not only the interlocutor in a situated event, but absent others, hypothetical (imagined) others (third parties of different sorts), groups, communities, norms of language, 'super-addressees' (Bakhtin, 1986) and so on.

This conception of sense-making suggests that the proponents of dialogism (e.g. Marková, Rommetveit and Valsiner among others) consider the human mind as 'social', in the sense that it is not an autonomously working system; rather, the human mind interacts with the minds of the other individual(s) present in the situated context and with the world. The term 'social mind' is used metaphorically to explain how the mind is understood to function during the process of sense-making (Valsiner & Van der Veer, 2000). Every product of the mind is considered the result of an interaction between the individual's mind, the mind of the other and the world in which the individual lives. This also applies when the interaction involves only the world, such as when an interlocutor is contemplating a question they want to ask. Meaning is seen as a joint construction between an individual's vision of the world and the visions of the others who are (or have been) interacting with him/her. So what each individual says/thinks is a joint construction. Linell (2009: 95) adds to this at least one constituent, namely collective culture(s) – in the present context, the Syrian Arab and Dutch cultures. To enable this joint construction, characteristics of the world itself are needed (Lourenço *et al.*, 2013: 422). These characteristics are not only physical world but also the knowledge which individuals have of the world. In the present study, the pre-encounter knowledge of all three interlocutors shapes the interaction at hand during the consultation. Lourenço *et al.* here echo the vision of Clowes (2007: 94), cited in Linell (2009: 12): 'insofar as there are such things as internal mental states that can be ascribed symbolic content, they exist and have that content only because they derive it from social and prototypically public interactions'.

4.3.2.2 Intersubjectivity and alterity in dialogism: Navigating the complexities of meaning-making

The next assumptions/principles of dialogism to consider are intersubjectivity and alterity. As a dialogist, Linell deals with the assumption of intersubjectivity as part of (or related to) the notion of other-orientedness (or 'orientation'). The latter refers to the interrelation between interlocutors during the process of meaning-making, in the study context, during the consultation. That is, in dialogism, meaning is made collectively by interlocutors during the interaction, and interlocutors are dependent on each other during this process. Unlike monologism, which forces one to choose between subjectivism and objectivism, dialogism concentrates on the other-orientation, which presupposes a different theorisation of reality. Dialogism theorises meaning-making (made during the consultation) from the perspective that the 'individual mind [of any attendee] evolves in constant interaction with others [the other attendees]' (Linell, 2009: 80). In this regard, Dufva (2004: 140) states that it is this interaction with the other that enables us 'to see wholes instead of fragmented and separate individual realities'. During the consultation, this means that the perspectives of, say, the applicant would be complemented by those of the INS and other attendees. As a result, all parties will come to hear and understand the views of others involved in the asylum procedure, leading them to re-evaluate their own thinking. Dufva and Linell seem to have the same theoretical position on this.

However, individuals taking part in an interaction have not only complementary perspectives but also differences which arise during the interaction (see Chapter 5). As Linell surmises, 'Other-orientedness has thus two sides: commonality and sharedness with others, and difference from others' (2009: 81). In the present context, such a commonality and sharedness is when, say, the applicant agrees with the INS, and a difference is when he does not agree with it. 'Commonality and sharedness with others' refers to *intersubjectivity* while 'difference from others' to *alterity*. These two concept feature prominently in my study and will be examined in relation to many of the examples in Chapter 5.

When individuals interact, they can be understood to generally assume intersubjectivity with each other, and the other parties make an effort to achieve this intersubjectivity (Rommetveit, 1974: 56): 'intersubjectivity must be taken for granted in order to be achieved'. The applicant must assume that he and the lawyer are aligned, collaboratively working towards a satisfactory conclusion of the consultation. However, they are also arguably aware of the differences, or alterity, between them. The lawyer and the applicant know that they do not possess the same knowledge or share the same cultural background. Alterity implies 'difference, multiplicity of meanings and opinions, open-endedness and unfinalizability', while intersubjectivity 'tends toward unity, closure, consensus and possibly and ultimately, by extension, even monologization' (Linell, 2009: 81). This goes for cross-cultural encounters too. For example, the case study is an encounter where the participants are meant to cooperate to achieve a mutual goal; however, the interlocutors know there is alterity between them. The interpreter is not called in without a reason. The point which needs to be made here is that Linell does not, as far as I have been able to ascertain, devote much attention to the fact that there are degrees to alterity and intersubjectivity in daily life. This is strange, as interlocutors vary in their tendency towards intersubjectivity or alterity depending on many variables that are found in daily interactions. I will now consider the notions of intersubjectivity and alterity in more depth, and explain their relevance to this study.

First, as has been pointed out in the discussion of the first assumption/ principle, the role of the other is important in the process of sense-making, a conviction which is accepted by all dialogists. In dialogism, generally, *intersubjectivity* is a term that is used to refer to the interrelationship of communicating individuals, during a consultation for example, with regard to cooperating communicatively during a social event, a consultation, with the aim of making sense of the world, that is, the material under discussion and the asylum procedure. Dialogism gives the 'other' an important role with regard to the 'acquisition of knowledge' (Lourenço *et al.*, 2013: 423) during the sense-making process, knowledge being what the interlocutors during such a legal consultation come to learn. Linell considers intersubjectivity a 'defining property of communication' (2009: 81) during interactions, such as consultations and hearing.

According to Clark (1996: 92–120), in order to be able to communicate, interlocutors have to have some knowledge they share, as well as some common assumptions and commitments (here, that the parties to the consultation have to agree that the applicant must be helped with his procedure). This opinion is shared by Rommetveit (1974: 56): without a shared basis, communication is very difficult, if not impossible. If the applicant wanted to go back to his homeland whereas the lawyer wanted to make the INS grant protection, the consultation might lead to nowhere. Again, the human mind does not produce ideas or generate knowledge as an autonomously working machine: it needs the other, the other interlocutor, in the process of sense-making. Put alternatively, the other is the 'main important source of information and of communication' needed by the human mind, making it logical that the mind is seen as a 'social mechanism' (Lourenço *et al.*, 2013: 423). Marková (2000: 419) refers to this when she describes a thought as a social product that have come into being during the social process of meaning-making. This means that what the individual knows/learns is a joint product between that individual and the 'outer world'. For this social process, the other, that is, another interlocutor, is needed, and as noted by Clark (1996) above, in order to be able to communicate interlocutors have to have some knowledge they share, alongside some common assumptions and commitments.

In this study I am particularly interested in ascertaining how much knowledge the interlocutors in the legal consultation share or do not share, and how this impacts the outcome. The 'other' is an essential factor in the process of communication: 'When we are in contact with the world we communicate and at the same time we elaborate thoughts. Our thoughts are a form of communication' (Lourenço *et al.*, 2013: 423).

In this study I am interested to know how the thought of the applicant developed during the interaction, especially in those instances where the material discussed by the lawyer was challenging. I am curious about the process that produced this 'social product'. This might explain why meetings and other social events sometimes take a longer (or a shorter) time than anticipated. In such meetings, people consider the perspective of the other and reformulate their own thinking, perhaps with new ideas. It also explains why intersubjectivity is so important with regard to communication. Rommetveit (1974: 56), working in 'social' social psychology (i.e. social psychology with a very strong sociological orientation), mentions that if intersubjectivity were not taken for granted at least at some level, interlocutors would find it extremely difficult to communicate at all.

Many scholars stress intersubjectivity as an important concept with regard to how meaning is made from the perspective of dialogism. For example, according to Graumann (1990: 111) and Marková *et al.* (2007: 21), Schutz, a social scientist who also worked in the tradition of 'social-social psychology', emphasised that reciprocity of perspectives is important. According to Linell (2009: 82), Schutz and Rommetveit consider intersubjectivity to have priority over alterity, a view which is discussed below. If it were the other way round, communication would be very difficult under any circumstances. However, Schutz does mention that 'socially shared knowledge is far from totally socially shared' (Linell, 2009: 82); in the present context, the lawyer and the applicant have very different backgrounds. Marková *et al.* (2007: 21) agree: '[T]his is to be expected because people have different biographies, experiences, and knowledge, and these differences amount to distances among people'. According to Linell (2009: 82), Rommetveit also refers to this 'differentiated knowledge', and he stresses that 'different individuals and groups have different amounts of shares, and not all shares are of the same value'. Perhaps reflecting this insight, in his later work Rommetveit seems to prefer, in relation to the process of sense-making, the concept of 'co-authorship' to that of intersubjectivity (Linell, 2009: 82), as it stresses the importance and relevance of the different perceptions of reality of different interlocutors. As shown, intersubjectivity does not mean that there is a linear relationship between the parties involved in an interaction; in Linell's words (2009: 81), because 'intersubjectivity is necessarily partial', it is important to discuss and incorporate the notion of alterity in the current study.

Second, the concept of *alterity* 'implies that the other often comes with a perspective on things talked about that is different from oneself's [*sic*] own' (Linell, 2009: 82). In the case study, the knowledge backgrounds of the lawyer and the applicant are vastly different, as mentioned to me by both. When individuals interact, in addition to the properties related to intersubjectivity discussed above, discourse is characterised by 'strains and tensions, differences between people and traditions, boundaries between communities (and reaching across these boundaries), knowledge, norms and expectations at variance', according to Linell's interpretation of Marková (2003: 103), with whom he agrees. In this study I was particularly interested in this notion for, as the consultation progressed, the applicant kept feeding 'correct' at places when the material afforded by the lawyer and translated by the interpreter was either dense or unclear. It is important to mention here that alterity is not theorised as a negative aspect of communication as much as a complementary feature of discourse. Quoting from Bakhtin (1981: 314), Linell mentions that 'this dialogic tension [...] permits authorial intentions to be realized'. This means that the 'tensions evoke thoughts in the self' (Linell, 2009: 83). Thus, alterity can be considered an essential component of talk during interactions. Alterity enriches communication rather than jeopardising it. Linell (2009) also noted that people do not always communicate in order to arrive at a common understanding: they often do it in order to find out what the differences are between them.

This theorisation opens up opportunities to study the talk utilised in immigration settings. While it would be a mistake to put too much emphasis on intersubjectivity and thus over-associate this discourse with 'consensus, communion and equality' (Linell, 2009: 85), the notion of alterity, which provides 'space for differences of perspectives and opinions, asymmetries and argumentation, competition and conflict, as well as misunderstandings and misalignments' (Linell, 2009: 85), can be very helpful when borne in mind during the analysis of immigration discourse. Many of the features mentioned characterise the discourse in immigration settings due to the differences in language and culture between the interacting individuals and the challenging nature of legal language for lay people. It is important to see how interpreters address these differences.

Furthermore, many of the meetings of immigration lawyers with their clients concern reports authored by the INS or a judicial entity. Often, these discussions are characterised by conflicting views of the INS and the applicant. Lawyers may want to contrast the opinions of the INS with those of the applicant in order to be able to defend the interests of the latter and rather than seeing these conflicting views as negative they think the difference 'brings in a "surplus" of vision, knowledge and understanding' (Linell, 2009: 83). The INS or the lawyer 'may see things from points-of-view that have so far been strange or unfamiliar' (Linell, 2009: 83). Furthermore, '[t]he other's discourse may function as a counterpoint, and [give] the individual opportunities for integration of others' knowledge' (Linell, 2009: 83). This is why the lawyer holds the meeting in the case study. He aims to confront the applicant with the opinion of the INS, as seen throughout the transcribed encounter. He will later write to the INS or the judge, giving the point of view of the applicant.

An interpreter often mediates these immigration encounters. Some misunderstandings will inevitably arise, perhaps due to cultural differences. In an interview with Ingrid Josephs, Rommetveit stated that 'in the most fruitful dialogues novel ideas emerge as a result of fruitful misunderstandings' (Josephs, 1998: 200). Approaching talk-in-interaction with a strong awareness of alterity can help identify such misunderstandings.

The notions of alterity and intersubjectivity are studied in the context of interacting with people. This brings me to the next assumption of dialogism: *interactionism*.

4.3.2.3 Interaction and cognition in dialogism

During the asylum procedure, interacting with the other is crucial for all parties. For the INS and the lawyer, interaction is necessary in order to understand the applicant's narrative of escape. Asylum-seekers (come to) know that they have to narrate their narrative in a way that satisfies the requirements of the potential country of asylum (PCA). They do this by interacting with a caseworker. I do not agree with the manner in which the INS understands communication (see Chapter 2) and instead use dialogism, which is a more modern, scholarly theorisation of how human beings interact during interactions in general and in asylum procedures.

In their review of Linell's book (2009), Lourenço *et al.* (2013: 423) argue that the 'construction of meaning is dependent on the interconnection with others, looking at both communication and cognition as interactional processes of knowledge acquisition'. Linell's view (2009) is compatible with this, and he mentions that '[one] difference between communication and cognition is that the former, by definition, involves *interaction*, especially interpersonal interaction' (original emphasis). Thus, one of dialogism's central assumptions/principles is that the sense-making involves interaction. When people communicate and think, during the sense-making process, they interact with others, sometimes on two levels, the communicative and the cognitive level, but sometimes only on the cognitive level. The others do not have to b human beings, as mentioned earlier, but can be 'other persons, other systems, other dimensions of one's self, others through texts and additional types of artifacts with "inscriptions", etc.' (Linell, 2009: 14).

Thinking (cognition), unlike communication, is not normally considered to involve interaction with the world, but from the perspective of dialogism, it does, 'albeit not always directly (i.e., not in each and every moment) with other human beings' (Linell, 2009: 14). Lourenço *et al.* (2013) do not offer any different views on this.

Potter (1998: 35) observes that discursive psychology, 'rather than treating cognition as prior to, and separable from, interaction', treats cognition 'as something that is managed in, constituted in, and constructed in interaction'. Linell and Potter seem to agree on this matter; the former, commenting on the latter, says that '[t]hinking is indeed (largely) "managed in, constituted in, and constructed in" languaging and semiotic processes' (Linell, 2009: 15). However, Linell makes the point that in dialogism, unlike in Potter's discursive psychology, interaction is not considered only in the sense of 'talk and publicly observable, external behavior' (Linell, 2009: 15), because people 'simply do not disclose everything they think'. I take the side of Linell (2009) because, as shown in Chapter 5, the interlocutor (the applicant) keeps many aspects of interaction to himself. In dialogism, thinking is theorised as being inseparable from the process of interaction, even if this interaction is not observable to others. Thinking takes shape during this interaction, when it is influenced by the other during the interdependent process of communication, and it influences the other during the same process.

4.3.2.4 Contextualism in dialogism: The role of dynamic contexts in sense-making

The assumption/principle of contextualism is about how knowledge is acquired and how it is 'interdependent' on the context (Lourenço *et al.*, 2013: 423) in which the interaction takes place. The asylum hearings and legal consultation occur in the specific context of the home country of the asylum-seeker and those of the PCA and the situated context. During the reflective interviews, the participants repeatedly referred to context in shaping how they understood a meaning or chose to communicate. Undoubtedly, context is central to dialogism in relation to sense-making. Linell, whose position on this matches that of Lourenço *et al.*, says that 'sense-making processes and situated discourse are *always* interdependent with contexts' (Linell, 2009: 16). Unlike in monologism, in the theory of dialogism contexts are important, a 'universal property' of the practices in which they are seen, and are dynamic, in the sense that they, like situations, 'dynamically change with the participants' communicative and cognitive activities' (Linell, 2009: 16). Contexts (as imagined) may be changed through interaction itself.

Affirming Linell (2009), Lourenço *et al.* (2013: 423) state that context is also a 'resource' used in sense-making. In dialogism, reality is theorised not only from the perspective of the individual taking part in the sense-making process but also takes into account 'the elements that are provided by this same reality' (Lourenço *et al.*, 2013: 423) that is being made sense of. These elements are related to the situated context. It is not only the situated context which is important, but also the general context in which an interaction takes place. In the setting of this study, context thus refers not only to the situated context, that is, the IME, but also the entire asylum procedure. This last will be discussed in more depth later on in this chapter.

One of the distinctions Linell (2009) makes regarding the types of context relevant to this study is the distinction between '*realized contexts*', which are those '*actually made communicatively relevant* by participants in situ' and '*contextual resources*', which refer to 'various meaningful phenomena which are (in one way or another) accessible and could potentially be made relevant' during the interaction (Linell, 2009: 16; all italics original). In this study, the first type would represent the 'material' which is made relevant during the IME, while the second would represent the 'material' which is there and which could be used during the interaction – for example, information which involves past events related to asylum. Regarding this type of context, Linell argues that it 'come[s] to life only when actively oriented to *in situ*' (2009: 17). While I agree with this, not all aspects of this type of context are retrievable, even if actively oriented to, during the IME – for example, the private material that is what the applicant thinks of the interpreter or the lawyer, or information regarding previous, relevant asylum-related events which the applicant wants to keep private.

Another scholar who expresses the importance of context in relation to understanding communication is the interactional sociolinguist John J. Gumperz (see Davitti, 2012). In his work *Discourse Strategies*, which addresses discourse analysis, he describes contextualisation as a process through which interlocutors in a conversation selectively emphasise certain aspects of their background knowledge to make them relevant, while simultaneously diminishing the importance of other aspects (Gumperz, 1982). It is important to be aware of these 'cues' when interactions like the IME are analysed. They can give interesting insights regarding how interlocutors understand what is being said and how they engage in meaning-making. However, in immigration settings, the interpreter and the applicant do not usually entirely share the same culture, even if they speak the same language, namely Arabic in this study.

Lourenço *et al.* (2013: 320) mention that although the 'image that we get of reality is constructed through the relationship with others and the use of language as a semiotic mediator', 'some elements that are taken into this construction exist in fact in the outer world'. Linell (2009: 54) stated that such elements involve information that individuals take with them into an interaction which belongs to traditions (see the discussion of double dialogicality in Section 4.3.2.10). Therefore, because there are different individuals with different histories and personal biographies, for sense-making to take place, the individuals who are in the process of sense-making need to communicate with one another. This brings us to the following assumption/principle of dialogism: communicative constructionism.

4.3.2.5 Communicative constructionism: Social co-construction of meaning in dialogism

Communicative constructionism deals with the social nature of sense-making. As mentioned earlier, meaning-making is not a process where interlocutors have ready-made thoughts which they simply share. Thoughts are co-constructed during the process of meaning-making. In the data collected during the reflective interviews, the participants regularly mentioned that they understood something because the other interlocutors had or had not said something; that is, they did not make meaning on their own, apart from the other interlocutors. On this level, the asylum hearings and the consultation are no different from any other daily interaction. Each interlocutor has a share in the development of these thoughts. In dialogism, the cognition of each interlocutor does not simply 'copy, reproduce or reflect a pre-given extra-discursive reality' (Linell, 2009: 19). Lourenço *et al.* (2013: 423) say that meaning-making is a shared activity in which individuals communicate using semiotic means, such that dialogism theorises reality as being there, 'outside the individual but [...] also built through communication with others'. Meaning is thus actively co-constructed by individuals in making sense of the world. According to Linell (2009: 19), the 'meaning of discourse and texts is (partly) accomplished in and through the active and formative sense-making which is part of the linguistic, cognitive and communicative processes themselves'. Arguably, it is more logical to say that these processes are constituents of the process of sense-making because, as Linell himself argues in his book repeatedly, sense is made of the world in relation to the interrelatedness of the human mind (cognition), the other (whom we communicate with using semiotic means) and the world. In the case study, the human mind is that of each individual during the hearing/consultation and the other interlocutor(s). Sense-making cannot take place if one of these interrelated processes is missing. Therefore, these processes and sense-making can be said to be interrelated.

Communicative constructionism concerns 'intersubjective co-construction with the help of others and artifacts' (Linell, 2009: 19). This stresses again the interdependence of the individuals in the process of sense-making. Thus, during the consultation the interlocutors construct meaning and make sense collectively. The individuals do not engage in sense-making in isolation from the outer world, or only with the other but, rather, do so also in relation to the situated context and the *pre-encounter knowledge*, that is, the sociocultural knowledge the person has (see below). In this case study, the interlocutors kept referring to past experiences and knowledge when explaining an 'action' on their part.

4.3.2.6 The complexity of meaning-making in interpreter-mediated encounters: A dialogical perspective

Above, the central assumptions/principles of dialogism have been introduced and evaluated. In the following sections, I will discuss the notions of 'meaning' and 'understanding' (and other interrelated notions). Meaning-making and understanding are central concepts to communication during the hearings and legal consultations in the case study. Assessing the credibility of the asylum account engages actively with these concepts.

Wadensjö (1998: 280), whose theoretical model draws heavily on dialogism, mentions that '[i]t goes without saying that interpreter-mediated interaction involves a certain lack of shared understanding'.

This lack could be large or small, depending on the applicant's aptitude in the language of the host country, and the content of the material dealt with during the IME. This lack of shared understanding is the fundamental reason why interpreters are called in. They are 'by definition placed in a position of promoting the primary interlocutors' mutual understanding' (Wadensjö, 1998: 280) in addition to solving translation problems (Roy, 2000: 31). However, this does not guarantee that the desired understanding takes place. Therefore, the second research question in this study is about investigating understanding on the part of the applicant (see Section 3.1.1). Understanding, or the lack of it, are not straightforward processes but are in fact rather complex. Understanding is not a stand-alone notion that can be addressed independently, as claimed by monologism. Dialogism addresses understanding differently, and its conception hinges on a number of ideas explored in this section.

In order to bring 'the cognitive revolution' back to its 'original impulse' and away from the 'computational metaphor', Bruner, a dialogist who works in the cultural psychology tradition, calls for returning to the 'central concept' of human psychology, which is '*meaning* and the processes and transactions involved in the construction of meanings' (Bruner, 1990: 33; original emphasis). Linell (2009), building on this, calls for the adoption of a new theory for the notions of meaning and understanding. He proposes a move away from the traditional monological approach to sense-making, according to which meaning is an entity which is born in the mind of the individual and belongs entirely to them (Linell, 2009: 221). According to this theorisation, other individuals/interlocutors have no share in producing meaning. The approach proposed by Linell is dialogism, which in its pursuit of understanding meaning does not draw on concepts that are used in the extreme cognitive paradigm (Bruner, 1990), such as 'stimuli and responses', or 'overtly observable behaviour'. These concepts would be used if a monological theorisation were adopted. Rather, dialogism adopts a 'theory of action', as it is called by Linell, whereby meaning is theorised by looking at the actions of the participants ('agents, or persons'), who are essential in the process of meaning-making (Linell, 2009: 221).

As mentioned earlier, in dialogism, unlike in monologism, meaning does not belong to one single individual nor necessarily to one single language system, that is, it is not made only by one individual; rather, it is co-constructed as a joint effort by interacting individuals. During this process, individuals act and interact (among other things with each other); and it is during these interrelated actions between individuals that meaning is co-constructed. This means that when individuals participate in a communicative event, meaning is made by an action on the part of an individual and a response to it on the part of the other individual (Wadensjö, 1998; Linell, 2009) in addition to orientation to cultural norms, or *situation-transcendence* (see, for example, Linell, 2009).

The process of meaning-making involves cognition (thinking) and communication. These 'involve interventions in the world, engaging with the world' (Linell, 2009: 221). Individuals intervene *in* the world (in a concrete situation) by performing an 'action'. This action is a 'semantic-pragmatic function of language and communication', as Linell says (2009: 221). Unlike in monologism, this action is not considered as a 'representation of the world' in dialogism (2009: 221), that is, the action is not given the status of an independent entity. Therefore, when this action has been performed, meaning has not been made yet. For meaning to come into being, another individual must react to this action. The individual has thus to engage *with* the world, that is (among other things) with another individual. To reiterate, individuals also communicate with non-humans (artefacts and norms, which can be regarded as abstract artefacts) in the process of sense-making.

Thus, from the perspective of dialogism, the action of an individual is not decisive in the process of meaning-making. Generally, when *action* is heard, *interaction* comes to mind (Linell, 2009: 221). When individuals interact, they achieve communication by interacting with each other. The *inter-acts* in which they are involved are the communicative acts by which they respond to and anticipate positionings by the other during conversations. Every basic action, with its content, performed by any individual is permeated by other-orientation (Linell, 2009: 221–222). Instead of communicative acts, monologists would talk about individual 'speech acts' (Searle, 1969; Birner, 2013).

The process of meaning-making involves at least two individuals engaging with each other communicatively (the role of *traditions* is left out here temporarily). There is internal dialogue too. During these interactions meaning is co-constructed. Meanings are not a phenomenon which is there, and which belongs to the individual, because the other individuals in the interaction also share it. The fact that meaning is made through interaction and that the one individual is dependent on the other in interaction during the process of meaning-making does not mean that agency in dialogical theory is downgraded – dialogical theory does not 'disavow the agency of the individual' (Linell, 2009: 222). By introducing the notion of co-construction with regard to meaning-making, dialogism, on the one hand, relieves a single individual of being ascribed sole responsibility for the production of meaning, while, on the other hand, it empowers the other individual, as they also take part in the co-construction of meaning. Similarly, researchers of talk-in-interaction (such as myself) are empowered. Instead of attempting to 'read' the mind of the individual, dialogism makes their task more realistic, as they can explore the manifest actions and interactions of the individuals involved. Meaning is easier to reconstruct by investigating the actions and interactions of those involved.

Theorising 'actions' from the perspective of dialogism, Linell states that they 'must be meant and understood' (Linell, 2009: 222). This statement, although somewhat obscure, can be interpreted to represent a basic theoretical assumption made to account for the efforts individuals make to understand meaning. Actions *can* be understood but there are no guarantees they always are. This explains why dialogism theorises misunderstanding. Linell (2009: 222) also states that '[m]eaning and understanding are absolutely central concepts in a dialogical approach to the world'. No reference is made to misunderstanding here, but I believe that it is implied. Bartlett, a dialogist working in the cultural psychology tradition, has a similar opinion to that of Linell regarding the importance of meaning and understanding. He considers 'every human cognitive reaction – perceiving, imaging, remembering, thinking and reasoning – as an *effort after meaning*' (Bartlett, 1932: 44, original emphasis). People want to understand.

As dialogism is about sense-making, Linell could not but address the notion of *understanding*. He states that '[i]f meaning is linked to action and interaction, the same applies to *understanding*' and '[u]nderstanding is closely linked to responding to situations and utterances' (Linell, 2009: 222, original emphasis), meaning that people try to make sense of/understand these situations and utterances. He follows this by saying that understanding 'involves being able to cope with situations, carrying out tasks, being able to explain and account for various subject matters, etc.' It is noticeable here that the abilities referred to are articulated in a way which suggests that misunderstanding/miscommunication automatically means the opposite, though this does not have to be the case, and in fact miscommunication is an essential part of sense-making.

Linell underlines that understanding is needed only for current practical purposes. Wadensjö clarifies this point: 'interlocutors engage in achieving *sufficient understanding of current activity*' (Wadensjö, 1998: 200, original emphasis). Sufficient understanding is needed for us 'so we can go on with our current doings' (Linell, 2009: 222). However, in some situations partial understanding is not sufficient for us to 'go on with our current doings'. Communication in talk-in-interaction can carry on without sufficient understanding having taken place on the part of one (or more) of the interlocutors of the meanings that is being negotiated, or even when parts of the communicative acts performed are miscommunicated, as seen in this study (see Chapter 5). Misunderstanding can take place on a local level (related to some communicative acts) or on a global level (related to large parts of the talk-in-interaction) (Wadensjö, 1998). It is time now to address the notion of understanding in more depth, illuminating its nature as theorised in dialogism.

As noted earlier, unlike monologism, which theorises meaning as a phenomenon encapsulated in an individual's mind, dialogism perceives meaning as being the result of situated communicative actions and interactions performed by individuals (Linell, 2009: 222). The semiotic resources of the language used during such interactions do not carry meaning per se; they carry *meaning potentials* (Linell, 2009: 222). Some of these semiotic resources are words. In her endeavour to develop a theoretical model for interpreting, Wadensjö (1998) affirms the view of Linell and other dialogists such as Bakhtin regarding this, and likewise explicitly states that these semiotic resources carry meaning potentials rather than meaning. Therefore interlocutors have a task to do when they interact.

When people enter a communicative situation, they try to make sense of it. In so doing, they influence and are influenced by the other individuals in that interaction. During the process of sense-making, when producing an utterance, speakers 'afford material for making sense' (Linell, 2009: 222); that is, they provide clues, linguistic and/or non-linguistic, which can be taken up by the participating individuals to make sense of what was said. This material is meant to guide 'the interlocutors in their efforts after meaning and interpretation' (Linell, 2009: 222). This material carries meaning potentials, which means that sense-making is not totally dependent for its creation on the speaker. The receiving interlocutor also contributes to sense-making by his or her 'uptake and interpretation, made manifest in his or her following utterance(s), that counts in the interaction as the communicated meaning' (Linell, 2009: 222).

The response shown by the 'receiving' interlocutor does not necessarily show understanding of the utterance voiced by the 'providing' interlocutor even when a sign of assent is made. An interlocutor *may* have misunderstood even though they give a verbal sign that they have understood it, as seen in this study (see Chapters 3 and 5). This tells us that the 'communicated meaning' could be perceived differently by the receiving and the producing interlocutors. We need to 'understand' how understanding is determined.

Sense-making is, as noted, a dialogical process. While contributing to meaning, interlocutors show how they understand each other's utterances; they thus 'interact' with the 'action' of their interlocutor. Therefore, it can be said that understanding is shown during the process of meaning-making when interlocutors try to make sense of the material which is provided by the 'other'. It is not only the speaker who determines meaning: 'the utterance is nothing more than a selection proposal, a suggestion' (Luhmann, 1995: 139). The listener also contributes to it by responding: 'that the listener contributes to meaning is a consequence of the responsivity permeating understanding' (Linell, 2009: 223). To reinforce his point, Linell (2009: 223) refers to the following statement by Bakhtin:

> Any understanding of live speech, a live utterance, is inherently responsive, although the degree of this activity varies extremely. Any understanding is imbued with response and necessarily elicits it in one form or another: the listener becomes the speaker. (Bakhtin, 1986: 68)

Due to the centrality of the notion of understanding in this study, it is necessary to contextualise the discussion of this concept as it is employed in this book. Sense-making is not always about understanding. Miscommunications can also take place, because the 'material' provided by each interlocutor does not hold meanings but only potential meanings. The information or messages conveyed by each interlocutor do not possess fixed meanings but hold multiple potential meanings that depend on the interpretation of the listener. Because of this variability, the possibility arises for misinterpretation or misunderstanding. Miscommunication is where the listener's interpretation differs from what the speaker intended to convey. Therefore, the interactions between interlocutors, such as an applicant and an interpreter, need careful examination to ensure that the meanings inferred are accurate. As such, the interactions of the applicant with the actions of the interpreter need to be problematised. By this I mean that although the interpreter is seen as empowered in this study, it is inevitable that he will sometimes misunderstand 'interactions' (the counterpart of the 'actions') made by the applicant. This makes it essential to check, where possible, whether the interpreter has inferred a meaning that is not based on a correct interpretation of the applicant's interactions. The applicant, too, can select potential meanings not meant/intended by the interpreter, as shown in Chapter 5. When responses are not what the speaker would wish or expect, the speaker may find it difficult to know whether the listener has understood the action (i.e. the speaker's utterance) or they may think the listener has when that is not the case. This very situation arose in this study (see Chapter 5).

The two central notions in Bakhtin's interpretation of 'understanding *in situ*' are: responding and anticipation (Linell, 2009: 223): 'When a listener attends to an utterance, especially if he is the addressee expected to respond in the following moment, he understands the utterance itself partly by anticipating what his response might be'. When listeners are passive or economical in their responses (like the applicant in this study), it becomes very difficult to reconstruct how they understood the speaker unless they are asked about this. In this study, the interpreter did not do this, leaving the matter of understanding ambiguous and underexplored. However the study's interview stage illustrates that (mis)understanding is a recoverable phenomenon.

4.3.2.7 Nature of talk in dialogism: Implicitness, vagueness and the dynamics of understanding

Meaning-making and sense-making are closely related to *talk*. A lot takes place during talk, during INS hearings and legal consultations, as in daily life. This section will discuss the characteristics of the domain of talk. This will help us further understand how sense-making develops and how the very nature of talk influences meaning-making during the asylum procedure. I will start with *implicitness*.

According to Linell (2009), not everything individuals want to say can be said explicitly. This happens a lot in the case study. Many assumptions, understandings and miscommunications remained under the surface of the IME (see Chapter 5). Further, unlike in monologism, in dialogism it is not claimed that utterances, which are constituents of talk, hold meaning. Rather, utterances 'prompt' individuals to make meaning. As such, the utterances produced by the speaker can be understood only when the context is known (Linell, 2009: 224). Thus, language itself can be understood as a tool that guides individuals to make meaning and to understand it. The fact that language is incomplete results in meanings being difficult to follow and understandings difficult to infer, unless the utterances are put in context. Context, then, serves as a guide through the jungle of possible meanings, to understand the situated meaning of an utterance, also called 'contextual meaning' (Wadensjö, 1998: 153). This entails that a 'considerable part of meaning in interaction is therefore *inferred*, implicit rather than explicitly expressed' (Linell, 2009: 224). This also features prominently in the case study. For instance, very often the applicant would say 'I assumed he meant' this or that. In light of these fundamental mechanics of language, which are made evident through dialogical approaches and obscured by monological approaches, it becomes clear that the manner in which a person conceives language has the ability to directly influence the outcome of communicative events. Accordingly, the choice of monological approaches among asylum institutions can, at the very least, be considered as having an active role in shaping the outcome of asylum applications – something at odds with the notion that an application succeeds or fails on the objective merits of the case itself.

In the simplest case, some information needed to make sense is not explicitly mentioned by speakers. Rather, the context in which the utterance is made is utilised by the listener to infer the possible meaning(s) aimed at by the speaker. According to Bakhtin (1981: xix), a 'unitary language is not something that is given, but is in its very essence something that must be posited'. The interlocutor engages in a task that they need to resolve. This is because, as mentioned earlier, the words of which utterances consist of do not hold meanings that are stable and permanent (but hold, instead, potential meanings). In this study, for example, the applicant would say 'when the interpreter said [...] I assumed he meant [...]', when in fact the lawyer had said something else through the interpreter. The listener/interlocutor becomes the speaker in the process of attempting to make sense of what is said, while responding to it in the process of meaning-making. By doing so, the speaker 'attributes sense to a word', or the words an utterance consists of (Wadensjö, 1998: 39) in the sense that their understanding of it is shown. Thus, when the speaker uses a word, they use it the way they understand it, they populate it with their own sense of it. This reflects the view of Bakhtin that understanding an utterance is a task *posited* and that interlocutors do not decode the talk of the other interlocutor in a mechanical way. Even then, as I show in this study, when something is said by a speaker it does not necessarily mean it reflects what the speaker thinks or understands. The applicant's utterance 'correct', often seen in the case study, does not necessarily mean that the applicant has understood and agrees with what had been said. His internal dialogue could still hold meanings that were not shown and did not reflect what the word 'correct' would normally indicate (see Chapter 5).

There are varying levels of difficulty in understanding and making sense of an utterance. The degree of difficulty of the task posited will depend (among other things) on the speaker's attitude regarding how they need/want to be understood by the listener. This will be dealt with in more depth in Section 4.5.1 because of its importance to this study. Linell (2009: 224), citing Rommetveit (1974), states:

> We assume [as interlocutors of an encounter] that we share a lot of knowledge and assumptions, which remain implicit or unquestioned in most communicative encounters. It would be unpractical, tedious and often mutually face-threatening if we were to make all our assumptions explicit; we are simply 'supposed to know' a lot in advance; intersubjectivity is taken for granted.

Some knowledge is certainly assumed in asylum contexts but much less than in many other contexts, because in cross-cultural meetings one of the interlocutors does not speak the language (well) and does not have (enough) legal knowledge. Further, especially early on, the asylum procedure is usually explained in detail because the applicant is expected to know little about it. This decreases with the passage of time because the applicant is supposed by then to have heard the information. Another point that needs to be addressed is that while attempting to prepare for the legal procedure, lawyers may choose to withhold some information from the applicant until the applicant has answered a question asked by the lawyer regarding their backstory, to avoid influencing what the applicant says. This illustrates Linell's insight that the amount of information displayed in utterances differs in different situations (Linell, 2009: 224), which is a manifestation of talk's characteristic of implicitness.

Another key characteristic of talk is its *vagueness*. According to Linell (2009: 226), '[i]mplicitness is also related to vagueness. There is normally a considerable amount of vagueness in normal language use'. The speaker cannot always be expected to be clear. The speaker cannot anticipate everything that is not known to the other interlocutors, and which needs to be mentioned. To do so would be impossible, and so talk is inevitably sometimes vague, but this is not necessarily unwelcome. Suchman (1987: 27), taking an anthropological approach to human action and communication, mentions that 'the prescriptive significance of intentions for situated actions is inherently vague'. Potter and Te Molder (2005: 29) underline in their book *Conversation and Cognition* Suchman's point of view:

> This vagueness is not a flaw when compared with full specification; rather the vagueness is precisely what makes plans useful for their projective and reconstructive tasks – they can be applied to an indefinite number of situations in deft and locally specific ways.

Thus, often, vagueness cannot be (entirely) anticipated. However, interlocutors generally expect that the listener will demand an explanation. For this reason, in asylum settings, applicants are expected to indicate that they need further explanation when they do not understand something, due to lack of background information and/or the complexity of legal discourse. However, the reality is sometimes more complex. What if, for instance, the applicant has miscommunicated the issue under discussion and thinks he *does* understand the rendition (as occurred in this study)? What if the applicant wrongly assumes that an interlocutor meant something? This is why I favour conducting interviews with the applicant when notions of meaning and understanding are dealt with, that is, when the topic of the study is sense-making. There are other situations where vagueness can be utilised from a strategic point of view. In immigration settings for instance, the lawyer may try to make the applicant release information to him without influencing the quality of that information or altering its content.

Ambiguity can also be related to implicitness (Wadensjö, 1998: 223). When a word is ambiguous (i.e. it can be interpreted in different ways), it can cause miscommunication on the utterance level. The speaker cannot be expected to be able, under all circumstances, to anticipate possible ambiguity. This also justifies conducting an interview with the applicant.

The individual participants in a situated interaction cannot fully anticipate what will be said by the other, and what they themselves will end up having said during this interaction. They are dependent on the other interlocutors in co-constructing meaning. Rommetveit (1974: 50–51) states that situated understandings are partially shared. They come into being dialogically, in a fragmentary way. This stance is shared by Wadensjö (1998). This partial and fragmentary nature of understanding makes us work with understanding 'for current (practical) purposes' (Linell, 2009: 226) and individuals must be 'content with understanding each other sufficiently well in order to proceed further in their communication or other current doings' (2009: 39). Wittgenstein (1953: 158), who worked on the philosophy of language, was one of the dialogists who took this stance. He linked situated understanding to the idea that 'Now I at least have a clue how to go on'. But what does this mean, exactly? It is as if interlocutors have a milestone by which to gauge these understandings and that they choose to stop understanding when the 'current (practical) purpose' does not require further understanding. I argue that interlocutors are, rather, thought to do their best to understand until they understand enough for 'current (practical) purposes' (Linell, 2009: 226). However, they can also choose not to stop engaging with further understandings on the basis that a better understanding is required of something. For example, the interlocutor can include a new dimension in the discussion and ask for a response to it.

Linell (2009) relates the notion of 'understanding each other sufficiently well' 'for current (practical) purposes' to the notion of 'difference that makes a difference', which is used by Bateson (1972: 99). This is to say, difference 'makes it possible to communicate something; it is the necessary prerequisite and product of movement and dialogue' (Linell, 2009: 84). However, interlocutors do not always interact with a practical purpose in mind, for example when the listener wants a piece of information for an unrelated subject. Interactions can also progress without that understanding being even partially achieved. The speaker may proceed knowing, or perhaps not knowing, that the interlocutor has not understood.

4.3.2.8 Miscommunication: Dialogical perspective on understanding and misunderstanding

Unlike monological theories of communication, which often associate misunderstandings only with the recipients of the utterance(s) (i.e. the listeners are assumed to have not understood what the speaker means, see: Linell, 2009: 227), in dialogism, misunderstanding is theorised as miscommunication, implying that misunderstanding is a 'joint' product between the interlocutors, as Wadensjö says (1998: 228). It has repeatedly been shown in empirical studies of misunderstandings in talk-in-interaction that miscommunication is generated 'collectively and reciprocally' (Linell, 2009: 228); Wadensjö (1998: 198) agrees with this, which is to be expected as she has stressed the benefits of dialogism for interpreting studies. According to Linell (2009: 228), miscommunications are often the:

> [...] products of the intricate interaction of participants' interpretations of various contextual affordances and of *each other's utterances*. When parties build new utterances, they sometimes exploit different parts of the semantic-pragmatic affordances of self's and other's prior utterances [...].

I argue that these contextual affordances can be related to the context of the interaction, but they can also be related to knowledge that was learned in prior interactions with the same interlocutors or with other interlocutors as I will show in Chapter 5. In asylum settings, the affordances exploited in a courtroom, for example, could be used later during an interaction with a lawyer. When the meaning learned in a previous context does not match the meaning in a situated context, miscommunications can take place (see also the discussion on *situation-transcending resources*, referred to as *pre-encounter knowledge* in this book in Section 4.3.2.9, and double dialogicality in Section 4.3.2.10).

Linell (2009: 228) states that '[m]iscommunication often involve [*sic*] mismatches of participants' purposes and situation definitions; it is not just utterances in themselves that can be "misunderstood," but rather utterances in relation to framing assumptions and expectations' (commas in original). I argue that these assumptions can relate to the role of the interpreter, that of the lawyer, etc. or simply to what has been said or not. 'Hence, miscommunication is dialogically generated and accomplished, in several respects' (Linell, 2009: 228). Wadensjö (1998) refers extensively to this. She introduces the useful analytical tool 'trouble sources' to account for those elements that cause miscommunication. This tool is adopted in this study.

Expanding on the notion of understanding, Linell (2009: 230) states that '[d]ialogical theories align with CA [conversation analysis] in regarding responses as embodying interpretations of prior contributions'. Yet, he argues, the contributions overtly shown in public discourse do not comprise all aspects of the understandings (or misunderstandings) of individuals: '[p]arties to communication conceal a good deal of those understandings, which are presumably present in their "internal dialogues"' (Linell, 2009: 230). I argue that this is understandable as the characteristics of talk (see Section 4.3.2.7 above) cause the interlocutor not to show all their understandings. The present study adopts the position of Linell in relation to understanding. Bearing this fact in mind, I consider it an essential theoretical basis for the manner in which data needs to be collected and dealt with. Further, I argue that due to the fact that 'speakers often "claim" understanding without "demonstrating" it' (Linell, 2009: 230) and that 'internal dialogue' forms a cornerstone of dialogical theory, excluding any attempt to reconstruct the meaning from the perspective of the recipient and the speaker would be a considerable impoverishment. It is not possible to claim that private understandings, that is, ones that are not shown in discourse, could be (fully) reconstructed by interviewing the involved participants. However, I believe that under the right circumstances and given the right approach, participants could be willing to disclose (some parts of) their understanding, which is generated through internal dialogue (see the details for this in Chapter 5).

4.3.2.9 Pre-encounter knowledge: The role of sociocultural resources in meaning-making

While meaning is being constructed during situated interactions in dialogism, the interacting individuals do not only depend on the *material* (so called by Linell, 2009) provided during the interaction itself – the utterances of the lawyer and the renditions of the interpreter in this study. They also appeal to the sociocultural resources they take with them into this interaction as I will show in Chapter 5. These resources are the 'language, concepts, knowledge about the world, identities and norms, etc., which govern expectations and efforts for meaning in concrete situations' (Linell,

2009: 49). These resources belong to *traditions*, which '[…] constitute the counterpoint of "situations"' (Linell, 2009: 49). Situations refer here to the '*specific occasions* or encounters, *specified in terms of particular times and places and specific participants* (speakers and recipients)' (Linell, 2009: 49, italics original). The term 'situation transcending knowledge/resources' (STK/Rs) will not be used in this book. Instead, the more accessible term *pre-encounter knowledge* will be used to refer to the '*situation-transcending, sociocultural practices*, to which participants in situated interactions orient in producing and reproducing activity types and other routines' (Linell, 2009: 50 italics original). Situatedness and situation-transcendence can be illustrated by almost any actual utterance or sequence of utterances as '[…] sense-making is always situated, *and* it is dependent on situation-transcending resources' (2009: 51).

Thus, when individuals interact, for example in hearings or legal consultations like that found in this study, they are not entirely dependent on current social interactions in meaning-making. They also appeal to the knowledge they already have that they bring with them, which belongs to their backstory or just to their past experiences in life. This is important for the current study, since it means that it is not enough to study the discourse utilised during the 'talk-in-interaction'. But how is this information, that is pre-encounter knowledge, acquired and how it is engaged with during the IME interaction during the sense- and meaning-making processes? When an individual acquires knowledge and skills from understanding something new, this new knowledge could be used in future situations. Something then has been 'learnt', and 'the concept of "learning" is intrinsically related to trans-situational changes over time' (Linell, 2009: 230). When information is provided to individuals in a learning situation, this information is thought (meant) to be of use for future situations, '[…] where learners get opportunities to account more extensively for their understanding […]' (Linell, 2009: 231).

An element of pre-encounter knowledge that deserves particular attention in the context of asylum settings is the biographical experiences of the interlocutors. Linell (2009: 53) refers to these as the biographical experiences of the individual: 'Each person develops individual points-of-view as a result of his or her biographical experiences'. This study places importance on these points of view as they can reveal very interesting insights into meaning-making and understanding with regard to one's own responsibility and that of the other. It is important to involve these points of view in the study as they are '[…] thoroughly impregnated by social and cultural interdependences […]' (Linell, 2009: 53). Although some of these points of view (perspectives) can be taken to be views shared by many people, they are sometimes '[…] partly unique to the individual, due to his or her specific life course' (Linell, 2009: 53).

Having introduced the notion of pre-encounter knowledge, now is an appropriate point to explain how situated meanings and those related to pre-encounter knowledge relate to each other during the process of meaning-making during interactions.

4.3.2.10 Double dialogicality: The interplay of situated interaction and pre-encounter knowledge

In studies like the current one, it is important not to look at the situated interaction as if it takes place in a vacuum (Wadensjö, 1998). While they are engaging in sense-making, people depend not only on materials that are purely related to the situated interaction but also resort to materials that belong to pre-encounter knowledge. Thus, during these interactions, each individual engages in two dialogues, an external one with the interlocutor(s) and an internal one, during which they engage with their own previous knowledge. Linell calls this process 'double dialogicality', and says it refers:

> [...] in the terms of Nystrand (1992), to the combination of interactionism and social (i.e., sociohistorical) constructionism. In and through communicative and cognitive activities, there is dialogue within both situations and traditions; participants in the activities in question engage in both situated interaction and sociocultural praxis. In one sense, the situated interaction (with its internal dialogue) and the various situation-transcending aspects [...] are features of the same comprehensive communicative project performed there-and-then [...]. (Linell, 2009: 52)

These two dialogues are part of the same interaction, that is, the parties interact with each other *in situ* and they orient to non-local aspects of the activity (situation-transcending aspects – pre-encounter knowledge); both orientations are part of the same physical activity. The situation-transcending aspects are 'non-local' in the sense that they have been established over a period that often stretches far back into socio-cultural history. Note that non-local aspects of this knowledge must be made locally relevant in the situated activity, or else they are simply irrelevant and ignored.

The concept of double dialogicality is useful in the analysis of discourse in asylum contexts. As has been shown in Chapter 2, the asylum process often entails engaging in numerous meetings with the representatives of various institutions. For instance, lawyers hold meetings with their clients with the aim of strengthening their legal position. The interlocutors engage in a discussion that addresses situational issues related not only to the context of the situated meeting but often also to life in their homeland. Individuals participating in the interaction do not involve themselves in such interactions 'empty-handed'; they take with them the knowledge they have acquired prior to the situated interaction. Both the situated meanings and the meanings related to the homeland are, then, dealt with in the internal dialogues of the participants. For example, when an applicant meets their lawyer, they will have very often heard parts of the information being discussed during earlier meetings. This means that in addition to the situated interaction, the interaction is also influenced by pre-encounter knowledge.

4.3.3 Summary of dialogical principles

In this section, I have discussed notions related to the theory of dialogism, which accounts for how meaning-making develops during interactions. This detailed account provides the theoretical grounding necessary for a comprehensive understanding of the theoretical approach adopted in the case study and the recommendations derived therefrom. This section serves as a crucial bridge between the introduction to theoretical foundations presented in Sections 4.1 and 4.2 and the subsequent application of dialogism in interpreting studies, particularly in its integration with Cecilia Wadensjö's theoretical model in Section 4.5.

It may be surmised, then, that dialogism is not merely as a single theory but a meta-theoretical perspective, particularly drawing on the work of Per Linell, who synthesises various strands of dialogical theories. The contrast between dialogism and monologism is crucial to the message of this book. Unlike monologism, dialogism underscores the dynamic and interactive nature of communication in IMEs.

Key concepts from dialogism, such as sense-making, intersubjectivity, alterity and contextualism, are foundational to the case study analysis in Chapter 5. These ideas are not merely theoretical but are deeply connected to the practical concerns of interpreting, particularly in high-stakes contexts like asylum procedures. As explored in Chapter 2, the design of asylum procedures, both in the studied context and more broadly across the Global North, does not account for these dialogical concepts and principles, but is underpinned by an inherently monological theorisation of language. This leads to a failure to account for numerous dynamics at play in IMEs, many of which have a direct (and rectifiable) impact on asylum procedures in terms of their success as a communicative, sense-making exercise.

4.4 Developments in Interpreting Studies

A better understanding of interpreters' work will lead to better outcomes. To this end, this section presents a brief overview of some of the more recent advances in interpreting studies, an academic field which has benefited greatly from the advances presented by dialogism and also the field in which this book seeks to make its core contribution. This has been reflected both implicitly and explicitly as the field of interpreting has developed. As the example of asylum procedures in this study shows, reforming practice through integration of these advances in theory holds the prospect of tangible improvements for interpreters and service users alike, as well as improved outcomes for communicative events that involve interpretation. The following sections explore this dimension of contemporary thought, with a view to highlighting the basis on which the recommendations in Chapter 6 are made.

4.4.1 Impact of insufficient understanding of the interpreter's work

A recurring theme in research in interpreting studies has been the unintended influence of interpreters can exert, often surpassing what end-users might expect or desire. For instance, Berk-Seligson (1989), in her study on Spanish–English bilingual police interrogations, observed that interpreters sometimes unintentionally altered a suspect's statement, influencing perceptions of guilt or innocence. I contend that if all involved parties truly understood sense-making and meaning-making, such undesired outcomes might be avoided. Users of interpreting services would know better what an interpreter does and interpreters would be less likely to make such 'mistakes'. In Berk-Seligson's context, the judiciary, by understanding the mutual influence of each party's contributions, would have been better equipped to support the interpreter.

Similarly, Reynolds (2020b) reported that lawyers found their authority 'moderated' by the interpreters. However, this moderation might not have occurred if the lawyers' and the interpreters' perspectives were grounded in the principles of dialogism. A thorough understanding of dialogism would have helped all parties to recognise their roles and counteract any undesired interventions from others. Smith-Khan (2017a, 2017b, 2017c, 2020) underscores this point. Had the lawyers in Smith-Khan's studies been well versed in sense-making and meaning-making, they would have been better positioned to ensure that interpreters did not undertake roles or tasks deemed to be the lawyers' sole prerogative, such as providing summaries, making unsolicited comments or engaging in side-discussions. Furthermore, the interpreters would likely have refrained from such interventions if they were more informed about the sense-making and meaning-making inherent to dialogism.

Xu (2020) conducted an observational study on 17 telephone-interpreted lawyer–client interviews in New South Wales, Australia, and examined the interactional management approaches of lawyers and interpreters when working together remotely. Her study yielded mixed results regarding interpreters' compliance with their code of ethics. While most interpreters followed normative practices, such as using standard first-person pronouns, there were many instances where interpreters assumed additional roles. The prevalence of these actions was attributed to insufficient training and credentials, and I would add that the challenging nature of remote interpreting, such as the absence of visual elements, may lead interpreters to act in ways they would not if they were physically present.

Interpreter visibility has been an important theme in interpreting studies for years. While this concept was more pronounced in research before dialogical theories gained prominence, its relevance has not diminished. Often, this visibility pertains to the interpreter's actions deemed unexpected or possibly unacceptable. In dialogism, visibility is not about the unexpected or unwanted. Instead, it refers to actions initiated by any participant within the IME. All interlocutors can opt to be visible or remain in the background. Here, the interpreter is considered one of the interlocutors, but this does not imply that all participants hold equal sway in the interaction. It is widely acknowledged that some users of interpreting services prefer (or even require) their interpreter to remain as inconspicuous as possible. While medical services, for example, might deem it acceptable for an interpreter to be 'visible', in other sectors, like the police, asylum institutions such as the INS and the judiciary, interpreters might be perceived as excessively visible if they do not translate in the first person or if they engage in side-conversations with one of the participants during the IME.

In the study by Xu (2020), interpreters primarily provided interpretations in the first person. However, the interpreter in my research either used the pronoun 'we' or left the pronoun unspecified. In Xu's study, interpreters occasionally interrupted their interpretation to facilitate communication. By doing so, they became 'visible' participants in the interaction, producing 'non-renditions', common in telephone interpreting, as noted by Xu (2020). Such visibility was not prevalent in my research. Interpreters in Xu's study often employed non-renditions to manage interactions, such as requesting repetitions when they had difficulty hearing the client due to technical issues. However, non-renditions also surfaced when interpreters offered their commentary or engaged in side conversations with one party and then neglected to relay the information to the other party. This behaviour contradicts the Code of Ethics of the Australian Institute of Interpreters and Translators. It should also be noted that in the research by Xu (2020), although lawyers advocated for an interpreter role that is 'impartial and faithful' and disapproved of certain types of interpreter interference, such as summarisation, few lawyers questioned or prevented interpreter interference during the observed interviews. Xu cites a study by Inghilleri that examined the provision of interpreting services within the British asylum system and observed outcomes that mirrored those found by Xu (2020). Through interviews with lawyers, Inghilleri discerned that many relied on interpreters to forge rapport and trust with their clients. As a result, they became receptive to an 'expanded' interpreter role. For instance, it became permissible for interpreters to address some of the client's queries directly, bypassing the lawyers, to elucidate the intent behind interviews, or even to suggest a particular phrasing for the lawyers' enquiries.

Zhan and Zeng (2017) explored the concept of visibility and pinpointed four primary functions of medical interpreters' text ownership:

attempting to expedite conclusions, 'redirecting turns, expressing solidarity, and educating the patient'. However, despite the interpreter's text ownership being intended to facilitate communication, the research by Zhan and Zeng suggests that increased visibility can obstruct the intended communication. This supports my argument: to facilitate an effective IME, all parties should profoundly understand their specific roles. This depth of understanding is contingent upon each party grasping how their counterpart in the IME conceptualises sense-making and meaning-making.

This brief review shows that there is a gap between advances in interpretation theory and workplace practices. This should be borne in mind in the following section, which will summarise the benefits of dialogism to the practice of interpretation. While I make specific reference to asylum settings, the ideas presented may be applied in any situations that entail IMEs.

4.4.2 From dialogism to dialogist interpreting

The conceptions of interpreter role and visibility outlined above largely originate from a monological perception of language and reality that is now outdated. In a dialogist approach to interpretating, all participants are active co-constructors of meaning and the interpreter's role in IMEs is more collaborative and less invisible. This approach leads to a better understanding of the interpreter's role, and so in turn helps to ensure that IMEs are successful, and will shift the analytical focus to why the interpreter acted in a particular way and whether the IME participants agreed upon such a role distribution.

The theoretical studies combined with my own first-hand experience as an interpreter in the Netherlands and the United Kingdom over two and a half decades illustrate how the interpreter's role is now more defined than it was during the 1980s and 1990s, but nevertheless remains somewhat fluid, especially within non-scholarly and educational sectors. For example, the expectations and perceptions of an interpreter's role in a legal setting can contrast sharply with those in a medical environment.

Importantly, until the end of the 1990s in the Netherlands, there was still no clear vision regarding the role of interpreters among practitioners and agencies. Understanding of the interpreter's work was based on common sense and knowledge of translation, communication and cognitive studies. The guidelines developed by prominent interpreting agencies were based on their unique understanding of the profession and client feedback. This lack of clarity was also the case for individual interpreters. Things started to change around 2005, when the Dutch government introduced a set of rules regulating the work and responsibilities of interpreters and their agencies. Now, interpreters seem more attuned to their roles and the expectations of service providers and end-users, such as lawyers or those who do not speak Dutch. However, interpreters need to exercise a degree of discretion since every interaction and end -ser is different. The beliefs and practices of interpreters in the Netherlands largely align with these new rules, partly because they all agree with these regulations but also because adhering to them ensures they receive assignments.

This said, it must always be appreciated that the extent to which interpreters comprehend and apply the guidelines and their associated concepts remains uncertain. Concepts such as 'sense-making' and 'meaning-making', along with related ideas like 'neutrality', 'objectivity' and 'non-bias', can be ambiguous and vary across cultures, and even fundamental concepts like 'professionalism' have cultural specificity (Rudvin, 2007). This once again demonstrates the need for a process within asylum procedures that has the ability to capture contextual information pertaining to conceptions of role in an IME, translation decisions and so on. Post-IME interviews, if routinely applied (or even only in audits), would do much to achieve this aim, while simultaneously furnishing the INS and the wider research community with an invaluable data source on the inner workings of IMEs.

In summary, the fluid understanding of the role of the interpreter originates from a lack of theoretical understanding of what interpreting is and entails, particularly among service users. The foggy has impacted the practice of interpreting, leading to unrealistic expectations of interpreters. Consequently, decades after the significant shift in the theorisation of the interpreter's role (Wadensjö, 1998), it is unsurprising that there is no consensus about the role of the interpreter, especially across different professional contexts. Even now, studies on how interpreters perform their tasks pose fundamental questions about the interpreter's role and how service users react. This lack of consensus is a core obstacle to the reform envisioned by dialogical interpreting.

In Section 4.5, I will explain how we can integrate these advances in interpreting studies and the dialogical principles discussed in Section 4.3 into the theoretical model of Wadensjö. As the next section will show, Wadensjö's model suggests that she did not unpack dialogism as much as I do in this study. According to Linell (personal communication), this is because dialogism was relatively new when Wadensjö used it in her research, and especially to the concept of pre-encounter knowledge. The next section therefore presents the analytical framework at the heart of this book's core endeavour: using dialogism to unpack the sense-making process in IMEs in asylum settings and finding practical recommendations to alleviate the deficiencies in their design.

4.5 Synthesising Core Theoretical Concepts: Monologism, Dialogism and Interpreting

To round off this review of the theoretical basis of this study, I will briefly recapitulate the central notions which it sheds light on:

sense-making, *explanations* and *assumptions*. These concepts will feature prominently in Chapter 5.

In dialogism, the concept of sense-making is theorised as encompassing the communication activity between the participants in a situated interaction (including the internal dialogue), the meanings the participants attribute to the situated interaction, and the pre-encounter knowledge. The pre-encounter knowledge is the sociocultural knowledge/resources interlocutors have access to before entering an interaction and which they can utilise during the interaction. *Meaning-making*, *understanding* and *miscommunication* (of particular importance to this study) are part of *sense-making*.

Dialogism calls for the perspectives of the interlocutors to be incorporated into the analysis of how sense-making developed during a recorded IME. In this regard, I believe that if the relevant parties are requested to reflect upon what Linell (2009: 13) refers to as their 'actions' and 'interactions' during the legal consultation, and the interrelated ones of the other interlocutors, and to explain these, the results will provide insights on the interrelationship between these actions and interactions and how they evolved during the overall sense-making process.

Taking as its starting point Wadensjö's (1998) model, my study enriches the analysis of the data with the notion of explanation, understood as the explanations which the interpreter provides when he is asked about the translation decisions taken during the IME. The word 'motivation' is sometimes used with the word 'explanation'. Sometimes the two words are used interchangeably in this book. The theory of dialogism helps me to conduct reflective interviews and to interpret this motivation (the third research question – see Section 3.1.1). It also helps to engage with the applicant during the reflective interviews conducted in an attempt to see if he understood the translations (second research question).

This study, thus, takes Wadensjö's approach a step further. This is essential because, as argued by other scholars (e.g. Fairclough, 1989, 2014; Meyer, 1998), analysis of transcribed data (even if the event was attended by the researcher, as was the case with Wadensjö) does not give access to enough information to reconstruct how the sense-making process evolved (even if complemented with interviews similar to those conducted by Wadensjö). For, as will be seen in Chapter 5, the sense-making process is heavily influenced by the pre-encounter knowledge and the interrelated *assumptions* on the part of the interlocutors regarding each other as interlocutors, the setting where the encounter takes place, the legal position of the applicant and the pre-encounter knowledge of the applicant.

In Chapter 3, I demonstrated that a text-based analysis of transcribed data does not effectively address my research questions. Consequently, in this chapter, I introduce the theoretical model of Wadensjö (Section 4.2) but incorporating additional elements of dialogism to align with my research agenda.

In this section, I present my thesis on how interpreters function according to the theory of dialogism. I argue that interviewing interpreters is essential for understanding their decision-making, which in turn provides insights into how my research questions can be most effectively answered. Building on the theoretical discussions above, I will lay down the theoretical foundations for the interpretation of the study data. I argue that:

(1) how the interpreter understands his role is interrelated to the nature of the 'material' he affords to the applicant;
(2) the nature of talk in general also influences the translation decisions of the interpreter;
(3) the characteristics of the profession of interpreting also influence how these decisions are made.

4.5.1 Understanding the interpreter's role: Navigating the complexities of translation and meaning-making in dialogism

In this section, I explore the intricate relationship between the interpreter's perception of their role as the speaker and the information they provide to the listener, who is the asylum applicant in the context of the present study). The research questions (see Section 3.1.1) focused on how the interpreter, acting as the 'speaker', executed the translations and how the applicant, as the 'listener', understood these renditions.

When people (such as the interpreter in this study) enter a communicative situation, they try to make sense of it. They influence and are influenced by the other interlocutors. When producing an utterance, the speaker affords materials for sense-making that are meant to guide 'the interlocutors in their efforts after meaning and interpretation' (Linell, 2009: 222). The receiving interlocutor (the applicant in the case study) contributes to sense-making by his 'uptake and interpretation, made manifest in his or her following utterance(s), that counts in the interaction as the communicated meaning' (Linell, 2009: 222). But how does this affording of material take place and what factors are taken into consideration?

Not everything that individuals want to say can be said explicitly (see Section 4.3.2.7). Contexts are always relied on by interlocutors to understand utterances (Linell, 2009: 224). They help understand the situated contextual meaning (Wadensjö, 1998: 153). 'A considerable part of meaning in interaction is therefore *inferred*, implicit rather than explicitly expressed' (Linell, 2009: 224, original emphasis). This helps the listener by providing context for the linguistic materials he 'gives off' (Goffman, 1961: 13). Even when this context is made clear, the listener will still need to solve a task (Bakhtin, 1981: xix). The degree of difficulty of this task will depend (among other things) on the attitude of the speaker with respect to how they need to be understood by the listener. In turn, the degree to which the interpreter deals with the task posited will depend on both their understanding of their role as an interpreter and their perception of their professional responsibility towards the applicant (in the present context). These two factors help us understand in the case study how the interpreter thinks he should best translate (the strategies he employs).

4.5.2 Influence of talk on interpreter decision-making

In relation to argument (2) set out at the start of Section 4.5, the nature of talk in general also influences how the translation decisions of the interpreter come into being. Generally, not everything that individuals (the interpreter and the applicant in my study) want to say can be said explicitly (Linell, 2009: 224). Because interlocutors cannot explicitly say everything and because talk is characterised by *implicitness* and *vagueness* due to its dialogic nature (see Section 4.3.2.7), interlocutors/speakers need to make choices concerning what they will say. In addition, the individual participants in a situated interaction cannot fully anticipate what will be said by the other(s). Rommetveit (1974: 50–51) states that situated understandings are not total or complete but partial. They are also fragmentary in the sense that they crystalise during sense-making; they are dialogically constituted. Finally, they are only partially shared; not everything is said. This nature of understanding makes us work with understanding 'for current (practical) purposes' such that individuals must 'be content with understanding each other sufficiently well in order to proceed further in their communication or other current doings' (Linell, 2009: 39). This applies also to interpreting.

4.5.3 The challenge of real-time translation: Internal dialogue, memory and the pressures of interpreter-mediated encounters

A discussion of 'internal dialogue' and its reconstruction is needed at this point because the process of meaning-making, during which interlocutors deal with the 'material' within an IME, requires that the interlocutors evaluate what they will say and re-evaluate their own thinking when the other interlocutor has presented how they think. In the context of this study, when the interpreter's translation decisions are discussed, it is my goal to understand how the interpreter made these evaluations and re-evaluations in his internal dialogue.

This investigation pertains to argument (3) – the characteristics related to the profession of interpreting also influence how these decisions come into being. The interpreter is expected to work in the 'here and now', that is, interpreting happens in real-time (Mason, 2001). Unlike in written translation, the clients of the interpreter are immediately present. These clients are having a conversation with each other but do not understand each other sufficiently without the aid of the interpreter, and they need to complete this communicative event within a certain amount of time. The interpreter has to adapt to the working space and conditions as soon as possible in order to be able to perform well. The interpreter also needs (and is perhaps expected) to match the speed with which the primary parties are communicating to avoid hampering the interaction. This means that the process of making sense (the evaluation and re-evaluation of the afforded material, that is, the internal dialogue) is put to the test. The interpreter generally does not have as much time as the primary parties when it comes to dealing with the materials being discussed, nor enough time (if any time at all) to revisit the translations just made (to correct or complement them). Talk is ongoing during IMEs – it is characterised by this *immediacy*.

Unlike a translator who works with written discourses, the interpreter is expected to be able to deal with the *unfolding nature of discourse* without too much 'disruption'. Such a disruption would be a request for time to rethink or check decisions. Interpreters are expected to produce translations smoothly and immediately. This is challenging, as it requires the retention of the material afforded by the other interlocutor(s) and the interpreter's own thinking during the process of meaning-making. The *memory* of the interpreter is burdened by these two characteristics of this type of interpreting. It is important that when strategies are investigated, the influence of the nature of the profession be given the attention it deserves when the data is analysed, which I do in this study.

To conclude this description of the effect of the nature of interpreting on the IME: the lawyer renders an original and expects the interpreter to produce a translation, while the applicant is waiting for the interpreter to offer the rendition. The interpreter comes under pressure to produce the translation both accurately and without much delay. This kind of interaction is thus generally characterised by its immediacy, which puts pressure on the interpreter to translate the communicative acts of the primary parties as efficiently as possible. This has consequences for the interpreter's cognition in terms of *memory*. This is the third factor found to influence the interpreter's ability to produce the renditions in my study. The interpreter is, as it were, at 'the mercy' of (in this case) the two primary parties (Al-Rubai'i, 2009: 329).

By analysing on the interrelationships between the interpreter's role, the nature of talk and the professional demands of interpreting, it is possible to identify key factors that influence the sense-making process during IMEs. The affording material, implicitness and the immediacy of interpreting shape the interpreter's decision-making and, ultimately, the success of communication in these settings.

4.6 Methodology: Post-Encounter Interviews in Asylum Procedures

This section will describe how I collected my data. Chapter 3 included some information on this topic, in terms of the coding process and the text-based data analysis process. An understanding of the overall data collection process used in this study is beneficial not only for the academically minded reader. Rather, sharing information on how to conduct post-encounter interviews is essential to the focus of this book, as it proposes the introduction of this supplementary method of information collection to the asylum procedure, to make it more equitable. Thus, this section serves as not only a methodological guide to the case study at hand, but also as a practical exploration of how post-encounter interviews may be implemented within asylum procedures (see Chapter 6). The level of detail given for the methodological considerations is sufficient to be of use to researchers, but may not be needed by the INS and similar organisations to design and plan their use of reflective interviews.

4.6.1 From text-based analysis to dialogist interpretation: Refining methodological approaches in asylum procedures research

Inspired by Wadensjö's work, I explored various avenues to address the research questions which emerged during my initial text-based analysis (see Chapter 3). These questions stemmed from a broader research puzzle – whether the applicant had understood the translated utterances. This in turn prompted questions about what motivated the interpreter's decisions and how these two interlocutors explained their sense-making and meaning-making. As demonstrated in Chapter 3, a text-based analysis did not and could not provide that information. I found that other theoretical frameworks, such as pragmatics and conversational analysis, also did not help me. This section retraces the steps that led to the formation of my overall methodological approach.

Wadensjö's use of dialogism was an inspiration during the formation of the case study. However, in designing this study, I needed additional tools to discuss participants' actions and interactions during the recorded IMEs. I investigated contemporary work by Linell on dialogism, an earlier version of which had inspired Wadensjö's own work. I turned to Linell's book (2009), which presents contemporary tools for conducting interviews. As this chapter has explored at length, Linell's theoretical grounding proved highly relevant. The theoretical framework for interviews was necessary to complement the interactional data and examine the motivations of the interactants.

My research questions required a qualitative approach to the data. Creswell (1994: 1–2) defines qualitative research as 'an inquiry process of understanding a social or human problem, based on building a complex, holistic picture, formed with words, reporting detailed views of informants and conducted in a natural setting'. The 'problem' in the case of this study was how the interpreter renders the lawyer's originals, and how or whether the applicant understands the originals through the translations. In relation to the second and third research questions, this enquiry requires, according to dialogism, just such a 'complex, holistic picture, formed with words'. The questions require that the perspectives of the participants be ascertained in interviews to determine whether the applicant understood the originals or not and to understand the perspective of the interpreter regarding the translation decisions he had taken. Qualitative methodology privileges individuals' lived experiences and improves our understandings of the worlds of the participating individuals (Marshall & Rossman, 2014). Moreover, '[*q*]*ualitative research is inductive*' (Taylor & Bogdan, 1984: 5, original emphasis).

The investigation requires an analysis of naturally occurring data. Following Hodkinson (2016: 99), I start with observable social phenomena and, through researching and analysing naturally occurring data, build broader theories of social life. I look for 'patterns and associations derived from observations of the world' (Snape & Spencer, 2003: 23).

Stake (2000: 19) observes that case studies help us grasp human affairs and deepen our knowledge of a subject. According to Yin (2003), a case study – whether single or multiple – may serve an exploratory, descriptive, or explanatory (causal) purpose. I use a descriptive case study, which, in Yin's terms, offers a full account of a phenomenon within its context. However, I argue that fully capturing every aspect of complex social interactions is, in practice, nearly impossible, even if theoretically attainable.

Recent scholarship has illuminated the complexities of language use in legal settings, particularly in contexts involving refugees and asylum-seekers. Esteemed contributions from scholars such as Jacobs, Maryns, Reynolds and Xu have profoundly advanced our understanding of narrative management, the discursive structure of legal consultations and the active roles of interpreters. Their work provides a robust foundation for exploring the intricate dynamics of communication within asylum procedures. The present study introduces a distinct focus by delving into often-overlooked communicative aspects of asylum procedures, especially those mediated by interpreters. It highlights the internal dialogues and unvoiced informational exchanges that are pivotal yet frequently disregarded in such consultations. Employing a novel approach I term 'dialogist interpretation', my work proposes methodologies addressing these hidden layers of meaning. This approach fills a notable gap in the academic literature and offers innovative perspectives on enhancing the fairness and efficacy of asylum procedures.

By integrating the empirical case study described here with theoretical insights, my research contributes new tools and perspectives that enrich the academic, legal and policymaking landscapes engaged in migration and asylum processes. The work examines the critical interplay of language, culture and institutional practices in legal settings and advocates for more nuanced approaches to training and practice in asylum procedures.

According to Matthews and Ross (2010: 128), '[t]he subject of the case may be a person, an organisation, a situation or a country'. In the case at hand, the subject may well be considered a combination of these. In the context of interpreting and translation studies, Susam-Saraeva (2009) states 'a case is a unit of translation or interpreting-related activity, product, person, etc. [...] A case can be anything from a translated text or author, translator/interpreter, etc. to a whole translation institution or source/receiving system'. The subject of the present study is an IME that takes place between a lawyer and a client.

Yin (2003: 13) points out that the case study method is used because it includes 'contextual conditions' in the analysis, and the context is an essential part of the phenomenon under investigation. Gillham (2000: 1) provides a useful definition of 'case study' that similarly emphasises the contextual factor: it is 'a unit of human activity embedded in the real world; which can only be studied or understood in context; which exists in the here and now; that merges in with its context so that precise boundaries are difficult to draw'. It is not clear whether these writers would consider pre-encounter knowledge to be a part of the context of a case study. Nevertheless, pre-encounter knowledge is here considered an integral part of how sense is made and how it develops. As sense-making is an inherent part of the case study, pre-encounter knowledge is considered to be so too, given that sense-making (including pre-encounter knowledge) is intrinsically embedded in the context in which the phenomenon to be studied is taking place (see Section 4.3.2.9). 'Context' refers not only to the place and time in which the case is studied but is also intrinsically connected to previous contexts. When sense is made during an IME, it is interrelated with sense-making processes which the participants had previously been involved in, for example in earlier meetings. In this study, the key method for determining participants' pre-encounter knowledge was through interviews.

Susam-Sarajeva (2009: 39) states that case studies have 'close conceptual and methodological links to "ethnography", "participant observation", "fieldwork", "qualitative research" and "life history"'. The main data I collected was produced through an ethnographic instrument (interviews) and is analysed within the qualitative research paradigm, and the case study method provided me with the possibility to 'render a "true to life" picture of what people say and how they act' (Taylor & Bogdan, 1984: 124).

A salient feature of case-study methodology is its capacity to investigate a select few units of analysis in considerable depth, thereby yielding extensive data that elucidate the distinctive characteristics of each unit (Swanborn, 2010). Case studies 'focus on the whole unit of analysis per se, paying attention not to leave out any relevant detail – and certainly not those which might contradict the initial hypotheses – and also making sure that one can still see the wood through the trees' (Susam-Sarajeva, 2009: 39). Moreover, case studies engage with naturally occurring instances, offering qualitative examinations of unstructured data (Hammersley & Traianou, 2012).

Context is central to this kind of research (Duff, 2012; Gillham, 2000). Susam-Sarajeva (2009: 39) indicates that case studies focus on the 'context in which the case is embedded and which can be highly pertinent'. In Chapter 3, the context of the recorded meeting was explained, while Chapters 1 and 2 frame the wider context of asylum procedures in the Netherlands and historically. Without a good understanding of the context, the whole recorded meeting would be difficult to understand and even harder to investigate. In addition, the collected data shows that it is not the only context which influences how sense is made during the IME. For instance, the interpreter changed his translation decisions according to the context in which he does his work (see Chapters 3 and 5). His understanding of his role as an interpreter is firmly connected to the context in which he is asked to perform. Further, he expressed the view that it is important to consider the type of applicant (i.e. their socioeconomic background and education) when he produces his rendition. This is also a context which has been found to influence the process of sense-making.

Interviews are the second key methodological element of this study. Research interviews are a 'conversation that has a structure and a purpose' (Merriam & Tisdell, 2015: 107) and are an ethnographic method used to collect primary data. Arksey and Knight (1999: 33) say that the interview is a 'powerful way of helping people to make explicit things that have hitherto been implicit – to articulate their tacit perceptions, feelings and understandings'.

Interview may be structured or semi-structured, non-directive or focused, or simply informal conversations. The interview is used in this study to collect data and for triangulation purposes, where 'triangulation' is 'the combination of methodologies in the study of the same phenomenon' (Jick, 1979: 602). The interviews thus ask questions arising from the transcribed data and serve to triangulate these data. In this study I utilised semi-structured interviews. Given their centrality to the data collection, and their close connection to the procedural reform recommendations made in Chapter 6, interviews will be explored in detail in the next section.

4.6.2 Reconstructing internal dialogues: Methodological considerations in post-IME interviews

Many aspects of the methodology used in this case study reflect the rigours of academic research; for practical application by an asylum institution, much of what follows is not pertinent.

When I conducted interviews with the interpreter, I sought to enable the interpreter to reconstruct the internal dialogue he had when interpreting during the IME in order to understand how his meaning-making process had led to his particular translation strategies and decisions. The purpose of the interview was to enable the interpreter to reflect on how the investigated renditions came into being, explore if he could remember this process and to consider what led him to take particular decisions. I asked the interpreter to describe which strategy, if any, he adopted towards a certain (part of a) rendition, that is, what led him to provide the translation in that particular way. This questioning was carefully calibrated to avoid undue criticality. My status as a former refugee helped me to absorb the material discussed during the recorded interview, and similarly my own work as interpreter helped me to ask the right questions without causing the interpreter to become defensive. If the interpreter or the applicant was unable to provide an explanation due to memory constraints, I asked them to reflect on *possible reasons*.

Regarding the reliability of the data, it is not possible to guarantee that an internal dialogue has been accurately reconstructed, or that participants were telling the truth. The interpreter cannot be expected to reconstruct every aspect of his thinking with absolute precision, especially as the interview took place some three weeks after the IME. Interpreting is cognitively taxing and stresses the human capacity for retention and recall. To mitigate this factor, I played the entire IME at the start of both reflective interviews to refresh the memory of both the interviewer and the applicant. For each question about a specific rendition, I played the relevant part of the recording.

4.6.3 Semi-structured interviews: Methodological reflections and practical approaches

As noted above, there are several types of interview: structured, semi-structured, unstructured, and non-directive (Clifford *et al.*, 2016; Conway, 2014). Gray (2009: 371) states that 'the choice of interview technique will depend in large part on the aims and objectives of your research'. Semi-structured interviews make it possible to probe the way the participant perceives the world (Galletta, 2013: 51) and allow respondents to expand on their answers (Gray, 2009). They offer some flexibility regarding the manner in which the topics are dealt with. According to Nunan (1992: 149), semi-structured interviews have been widely used in applied linguistics. While they allow for control, because there is no predetermined set of questions the researcher remains free to pursue unexpected elements that emerge. Seidman (2006) advises that 90 minutes should be allowed for a semi-structured interview, and that three interviews are wanted. I do not agree with this. The key thing is to give respondents sufficient opportunity to make informed responses. A balance is needed between the goals of the study and the interests of the respondents

I followed the advice offered by Wengraf (2001: 9) that the interviewer should arrive well ahead of the scheduled time of the interview to ensure that it is conducted in a stress-free and unhurried manner. As Gray (2009: 379) suggests, before the interviews the interviewees were contacted to ask them if they were still prepared to participate, and still remembered the date, time and place. On the day of the interview, I made sure that I had everything I needed ready.

At the start of the interview, as advised by Gray (2009: 379), I provided the interviewee with an explanation of its purpose. (I had also done this on the day of the recorded IME and when the participants were contacted to consider participating in this study.) The interviewees were informed why this specific information would be collected and how it would be used, and were given the opportunity to ask questions. I ensured that the participants understood what the interview was about and used an example to show how the interview would be conducted. This was also an opportunity for me to reflect on my own functioning, in that I tried to find out whether my approach to interviewing was adequate.

The applicant was explicitly requested to indicate if he had understood something directly from Dutch, thus not via the interpreter, whether partly or completely. Whenever I sensed that that might be the case, I checked by asking the applicant.

Gray (2009: 380) states that rapport must be established with respondent during interviews. He says that '[r]apport means an understanding, one established on a basis of respect and trust between the interviewer and respondent'. He further argues that '[t]o establish a rapport it is particularly important to make the respondent relaxed and to get the interview off to a good start'. Accordingly, I explained to each participant the manner in which the interview would be conducted, how much time it was expected to take, which issues would be the focus of attention, and the areas questions would be asked about. The participants were assured that participation and recording were voluntary, and that the content of the interview would remain strictly confidential. The participants were told that they could ask questions at any point.

Following Patton (1990), I made clear at the beginning of the reflective interview why the participant was being interviewed.[1] I also explained to the applicant why he had been chosen for the interview, that is, that the initial suggestion had come from the lawyer. The interpreter had

1 I informed them about my background as a doctoral researcher and elucidated my research questions. I ensured that the participants understood that the research was not centred on them as individuals. The focus was on whether the applicant understood the translations provided by the interpreter, and on the interpreter's decision-making in translation. This information, along with other relevant details, was also provided in writing, and participants were asked to sign an informed consent form before participating in the interview, in accordance with the ethical requirements of the Ethics Committee of the University of Leeds. This information had also been conveyed when the lawyer introduced me to them, prior to recording the consultation a few weeks earlier. To avoid influencing the legal consultation that was about to commence, I refrained from discussing the research questions with the participants at that time. The recording was done in my absence, after a brief consultation between the lawyer and both the applicant and the interpreter.

immediately agreed to participate in the research. Interviewees were told that their genuine opinions were required, not opinions they thought I would like to hear. During the interview, I tried not to show any emotions (for example looking surprised) and to avoid giving hints about possible answers. I did my best not to show any sign of irritation even if there was a reason to, for example when the interviewee talked slowly and/or in a verbose way. Gray's (2009: 382) checklist of dos and don'ts of interviewing was taken into consideration.

The following sections address the practical process of approaching the participants.

4.6.4 Methodological considerations in interviewing the applicant for reconstructing interpretive decisions

Interviewing is challenging. Maxwell states that '[t]he development of good interview questions [...] requires creativity and insight, rather than a mechanical conversion of the research questions into an interview guide [...] and depends fundamentally on your understanding of the context of the research' (Maxwell, 2013: 101). Researchers with an agenda like mine cannot go to an interview with a fixed set of questions. With semi-structured interviews, 'improvisation may be the key to success' (Gray, 2009: 382). Arksey and Knight (1999) provide some tips, from which the following were adopted. The questions were varied in order 'to fit the flow of the interview'. Care was taken to make the questions sound natural by varying the phrasing and a neutral tone was used to avoid leading the participant in any particular direction. Following Gray (2009: 383), when questions were formulated, I attempted to avoid language which contained jargon or was prejudicial. I also attempted to avoid ambiguous language and leading questions.

Thus, the questions did not take one definitive and static linguistic form but depended on the context. For example, questions about the originals might be formulated as follows, in Arabic: 'What is the lawyer telling you here?', 'What did you understand here?', 'What did the lawyer want you to know here?', 'What did he want you to understand here?'

At the beginning of the interview, I asked the applicant to listen to the whole recording, in one go, without questions from me, in order to give him a chance to remember the details of the meeting. The applicant welcomed this. After this, I replayed the recording and stopped whenever I had a question. Depending on the context of each question, the part of the audio-text which the question was about was sometimes repeated, either by replaying or by reading aloud from the transcript. The choice depended partly on whether the applicant asked for the question to be repeated or not, and whether I thought this was needed.

Some of the questions were about whether the applicant knew what was meant by a specific element of the text; for example, the word 'istitna'iyya' ('exceptional') is generally not used in colloquial Arabic, but is, rather, Modern Standard Arabic. This was necessary to check whether this had influenced the understanding of the remaining parts of the utterance. Again, sometimes I would replay the audio text to ensure that the applicant had heard it well (or remembered exactly what the question was). In some cases, when I realised that the applicant had not answered correctly, I thought he should double-check to see if he really had not understood. I asked the applicant not to try to please me by giving an answer he thought I would like to hear. The applicant promised he would not do so. Then he told me that he had understood the question the way I explained it. In the second example, I tried to get the information from the applicant by asking 'wh-' questions – 'who', 'when', 'where'.

The applicant's meeting with the lawyer had been two weeks before the interview. Also, the material discussed during that meeting was largely not new. Nevertheless, the applicant did not have a legal background, and so remembering the technical legal material might have been challenging (an example is given in Section 5.2.1). Thus, when the applicant was unable to reconstruct a rendition, especially one which contained legal information, this does not necessarily mean that he did not understand it.

The process of assessing understanding was a delicate one. Every piece of information released during the interview had the potential to lead the applicant in a certain direction. Further, the information handled during the IME could have been mentioned during previous meetings with the applicant, or by the lawyer, the INS, the COA (Central Opvang Asielzoekers – Central Agency for the Reception of Asylum-Seekers) and other institutions, although from different perspectives and for different reasons.

During the interview with the applicant, it was deemed unreasonable to present questions in a direct or standard way, such as 'How do you understand this?' Rather, I needed to be creative in terms of my phrasing to avoid an unhelpfully interrogative tone. 'What is the lawyer saying here?', for example, is another way of expressing the same thing. Nonetheless, I tried as far as possible to standardise the process of asking the questions, particularly regarding their formulation and the way in which the applicant was exposed to the original and the rendition under investigation. Thus, I tried wherever possible to stay close to the original formulation of the rendition under investigation, that is, how it was uttered by the interpreter. Sometimes, I had to repeat a question or a rendition due to concentration-related constraints. Also, the length of these renditions and originals had an influence on the exposition strategy. When a certain rendition was found to be too long by the applicant, it was divided into parts. Given that the applicant could not possibly remember the meeting with the lawyer in its entirety, or all the renditions I wished to enquire about, I did my utmost to prepare the applicant ahead of the interview and he reported an acceptable understanding of what would happen. He was also asked to indicate any points where he needed more explanation. Through this combination of measures, I provided a structured approach to assisting the applicant's recall.

During the interview, whenever the applicant indicated that he did not understand a rendition, or part of it, or did not remember whether or not he had understood it during the IME, he was asked to reflect on this. I asked the applicant to try to remember if he understood during the meeting with the lawyer. Where he was not able to remember this, he was asked to answer the question based on his current listening (i.e. during the interview with me).

I believe that the explanations provided by the applicant have a high credibility, given that he was a willing participant in the study and had the right to withdraw whenever he wanted.

Due to time constraints, choices had to be made regarding which renditions would be discussed. There were some 110 renditions in the IME, and questions were asked about 39 of them. The selection of renditions and originals to enquire about was based on the micro-analysis of the transcription. First, the renditions where it seemed obvious that the applicant did understand the original were selected; Conversely, where there were no reasons to suspect any misunderstanding, no questions were asked or prepared. Where, for example, the rendition was not produced in a clear way, or where technical terminology was used, or where the legal procedure was being discussed, questions were formulated in order to investigate whether understanding had taken place or not.

4.6.5 Interviewing the interpreter: Balancing professional integrity and sincere reflection

Following the micro-analysis of the IME transcript, a reflective, semi-structured interview was conducted with the interpreter. The purpose was to probe his internal reasoning processes and explore how meaning was co-constructed at specific moments of the interpreted exchange. As in the interview with the applicant, the interpreter was afforded space and time to speak freely, with an emphasis on maintaining his professional integrity while encouraging honest reflection.

The setting was quiet and comfortable, arranged to ensure that the interpreter felt at ease. He was assured of full confidentiality, and it was reiterated that his responses – whether critical, uncertain, or speculative – would not affect his professional standing. At the start of the interview, the entire IME recording was replayed without interruption to facilitate memory recall, and the interpreter was given a full transcript to consult during the discussion. When direct recall was not possible, he was encouraged to describe what he would normally do in comparable circumstances. This enabled reflection not only on remembered decisions but also on normative routines and strategic habits.

Some of the interpreter's responses were immediate and assertive; he indicated on several occasions that he remembered exactly what his decision-making had involved. In other instances, he expressed uncertainty and provided multiple possible explanations. Such responses were not treated as equivocation but rather as layered reflections. Renditions for which more than one explanation was given were classified under multiple analytical categories (see Appendix II).

The questions used in the interview emerged from prior transcript analysis and were varied in type. Some focused on specific lexical or syntactic choices, beginning with the Dutch source phrase and inviting the interpreter to elaborate on how he arrived at the target rendition. Others were broader, inviting reflection on his perceived responsibilities toward each interlocutor, the influence of prior expectations or constraints, and his overall approach to role performance. Importantly, the phrasing was kept deliberately open and neutral, avoiding any language that might suggest criticism or imply a preferred answer. For example, rather than saying, 'Why didn't you interpret that part this way?', the interpreter was asked, 'Can you explain your thoughts when you decided to translate this original phrase?' – a formulation designed to invite explanation rather than judgement.

The interaction was conducted with attention to tone, pacing and responsiveness. The interpreter was reminded throughout that he could ask for clarification, pause the discussion, or take more time. At no point was he pressured to respond hastily. In moments of hesitation, he was invited to imagine how he might typically handle similar situations, thereby transforming memory lapses into productive hypothetical reflections. This proved especially useful when the interpreter could no longer recall a specific moment but was still able to articulate plausible reasoning strategies. In this way, speculative responses were not only accepted but actively encouraged as insight into the interpreter's professional habitus.

It was recognised that, given the evaluative nature of some questions, the interpreter might have felt that his competence was being scrutinised – particularly as he was a freelance interpreter who was dependent on further professional assignments. Nonetheless, he responded confidently and, on multiple occasions, expressed critical views of the interlocutors, including the lawyer. From my own experience as an interpreter, such openness is uncommon and suggests a high likelihood that the interpreter was answering sincerely.

To ensure data reliability, a form of triangulation was applied. The interpreter's responses were compared with the original audio recording and, where applicable, cross-checked with the lawyer's reported intentions. When uncertainties arose, relevant segments were replayed or read aloud again to minimise misinterpretation. This practice ensured that short-term memory gaps or environmental distractions did not compromise the accuracy of the interpreter's reflections.

Throughout, the aim was not to assess fidelity or accuracy per se, but to reconstruct the interpretive logic behind translational choices. By combining systematic preparation, flexible interviewing, and a neutral, dialogically attuned stance, the interview served to illuminate how the interpreter navigated competing demands, negotiated meaning, and rationalised his strategies within the constraints of the IME context. The insights derived from this reflective account are integral to the analysis presented in Chapter 5.

4.6.6 General questions

In addition to asking the interpreter and applicant questions related to specific issues found during the initial micro-analysis of the transcribed data, I asked both questions of a general nature. I sought to enrich the data which was gained from the IME by attempting to add an extra dimension to it: the applicant and the interpreter were asked to express their views on topics which could not be derived from the data recorded during the IME, or from the data collected during the interviews when asking questions about the renditions. These topics included the following:

- The applicant was asked about his understanding of the role of the interpreter and his own share of responsibility in sense-making.
- The interpreter was asked about his understanding of the role and responsibility of the applicant regarding the process of sense-making. I also investigated the role of the lawyer from the point of view of the interpreter.

As will be seen in Chapter 5, the opinions of the participants are not always compatible when it comes to the understanding of each other's role and the responsibility for translating the originals of the lawyer.

4.6.7 Insights from informal interactions: The role of corridor conversations in data collection and analysis

In addition to interviews, I benefited from another source of information, namely 'corridor conversations'. Such interactions are not actively sought by the researcher. Such information was beneficial to the case study, mainly in taking methodological decisions, but also during the analysis. For example, the lawyer mentioned that he utilises a lower register (e.g. less formal language/jargon) when he discusses the legal procedure and backstory with many applicants. He anticipated that if he utilised a higher register, many applicants would encounter difficulties in understanding the information, as legal language is challenging for many people. I benefited from this information during the micro-analysis and also while preparing the interviews. It helped explain some of the linguistic choices made by the lawyer during the IME.

4.6.8 Complexities and solutions to triangulation in interpreter-mediated research

Generally, IMEs are more complex than monolingual encounters, and so discourse-analytical studies of IMEs based on one single source of information can miss important information. Triangulation is therefore essential: '[t]he logic of triangulation is based on the premise that no single method ever adequately solves the problem of rival explanations' (Patton, 1999: 1192). The different sources of information 'reveal different aspects of empirical reality' and so provide the researcher with more tools for his research (Patton, 1999: 1192). Triangulation entails gathering information through a variety of sources and methods – each tied to the same event – which enhances reliability by exposing different facets of the empirical reality (Maxwell, 2005; Gray, 2009; Walliman, 2006).

There are several types of triangulation. That is used in this study is what Pöllabauer (2006: 236) calls 'triangulation of methods'. This qualitative, empirical piece of research is conducted using different types of primary data: recordings of an IME and two post-IME interviews. The term 'primary data' refers to information that has been observed, experienced or recorded in close proximity to the event (Walliman, 2006). The third source of primary data was the corridor conversations with the lawyer. As noted above, these comments were minimal but important. Triangulation enhances (but cannot guarantee) reliability. When methods are combined, one method will compensate for the weaknesses and blind spots of the other (Flick, 2006: 37). This was the case in this study, as will become clear in Chapter 5.

The transcribed data collected from the recorded meeting was analysed with the aim of investigating the renditions of the interpreter. Where there was a reason to suspect that a translation might not have been understood, this was marked and questions were formulated about it. During the interview with the applicant, I asked questions to explore whether or not the originals were understood. The interpreter was also interviewed with the aim of exploring the motivation behind the translation strategies/decisions used. I designed the interview to ask the interpreter to reflect on these strategies. The questions directed to the interpreter explored how decision-making regarding the strategies/decisions took shape.

Close analysis of the recorded IME was triangulated with the information collected during the meeting with the interviewed participants, and to lesser extent the corridor conversations. I also went a step further: during each interview, a biographical history was elicited from the participant, whether applicant or interpreter. That of the interpreter contains his understanding of his duties/responsibilities as an interpreter, on the one hand, and how these relate to those of the lawyer and applicant in relation to 'miscommunication', and to achieving 'shared understanding', on the other. That of the applicant contains his views on the responsibilities of the interpreter. Information about the education of the interpreter and the applicant was also collected during the interviews.

I contend that these procedures strengthened the study, as they reduce the risk that conclusions will reflect only the systematic biases or limitations of a single source or method and enable a broader, more robust understanding of the issues under investigation (Maxwell, 2005).

The triangulation used in this study appears to be innovative, as I have not found other studies with a similar research agenda that have adopted reflective/retrospective in-depth audio-recorded interviews in the manner utilised here. This triangulation involved recording a real interpreter-mediated legal consultation in an asylum procedure within a lawyer's office and applying a fine-grained text-based analysis, combined with reflective interviews. Nor have I come across any study where the interpreters were confronted with their translations at the word, expression, sentence and utterance levels, and were asked linguistic, translational and policy-related questions about them. Additionally, I spoke semi-formally with the lawyer in brief sessions before and after recording the IME, and later, after I had recorded my post-reflective interview and started the analysis, to gain his views on the work of interpreters as professionals and how he believed interpreters should conduct their work. During these interviews, the lawyer discussed his communication strategies with this particular applicant and how he thought he should handle the sense-making and meaning-making processes during the consultation.

As a final reflection, conducting this type of study proved challenging, and I believe such research is rare due to the difficulties in accessing necessary resources. I had to adhere to the stringent ethical requirements of the University of Leeds. Additionally, it was crucial at the outset and throughout to demonstrate to the lawyer that I was a serious researcher affiliated with a reputable research institution. Moreover, the lawyer needed to have an interest in research related to interpreting studies, and I had to assure him that his contribution would not be a waste of time, as lawyers in the Netherlands are consistently busy. I ensured that the data would be handled with the utmost confidentiality. We discussed the methods for recording the data, its transport to the UK, storage practices and access policies. In fact, I had approach several lawyers previously, who had declined to participate for various reasons. For example, one declined because she wanted detailed answers to her queries before I was able to provide them.

Overall, the case study was something of an experience in prototyping: taking existing theoretical tools, modifying them and then meticulously assembling a research case and analysing the results. As Chapter 6 will show, reflective interviewing need not be so laborious; rather, the meaningful insights of the reflective interviews (presented in Chapter 5) might be achieved at a fraction of the effort used to design this case study.

4.7 Conclusion

This chapter has laid the theoretical groundwork essential for understanding the complex dynamics of IMEs in asylum procedures. By integrating advanced frameworks, particularly dialogism and Wadensjö's interpreting model, we have ventured beyond traditional approaches to uncover the intricate layers of communication that impact the fairness and transparency of these processes.

Central to our discussion was the shift from a monological to a dialogical perspective of interpreting, highlighting the active role of interpreters in co-constructing meaning within IMEs. This shift foregrounds the nuanced interplay of pre-encounter knowledge, intersubjectivity, and alterity, thus offering a more holistic understanding of the communicative challenges faced by asylum seekers, interpreters, and legal representatives.

The incorporation of dialogism, as theorised by Linell, provided a robust framework to explore how meaning is dynamically constructed through interactions influenced by sociocultural contexts. This perspective underscores the significance of reflective interviews as a methodological tool, allowing for a deeper exploration of the interlocutors' experiences and perspectives during legal consultations and hearings.

In the context of the problems identified in Chapters 2 and 3, dialogism offers transformative solutions. Chapter 2 highlighted the symbolic power dynamics and inequalities within asylum procedures, while Chapter 3 detailed the complexities of IMEs and limitation of purely textual approaches to studying and evaluating them. Dialogism addresses these issues by fostering an environment where all voices are heard and valued, thereby dismantling power imbalances and allowing for a more empathetic and comprehensive evaluation of asylum claims. This perspective ensures that the asylum process becomes more transparent and fair, aligning with the book's overarching goal of enhancing equity in these procedures.

Our theoretical exploration also emphasised the critical need for considering the context in which communication occurs, recognising that meanings are not static but evolve through situated interactions. This understanding is crucial for addressing the systemic inequities present in asylum procedures, as it allows for a more empathetic and comprehensive approach to evaluating asylum claims.

In advancing these theoretical insights, we have prepared the groundwork for the practical applications to be discussed in subsequent chapters. Chapter 5 will delve into detailed interviews, further examining the issues raised, while Chapter 6 will present concrete recommendations aimed at enhancing the equity and effectiveness of asylum procedures.

Ultimately, this chapter reaffirms our central thesis: a thorough revaluation of existing communication practices within asylum procedures is indispensable. By refining our analytical tools and embracing a dialogical approach, we can significantly improve the fairness and transparency of these procedures, ensuring that all parties involved are better understood and more equitably treated.

5 Enhancing Equity in Asylum Procedures: The Dual Role of Retrospective Interviews in Research and Practice

This chapter illuminates the gaps in understanding and information within asylum procedures through an in-depth analysis of the case study introduced in Chapter 3, where it was demonstrated that the monological understanding of communication within interpreter-mediated encounters (IMEs) inherently engenders the loss of information in asylum procedures and so can prejudice the outcomes. The chapter therefore advocates for the integration of dialogist principles into interpreting practices so that consideration is given to the perspectives of all interlocutors involved, ensuring that the communication process is more inclusive and reflective of the complexities inherent in IMEs. This chapter demonstrates how retrospective interviews can reveal this essential yet often overlooked sense-making material, critical for fair and accurate credibility assessments. The chapter showcases the ability of reflective interviews to provide rich information about how sense-making occurs during IMEs.

Furthermore, the chapter aims to equip researchers in the field of interpreting studies with an additional methodological tool. By introducing and validating the use of reflective interviews, the case study analysis in this chapter offers a robust framework for analysing communication within a range of IME settings, including asylum procedures, and particularly during legal consultations. This methodological advancement fosters a deeper understanding of the dynamic interplay of language, culture and power in asylum settings.

The chapter thus contributes to a broader scholarly and practical understanding of the intricacies involved in asylum procedures. It emphasises the need for nuanced, dialogically informed approaches to better serve asylum-seekers and promote a more equitable asylum process. The suggested reforms will benefit other key stakeholders, such as the Dutch Immigration and Naturalisation Service (INS) and the judiciary, by reducing appeals, enriching the data available for caseworkers and decision-makers, and reducing the communicative hurdles inherent to IMEs. Moreover, these reforms do not inherently entail greater permissiveness in granting applications.

5.1 Introduction and Summary of Findings

Reflective interviews can yield rich information about how sense-making occurred during a given IME. The overall message of this chapter is that in certain cases an ethnographic tool has to be used to investigate the communication and sense-making processes of IMEs, otherwise important information can go unnoticed, which, in the asylum context, may have major consequences for the credibility assessments. In Chapter 2 has shown how crucial credibility assessments are for every asylum applicant. The information loss caused by monological approaches to communication – those that place all responsibility for sense- and meaning-making on entextualised talk produced during IMEs – represents a needless but rectifiable impediment to the overall integrity of decision-making in such procedures.

To first research question (Section 3.1.1) of the case study is: How does the interpreter render the originals of the lawyer? I present the findings related to this overarching research question in Section 5.1.1. Sections 5.2 and 5.3 deal with the second research question: Does the applicant understand these originals (via the renditions), and what can be learned from the applicant's answers in terms of the sense-making processes and meaning-making processes? This data was collected during the reflective interview with the applicant. To help answer this question, I present four categories which I have developed for analytical purposes regarding understanding and miscommunication on the part of the applicant. These are: 'originals understood', 'originals miscommunicated', 'originals partly understood' and 'originals partly miscommunicated' (for further details on the conceptualisation of these categories, see online Appendix II). The last two categories will not be discussed in separate (sub-)sections, but as part of the first two categories. In dialogism, misunderstanding (itself a monological concept) is theorised as a joint product – *miscommunication*.

The third research question is: How does the interpreter explain his translation decisions, and what can be learned from his answers in terms of the sense-making and meaning-making processes? This question holds significance beyond a better understanding of the practical considerations of interpreting in asylum settings, by bringing together an analysis of the perspectives and sense-making experiences of all the primary interlocutors in the studied IME. It is addressed in Sections 5.4 and 5.5.

First, Section 5.1.1 presents a summary of the case study data.

5.1.1 Renditions made: Data summary

A breakdown is given here of the renditions produced in the IME between the applicant and his lawyer. A micro-level analysis of the transcript identified 110 renditions. A full presentation of the data can be found in online Appendix II. Table 1 presents a summary categorisation of the renditions. This chapter analyses where textual analysis (i.e. analysis without the benefit of post-IME interviews) identified areas where the sense-making process between interlocutors required investigation.

As Table 1 depicts, 86 of 110 renditions produced in the studied IME fell within the categories developed by Wadensjö (1998). The rest (24) fell within the additional categories I have developed for this study (see online Appendix II). I have utilised the taxonomy of Wadensjö (1998) here, intending to show how these renditions relate to the originals produced by the lawyer. For example, when I say that a rendition (a translated utterance) was a 'close' rendition, this means that the rendition (the translation) was close to the original utterance of the lawyer in terms of both content and style. The results show that while 'close renditions' constitute the largest group, they represent less than 36% of the total number of renditions. The rest are all divergent renditions. The information in Table 1 provides the backdrop to the analysis in this chapter.

Table 1 Taxonomy of renditions using the categories of Wadensjö and Mizori

Category	No. of renditions	Percentage
Wadensjö's categories		
Close renditions	39	35.45%
Reduced renditions	24	21.81%
Expanded renditions	9	8.18%
Substituted renditions	5	4.54%
Summarised renditions[1]	5	4.54%
Two-part renditions[2]	2	1.81%
Zero renditions[3]	2	1.81%
Additional categories (Mizori)		
Reduced + substituted renditions[4]	12	10.90%
Only substituted renditions[5]	7	6.36%
Expanded + substituted renditions[6]	5	4.54%

1. A 'summarised rendition', as categorised by Wadensjö, is 'text that corresponds to two or more prior "originals". In some cases, it may consist of constituents related to two or more "originals" provided by one and the same interlocutor. In other cases, the "summarised rendition" corresponds to two or more utterances voiced by different individuals. Sometimes an interpreter's utterance and an "original" can together provide the information summarised in a succeeding "rendition"' (Wadensjö, 1998: 107).

2. 'Two-part' or 'multi-part renditions' are defined as follows: 'The text of a "two-part rendition" consists of two interpreter's utterances corresponding to one "original", which is split into parts by another interjected "original" utterance, the prepositional content of which is not reflected in the "rendition"' (Wadensjö, 1998: 108).

3. 'Zero renditions' are defined as follows: 'When comparison starts out not from the "renditions" but from the "originals", looking for correspondences among interpreters' utterances may result in cases of "zero rendition", that is, cases when "originals" are left' (Wadensjö, 1998: 108).

4. This category contains renditions where there is at least one item which is 'reduced' and one item which is 'substituted'.

5. This category contains 'renditions' where there is at least one 'substitution'.

6. Such renditions contain some 'reductions' and at least one 'substitution'.

Section 5.2 examines the impact of these renditions on the understanding of the applicant. Section 5.3 examines cases where these decisions appear to have led to partial understanding or miscommunication. Sections 5.4 and 5.5 explore the interpreter's response as to why he took certain translation decisions. The interpreter generally considered staying close to the originals to be less important than 'making the applicant understand', and he found that it is important to adapt the translation to the needs of the applicant. On his part, the applicant was found to be actively participating in the realisations of the renditions by his assumptions and so on during the meeting.

5.2 Originals Understood

To recap, during the recorded IME the lawyer is preparing himself and the applicant for the possibility that the INS may decide again to refuse to grant the applicant international protection. The applicant had at this stage already been granted 'subsidiary' asylum permit. To this end, during the encounter, the lawyer performed, among other things, three interactional goals: (1) he discussed with the applicant the legal process in which the latter had been involved from the date of submission of his asylum application a few years earlier; (2) he revisited the backstory of the applicant and read (parts of) it out; and (3) he asked the applicant about his backstory.

Ninety-three renditions of the 110 originals (i.e. the lawyer's original utterances) were concluded by me to have been understood by the applicant (84.54%): 12 of the understood originals belonged to the first interactional goal, 45 to the second and the rest (36) to the third. The total number of renditions (interpreter's translations) involving the first interactional goal was 18, the second 48 and the third 39. This shows that 66.66% of the first type of renditions were understood, 93.75% of the second type and 92.30% of the third type. The remaining originals (5) were not directly related to the topics mentioned (see online Appendix II).

To recap briefly the discussion in Chapter 4, dialogism theorises meaning as being co-constructed by all interlocutors. Each engages in his internal dialogue with the 'material' afforded by the other interlocutor(s). 'Material' is understood as being everything that comes from the other interlocutor(s) during the interaction/encounter. It can be verbal or visual information or both. The interlocutor evaluates this material and re-evaluates their own thinking. Their response then represents their understanding. This process is influenced by the context in which the interaction takes place as well as pre-encounter knowledge. In the context of this study, pre-encounter knowledge is the relevant knowledge each interlocutor has gained in their life before participating in the IME, for example the knowledge the applicant has gained about the asylum/immigration process during his prior meetings with the lawyer. Similarly, the knowledge of the interpreter and the lawyer regarding the asylum process, past cases, the situation in Syria and the disposition of the INS (to name but few examples) have a significant bearing on is said during the IME.

Thus, three main things need to be taken into consideration in the analysis: what the interlocutors say to each other during the encounter; the knowledge and meanings attributed to the context within which the encounter is taking place; and the pre-encounter knowledge of the participants. Sometimes the applicant's sense-making depends not only on the renditions but also on his pre-encounter knowledge. As will be observed in the following discussions, conclusions based on transcribed data only can sometimes be impoverishing or misleading, and it is necessary to consider the applicant's perspective.

The following subsections are organised and titled around the communicative phenomenon which requires extra investigation. In each case, the original was understood by the applicant, but not in a manner that a direct textual examination of the renditions can wholly explain. The excerpts examined in each are examples of the far-reaching influence of context and pre-encounter knowledge on sense-making, and highlight the shortcomings of monological design in capturing this. The excerpts retain the numbering used in Chapter 3. In some cases, additional supplementary excerpts are provided as well. In this chapter excerpts are explored thematically, rather than chronologically. Once again, it must be borne in mind that the excerpts are not self-contained phenomena but represent a referential aid to facilitate analysis.

5.2.1 Applicant says 'yes', assuming that the interpreter meant what he himself had gone through

In Excerpt 8, which is part of the second interactional goal of the IME, the lawyer is revisiting the backstory of the applicant. In turn 123, the lawyer is recounting how the backstory goes according to the report in front of him. It reads that the applicant and his girlfriend were released by the police after they were given a warning and that after this the applicant did not seek to contact his girlfriend for a few weeks. In his translation (turn 124), the interpreter substituted 'you too did not seek to contact her' for 'there was no contact between you and her'. I wanted to know if the applicant had understood the original as produced by the lawyer via the rendition, especially because he had agreed to this divergent rendition, as shown in the text in turn 133.

At the beginning of Excerpt 8, the applicant did not understand the entire rendition, let alone notice the substitution (see his response in turn 125: 'no (.) e I didn't understand you the question'). This could explain why he did not notice the substitution. After the interpreter indicated to the lawyer that the applicant did not understand the rendition and that he

Excerpt 8

123 Lawyer: ok (..) e:mm (..) nou uiteindelijk hebben ze jullie laten gaan met een waarschuwing en heb je ook aantal weken geen contact met haar gezocht.
Lawyer: ok (..) e:mm (..) well eventually they let you go with a warning and you too did not seek to contact her for a number of weeks.

124 المترجم: وفي النِهاية أعطوكو تحذير و و و إي إي خلّوكن (.) تمشو (.) وانت لمدّة (.) عدّة أسابيع بعد ما كان في هالموضوع (.) اتصال بينك وبينا.
Interpreter: and in the end they gave you a warning and and and e e they let you (.) go away (.) and you for (.) several weeks after this thing (.) there was no contact between you and her.

125 اللاجئ: لا (.) إي ما فهمت عليك السؤال.
Immigrant: no (.) e I didn't understand you the question.

126 Interpreter: Ik zal het herhalen meneer heeft het niet begrepen.
Interpreter: I will repeat the gentleman did not understand it.

127 Lawyer: ja
Lawyer: yes

128 المترجم: بعد ما أعطوكن تحذير (.) تركوكن.
Interpreter: after they gave you a warning (.) they let you go.

129 اللاجئ: مين أعطانا تحذير؟ (..) الشرطة يعني؟
Immigrant: who gave us a warning? (..) You mean the police?

130 المترجم: إيه
Interpreter: yeah

131 اللاجئ : إيه إيه
Immigrant: yeah yeah

132 المترجم: =وبعدا (.) عدة اسابيع بعد هالحادثة (.) ما كان ما كان في إتصال.
Interpreter: = and after that (.) a number of weeks after this incident (.) there was no there was no contact.

133 اللاجئ: صح.
Immigrant: that is right.

134 Lawyer: en toen heeft ze jou opgebeld (.) en gevraagd waarom je haar niet meer wilde zien.
Lawyer: and then she phoned you up (.) and asked why you no longer wanted to see her.

135 المترجم: وبعدا هي تلفنت لك وقالت لك ليه ليه ما بدك (.) تشوفا.
Interpreter: and after that she phoned you up and said to you why why you do not want (.) to see her.

136 اللاجئ: صح.
Immigrant: correct.

was going to repeat it (turn 126), the interpreter engaged in a side-sequence with the applicant in which he explained to the applicant step by step what the lawyer had just said (turns 128–133). The interpreter then reproduced the substitution: he did not change it to a close rendition. A close rendition is when 'the propositional content found explicitly expressed in the rendition must be equally found in the preceding "original", and the style of the two utterances should be approximately the same' (Wadensjö, 1998: 107). The applicant, for his part, did not intervene to correct the interpreter (by explaining that it was *he* who did not seek contact). He restricted himself to saying 'that is right' (turn 133).

Without the post-IME interview, the applicant might appear not to have noticed the substitution, or had noticed it but thought that he knew enough 'for current (practical) purposes' (Linell, 2009: 226). From turn 135 onwards, after the side-sequence has ended, it becomes clear that it was indeed the applicant who did not seek contact with his girlfriend. His girlfriend called him and asked him why he did not want to see her. It is possible that the applicant might have felt here that there was no need to raise any more questions, if he had indeed become aware of the substitution. However, the question remains as to why he did not react during or directly after the preceding side-sequence if he had become aware of the substitution. Was it again that he thought that he knew enough for 'current (practical) purposes'? Or might there have been something else?

The post-IME interview shows that there is another dimension to this. When I asked the applicant to recount if and how he understood this rendition, the version the applicant produced for me corresponded with the original, rather than with the rendition (i.e. he was the one who did not seek contact with the girlfriend). When asked why he did not intervene when he heard the rendition, he said that he *assumed* that the interpreter meant that it was the applicant who did not 'seek contact'. During post-IME interview the applicant might not have remembered what had happened during the encounter two weeks earlier and gave this answer only to please me. However, this is not the only case elsewhere in the data where the applicant provides a similar reason (see the following paragraph). Therefore, the fact that the applicant provides such an explanation on several occasions in the post-IME interview might indicate that he was being honest when he was providing this explanation. Again, this was not the only case where the applicant did not intervene and *assumed* things. In the following paragraphs, this tendency on the part of the applicant to assume things will be analysed in greater depth.

There are seven instances (including the above) where the applicant agrees to the informational content of a rendition during the IME but where this content, when probed, does not correspond to the informational content of the rendition produced by the interpreter. In other words, seven instances emerged where the applicant comprehended and agreed with information that reflected the lawyer's original which was not found in the interpreter's divergent renditions. During the post-IME interview with the applicant, each time I asked him to explain why he had agreed with one of these seven renditions the applicant said, after understanding the point under discussion, that he *assumed* that the interpreter *meant* the version as he, the applicant, understood it and agreed to it. In each of these seven cases, the applicant said that the version he agreed to corresponded with the truth as he knew it, that is, to reality – 'reality' being related to the world as he knew it or had experienced it before entering the IME. Thus, in the case of Excerpt 8, the reality was that during the incident involving the applicant and his girlfriend, it was *the applicant* who did not seek contact.

How can I explain this theoretically? The applicant seems to be engaging in his *internal dialogue* with his pre-encounter knowledge. He seems to *assume* 'things' not necessarily mentioned in the rendition by the interpreter. It cannot be ruled out that this is not the only explanation – for example, his knowledge of Dutch might have helped him understand more than was said in the renditions. However, this is not very likely because his knowledge of Dutch was limited. At the very beginning of the post-IME interview with the applicant, when I asked him some general questions about his background, he mentioned that he did not know much Dutch and had attended only a few months of lessons. Thus, it is more probable that he was indeed making these assumptions by engaging his past knowledge. But what could be the explanation for making these assumptions?

It seems that, in this regard, the applicant was assuming the intersubjectivity of his interlocutors, probably by being relatively uncritical, and that each time he thought (in the seven cases referred to here) that he *knew enough for practical purposes*. Understanding, according to dialogism, 'involves being able to cope with situations, carrying out tasks, being able to explain and account for various subject matters, etc.' (Linell, 2009: 222). The applicant might indeed have thought that he knew enough to carry out the tasks expected from him on the part of the lawyer, which were, among other things, answering questions with regard to his backstory. After all, according to dialogism only partial understanding is intended and is needed only for *current practical purposes*.

The data shows that the applicant understood six of these seven originals. It is important to note, however, that the manner in which this applicant dealt with the pre-encounter knowledge cannot be taken as an example of how other applicants would act. Nevertheless, I argue that it is important to include pre-encounter knowledge in the analysis in such situations.

5.2.2 Understanding something the interpreter has not said

In this section, I discuss another grouping of renditions which show the influence pre-encounter knowledge has on sense-making during such an encounter, and again argue that the applicant is not always solely dependent on the renditions. The grouping 'understanding something the interpreter has not said' (see online Appendix II) reflects where the applicant engages in his internal dialogue information not mentioned in the rendition. This information also belongs to the pre-encounter knowledge.

In Excerpt 2, after having reminded the applicant about how the debate between him and the representative of the INS in front of the judge had developed, which constituted the first interactional goal of the lawyer during the IME, the lawyer revisited the backstory of the applicant,

Excerpt 2

51 Lawyer: goe:d e::: ok e: nou je hebt in jouw interview e: verteld (.) dat (.) jij samen (.) met jouw neef die hier nu even niet is maar wie ik nog een gesprek ga hebben (.) dat jullie samen naar Nederland zijn vertrokken= omdat jullie samen problemen hebben gekregen in Syria.
Lawyer: goo:d e::: ok e: well you said in your e: interview (.) that (.) you together (.) with your cousin who is not here right now but with whom I will have a conversation (.) that you together departed to the Netherlands=because you together got into troubles in Syria.

52 المترجم: انت (.) حكيت في المقابلى (.) انّو انتى إي في وقتا غادرت إي البلد (.) مع ابن عمك أو ابن اخوك (.) الي اليوم مو معانا ابن عمك إي: غادرتو إلى هولندا=لأنو انتو الإثنين تعرّضتو إلى: مشاكل.
Interpreter: you (.) said in the interview (.) that you e at the time left e [your] country (.) with your cousin or your nephew (.) who is today not with us your cousin e: you left to the Netherlands=because both of you got into: troubles.

53 اللاجئ: °صح°
Immigrant: °correct°

54 Interpreter: klopt
Interpreter: correct

55 Lawyer: e:m ik heb begrepen dat e: tus ik heb het verhaal zo begrepen= jouw vriend**in** (.) of nee jouw jouw neef had een vriendin e: een meisje leren kennen .hh waarmee e: ja die wat aanrommelde [*Laughs nasally*] om het zo maar te zeggen .hh (.) en (.) en op een gegeven moment heeft **jou** neef aan jou gevraagd om mee te gaan= zodat het meisje **ook** een vriendin mee zou nemen (.) en dan zou het allemaal wat minder (..) opvallen.
Lawyer: e:m I have understood that e: tog. I have understood the story in such a way=your **girl**friend (.) or no your your cousin had a girlfriend e: had met a girl .hh with whom e: yeah he used to mess around a little bit (*chuckles*) to put it this way .hh (.) and (.) and at a given moment **your** cousin asked you to accompany [them]=so that the girl **too** would take along a [girl] friend (.) and then things would be less (..) noticeable.

56 المترجم: يعني: (.) حسب ما هوى (.) فهم انّو ابن عمك (.) كان عندو رفيقة: (.) وعمل معا شغلا:ت، (.) وقال لك قال لك انّو تجي معو مشان هي كمان تجيب رفيقتها معا= مشان تغطو على هالموضوع.
Interpreter: yaʕni: (.) according to how he (.) has understood your cousin had a girl:friend (.) and he did things to her (.) and he said he said to you to come with him so that she too brings her [girl] friend with her=so you cover up this thing.

57 اللاجئ: أختا أختا.
Immigrant: her sister her sister

which is his second interactional goal. In the first turn (turn 51), the lawyer mentions, among other things, that, according to the report he is citing, the applicant came to the Netherlands together with his cousin because they got into trouble together, meaning they got into the same problem. Even though the interpreter reduces ‘together’, the applicant says ‘correct’ and does not say anything about the reduction.

Without the post-IME interview, it would be difficult, if not impossible, to know how the applicant understood the original. Was the applicant aware of the reduction when he said ‘correct’ in turn 53? If so, what made him accept the rendition? Could it be that he decided at that point to infer the presence of the reduced item in his evaluation (in his internal dialogue) even though he was aware it was not there? Or he might have felt he knew enough for 'current (practical) purposes' and did not think that the reduction was a problem. Or perhaps he simply was unaware of the reduction.

It is also possible that during the IME, the applicant had felt that there was something missing but thought that it was acceptable when the rendition in turn 56 was produced, where it becomes more or less clear that the applicant and his cousin had the same problem. Probably, he just felt that the rendition in turn 51 was acceptable for current practical purposes and there was no need to correct it, especially given that this was not the first time that he had a meeting of this kind with the lawyer. That said, the applicant was not always tolerant of divergent renditions. This may be seen in the next rendition, where the interpreter produced a substituted rendition and the applicant intervened and corrected the interpreter: the person concerned is the sister of the girlfriend of his cousin, not her friend (turn 57). This might be an indication that when an integral part of the rendition was not right, the applicant did intervene to correct the interpreter. But was the reduction in turn 52 not important and did it not deserve to be corrected? I would claim it was and did.

Until now, the above discussion has been based on the transcribed text alone. The post-IME interview shows that the applicant understood the rendition under discussion (turn 51 in Excerpt 2) in a way that does not reflect how the rendition was produced, but rather how the *original* was produced. When I asked him about how he understood the rendition, the applicant reproduced a close version of the original. When I drew his attention to the reduction made by the interpreter, the applicant indicated that he had *assumed* during the IME (during which he had indicated that the rendition was correct, as shown in Excerpt 2) that the interpreter *meant* by the rendition how things had happened as experienced by him in reality (i.e. the applicant had *assumed* that the interpreter had produced a close rendition, not a reduced one). He indicated that he understood the rendition in a way which corresponds to the *truth*, this truth being reality as he knows it as an applicant: that he and his cousin had encountered *one and the same* problem.

This shows again that the pre-encounter knowledge had an influence on how meaning was negotiated during the IME. It seems that the applicant was not dependent solely on the rendition, but that his pre-encounter knowledge also had an influence on his understanding. In all probability, while evaluating his thinking in his internal dialogue, he *assumed* that the interpreter had included the reduced lexical item in the rendition.

Once again, the influence of pre-encounter knowledge on the creation of meaning during this IME can be observed, with the notion of intersubjectivity appearing to have played a role. The applicant again seems to assume intersubjectivity on the part of the interpreter. He does not seem to take a critical attitude to the rendition. Was the asylum applicant aware of the specific and highly demanding credibility requirements of the asylum procedure? I believe so, but have no evidence for it. The applicant did tend to assume intersubjectivity rather than alterity. This might be a personal trait. It is also possible that the fact that he already had a residence permit played a role in him being less critical. Previous experiences with other interpreters might have also played a role, in that he had had positive experiences – although the applicant indicated at some point that he had noticed that not all interpreters produced close renditions, but rather reduced ones, which he did not approve of (Mizori, 2017).

We have two cases of this type in the data discussed with the applicant. There may be more, but these two appeared in the data during the post-IME interview with the applicant.

5.2.3 Understanding the original directly via Dutch

In this section, I pursue the discussion of the influence of pre-encounter knowledge on the process of meaning-making during the IME. The aim is to show that the rendition seems not to be the only source of understanding the original for the applicant. He seems to involve the pre-encounter knowledge in his internal dialogue during the process of sense-making.

In Excerpt 3, the lawyer is again revisiting the backstory of the applicant, which is his second interactional goal during the IME. In turn 68, he asks the applicant if the girl he had a relationship with was 'nice'. The interpreter makes a substituted rendition. He substitutes 'nice' with 'beautiful' (turn 69). During the post-IME interview with the interpreter, he stated that he did not have a better solution during the IME and, in hindsight, 'ḏarīfa' ('pleasant, charming') would have been better. The applicant responds with '[she] was beautiful yes' (turn 70).

Based on a purely textual analysis, it would not be possible to conclude whether or not the applicant was aware that a divergent rendition had been produced. His response (turn 70) corresponds to the rendition and not to the original. Nor is it possible to know how the applicant interpreted f the lawyer's chuckling (turn 71), or whether or not the applicant was aware that the Dutch rendition in turn 72 corresponded to the original of the lawyer in turn 68.

Excerpt 3

68 Lawyer: 't was een leuk meisje.
Lawyer: she was a nice girl.

69 المترجم: كانت إي: صبية: حلوى:؟
Interpreter: she was e: a beautiful gi:rl?

70 اللاجئ: كا:نت حلوة نعم .
Immigrant: Was beautiful yes.

71 Lawyer: [*Chuckles*]
Lawyer: [*Chuckles*]

72 Interpreter: 't was een leuk meisje.
Interpreter: she was a nice girl.

When I asked him about this substitution during the post-IME interview, the applicant mentioned that he was aware that the Dutch word 'leuk' did not mean 'beautiful' but, rather, 'nice', but he chose not to correct the translation because he understood the original directly from the lawyer whose version of the account corresponded with *reality/truth*. He said he thought there was no need to correct the interpreter and that he himself used the word 'beautiful' because it was used by the interpreter, on whom he was relying.

It is noticeable that the interpreter translated the confirmatory response of the applicant with a divergent rendition that corresponded to the lawyer's original (turn 72). He did not produce a close translation of the applicant's response; rather, he substituted it with 'nice', which corresponded with the lawyer's original. This shows that he knew that his rendition did not reflect the lawyer's original, something the interpreter admitted during his post-IME interview.

In this example (as in the previous sections), the applicant does not depend solely on the rendition during the sense-making process. At least in the one case shown here, the applicant indicated that he understood the original directly from the lawyer. The applicant's knowledge of Dutch is part of his pre-encounter knowledge. It is not possible to know how many more times (if at all) the applicant understood the original directly from the lawyer via Dutch, whether partly or completely. He did not mention other cases and I did not ask about this, in order to avoid leading questions. I did ask him at the beginning of the post-IME interview to mention if he understood any utterances directly from Dutch. He agreed, while acknowledging that his knowledge of Dutch was modest.

5.2.4 The applicant not being able to say 'something' related to pre-encounter knowledge but recognising it when mentioned

In this section, I discuss an instance in which it can be seen that the applicant cannot always be expected to express pre-encounter knowledge. If I had been inattentive, I could too early have concluded that the original had been miscommunicated. During the IME, in turn 30 from Excerpt 1, which is part of the first interactional goal of the lawyer, the lawyer indicates that it seems that the INS does not consider the backstory of the applicant 'sufficient' for international protection. He mentions then that the problem is that he and the applicant do not know why the INS thinks this and that the INS must explain its original decision. The lawyer complains that this means he is unable to provide counterarguments. He says that the fact that the applicant has not been granted international protection will have serious consequences for his residence position in the future. The applicant says 'correct'.

At face value this interaction leaves some questions related to understanding/miscommunication unanswered. Meaning-making can progress

From Excerpt 1

29 Intepreter: =klopt
Interpreter: correct

30 Lawyer: want mijn standpunt e: (.) is dat bekent dus **ei**genlijk als als ss je zo een besliss-ing neemt (.) dat ze jouw asielverhaal (.) e on voldoende vonden= wat je hebt verteld .h= maar wij weten niet waar**om** en dan moeten nog op kunnen reage:ren .h = omdat het grote gevolgen heeft voor jouw e::: verblijfspositie in Nederland.
Lawyer: for my point of view e: (.) is that means thus **ac**tually if if ss you take such a decision (.) that they consider your backstory (.) e insufficient= what you said .h= but we do not know **w**hy and we must then be enabled to res:pond to it [the decision] .h = because it has big consequences for your e::: residence position in the Netherlands.

31 المترجم: يعني هوّى (.) وجهة نظروو (.) إنّوو (.) هنّى (.) في هالحالى (.) قرّروا بانّو قصّة اللجوء تَبعك مَنّا كافية (.) وفي هالحالى (.) بدّون يقولولْنا لَشو (.) شو السبب مشان نقدر كمان نقدم بردّ على (.) هالموضوع= لأنّو هالشي ممكن يكون إلُه (.) عواقب (.) او تأثي:ر (.) على (.) إقامتك في هولندا.
Interpreter: yaʕni he (.) from his point of view (.) that (.) they (.) in that case (.) decided that your backstory isn't sufficient (.) **and in such a case** (.) they must say to us **for what** (.) **what is the reason** so that we can also submit a response (.) regarding this subject=for this thing can have (.) consequences (.) or influen:ce (.) on (.) your residence in the Netherlands [*Interrupted by immigrant*].

32 اللاجئ: صح
Immigrant: correct

differently from expected and what is uttered is not necessarily what is meant. Investigations into such utterances can reveal interesting information, as I will show in this section.

The previous sections showed how the applicant sometimes involved in his internal dialogue material which was not said by the interpreter but was *assumed* as having been meant by the interpreter. The applicant also incorporated material which was physically not present in the rendition but similarly assumed, or material which was directly taken from the original Dutch, not the rendition. All three possibilities align with the informational content of the lawyer's original. These materials aligned as well with the applicant's pre-encounter knowledge. Pre-encounter knowledge provides interesting insights into how the applicant's sense-making process in the IME. Nevertheless, this does not mean that the applicant can be assumed always to be able to say or show how he utilised it in his internal dialogue (as he did in the previous sections). In some cases the applicant might have understood the original without being able to show this, especially where the informational content concerned legal procedures.

For example, in turn 30 of Excerpt 1, the applicant was unable to show he understood the original. He sounded as if the informational content was somewhere in his mind, but he could not express it. It was as if he thought that he and his lawyer were expected to take the next action – that is, to convince the INS that his backstory was credible – while the original read that it was the INS which must state why they thought the backstory of the applicant was 'insufficient'. It was as if the applicant had not understood the original. If the original was of a general nature, in the sense that the content discussed was non-procedural, I would have characterised it as 'not understood'. However, because of my insider knowledge as an interpreter, this did not surprise me; legal and procedural originals can be challenging to deal with for some applicants.

When I noticed this, I proposed replaying the relevant part of the recording, to which the applicant agreed happily. During the second attempt, the informational content sounded more solid when mentioned by him. He sounded more confident. But still, while expressing the content in turn 30, he did not sound very sure about who was responsible for which task. It was as if he was seeking confirmation from me. At this point he mentioned much content that corresponded with the original, giving me the impression that his inability to show understanding was due to the complexity of the materials rather than him not having understood it. To ensure that I could make a decisive judgement for the sake of categorising whether or not the applicant had understood the original, I decided to explain the content in my own words and to see how the applicant would respond. When I did this, the applicant confirmed that this was the way he had understood the information during the IME and that he was finding it difficult to express the information in the way a researcher does. I therefore believe that the applicant had largely understood the original when he agreed to this (turn 32). His inability to say clearly how he understood this original could arguably be attributed to him being not empowered (the applicant had enjoyed only a few years of education, as he himself had said at the beginning of the post-IME reflective interview). Again, the applicant recognised the information and said that he indeed understood it the way it was mentioned by me but was unable to express it the way a researcher would, as he put it, meaning that he encountered difficulties in expressing the informational content.

5.2.5 Original understood: Summary

To summarise, sometimes the applicant was unable to clearly say what he had understood and I was unsure whether this was because he did not understand the rendition under investigation or whether it was because he encountered difficulties in expressing his thoughts with regard to it. For this reason, I asked targeted questions and, when needed, replayed the informational content in order to probe whether or not the applicant had understood the particular rendition(s).

It could be said that the applicant was encountering difficulties in expressing the informational content in the rendition because it was technical, about the legal asylum/immigration procedure. The fact that the applicant understood the information expressed in the rendition when recounted by me is easily explainable. The applicant probably had understood the information in a general, vague way but not as clear as 'normal', everyday talk. The legal nature of the information arguably adds to such 'vagueness', which is a characteristic of talk in general (Section 4.3.2.7). The applicant was not able to reproduce this kind of language clearly and independently but was able to recognise it when reproduced by me. This was probably because he had heard this information in previous meetings with the lawyer and/or organisations such as the INS, the court or the Central Reception for Asylum-Seekers, or in the IME under investigation. That is, the information was not new to him. Therefore, the knowledge interlocutors have prior to the encounter under investigation needs to be taken account of. The analyses would have been impoverished if I had not 'dug' further, that is, if I had not intervened when the applicant seemed not to have understood the renditions under investigation. The applicant would not have been able to indicate that he did understand the informational content and I would not have had the opportunity to find out that the applicant was not solely dependent on the information he was given during this the IME under discussion, but that previously gained knowledge helped him. It would also not have been easy, or perhaps even possible, to find out that the applicant's supply of the word 'correct' did not necessarily mean that everything had gone well with regard to understanding.

Section 5.2 has demonstrated how dialogism provides a means by which we can understand *how* the applicant successfully understood so many originals (93 out 110), including several key examples where the content of renditions (taken at face value) did not require the information to fully reflect the original. Pre-encounter knowledge is a significant influence in the applicant's internal dialogue. In the following section, I will move on to those cases where understanding proved to be challenging. I will discuss the possible reasons for this, and show that pre-encounter knowledge does not guarantee understanding on the part of the applicant.

5.3 Originals Miscommunicated, Partly Understood or Partly Miscommunicated

In this section, I discuss the findings related to those originals which were miscommunicated, partly understood, or partly miscommunicated. Information is provided on possible reasons why the applicant found understanding some originals produced during the IME challenging. I show that information related to pre-encounter knowledge does not always help the applicant understand the originals. As in Section 5.2, the discussions are categorised according to the nature of the miscommunication. They are presented in the order in which they were discussed during the post-IME interview with the applicant, and this does not reflect their relative importance.

5.3.1 Complex legal language

Asylum-related legal terms, notions and talk had an influence on sense-making during the IME. The applicant might not have understood an original even if he gave a confirmatory answer to a rendition. Sometimes, a possible linguistic 'trouble source' (Wadensjö, 1998) found in the transcribed data of the IME can lead to the discovery of a flaw in the understanding not only of the piece of talk probed but also of other originals. If I had not interviewed the applicant, I would not have known this.

In Excerpt 1, which is a part of the first interactional goal of the lawyer (see Section 3.3.1), the lawyer is discussing the legal procedure and explains to the applicant the benefits of getting international protection (i.e. a full asylum residence permit rather than the subsidiary one he had been granted; see turn 33). He then explains that the applicant has apparently won the appeal the lawyer had lodged, because the deadline imposed by the court on the INS for lodging a higher appeal has expired (turn 39). After that, the lawyer explains to the applicant that the INS is now expected (by court order) to take a new decision within a few days on whether or not it will grant the applicant the residence permit he wants (turn 41). In turn 44, the lawyer tells the applicant that he is very curious what this decision will be. In turn 45, however, the interpreter produces a substituted rendition of this. The lawyer says: '.hh thus I am very curious (.) whether it is going to happen', while the interpreter, interrupting the lawyer at the word 'whether', produces the following rendition: 'so he is longing really longing (.) [to know] what is going to happen'. The translation suggests more that the lawyer is feeling excited about the outcome of the expected decision on the part of the Dutch INS, rather than curious. As noted in Section 3.3.1, without dialogism and the perspective of the applicant, the applicant seems to show his appreciation of the lawyer and says that the lawyer has done everything that he could have done (turn 46). I sensed a possible 'trouble source' here. It was not clear to me whether or not the applicant had really understood what the lawyer had just said. In addition to the interpreter producing a substitution ('curious' is substituted with 'longing'), the applicant did not provide a (verbal) response when the lawyer was talking about technical issues related to the legal procedure (see turns 37 and 39). The applicant also showed minimal response when a rendition was made, which was not translated by the interpreter (turn 43). Having noticed this during the initial analysis of the transcribed text, I decided to probe this during the post-IME interview with the applicant. I wanted to know how the applicant had understood the original. The interview showed that the applicant had miscommunicated the original in which the lawyer said that he was curious about the decision of the INS. The applicant indicated that he thought that the related rendition meant that the lawyer was *optimistic* about his legal procedure, not *curious*. It made the applicant think, according to the applicant, that the lawyer was eager, in the sense that he was optimistic.

This instance is not the only one of this type, as revealed in the post-IME interview with the applicant. While this category contains

From Excerpt 1

33 Lawyer: .hh em: (.) want op het moment dat wij gelijk krijgen (.) en dat je **toch** een verblijfvergunning krijgt (.) met datum ingang e: jouw asielaanvraag (.) dat betekent dat je komende **juni** (.) al asiel onbepaalde tijd kan aanvragen en ook je Nederlandse paspoort kan krijgen.
Lawyer: .hh em: (.) for the moment that we are said to be right [by the court] (.) and that you nonetheless receive a residence permit (.) with a start date e: [which is] your asylum application [date] (.) this means that you coming June (.) already can apply for a permanent asylum [residence permit] and you can also get your Dutch passport.

34 المترجم: لأنّو إذا (.) إحنة (.) إي أخذنه (.) اللي بَدنا إيّاه (.) وَ وَ إعترفوا بأنّو (.) تاريخ الإقامى تبَعك (.) هو نفس (.) تاريخ (.) طلب اللجوء (.) ففي=هالشي معناه إنّو في شهر ستّى الجاي، من حقّك انه تقدم بطلب للحصول على إقامى مفتوحة، (.) وَفينك انّو تقدم على إي (.)البَسبور= على الجنسية.
Interpreter: Because if (.) we (.) e took (.) what we want (.) and and they admitted that (.) your residence [permit] date (.) is the same as (.) the date of (.) the asylum [application] date (.) in this=this thing means that in month six which is coming you have the right to apply for an open-ended residence [permit] (.) and you can apply for a e (.) the passport=for the nationality.

35 اللاجئ: صح
Immigrant: correct

36 Interpreter: klopt
Interpreter: correct

37 Lawyer: .hhh nou die beslissing van de rechtbank was op 15 oktober (.) en de IND had vier weken de tijd om daar tegen in hoger beroep te gaan.
Lawyer: .hhh well that decision of the court was on October 15 (.) and the INS had four weeks to lodge a higher appeal against it.

38 المترجم: قرار المحكمى كان صادر في 15 عشرة (.) ودائرة الهجرة والتجنيس كان الا (.) اربع اسابيع من الوقت (.) مشان تتقدم بإستئناف في المحكمة العليا.
Interpreter: the decision of the court was issued on October 15 (.) and the Immigration and Naturalisation Service had (.) four weeks of time (.) in order to lodge an appeal at the Higher Court.

39 Lawyer: nou die zijn voorbij, (.) en ik heb niks gehoord (.) dus ze zijn niet in hoger beroep (.) gegaan.
Lawyer: these have passed (.) and I have heard nothing (.) so they have not lodged an appeal (.)

40 المترجم: الأربعة أسابيع (.) مرّوا (.) وخلصوا (.) وهو ما سم. شي فمشان هيك (.) دائرة الهجرة والتجنيس ما قدمت إستئناف في المحكمة العليا.
Interpreter: The four weeks (.) have pass.. (.) and come to an end (.) and he has not (heard?) anything and this is why (.) the Immigration and Naturalisation Service has not lodged an appeal at the High Court.

41 Lawyer: de rechtbank heeft ook gezegd dat ze binnen zes weken nieuwe besluit moeten nemen en **dat is** komende disnsdag.
Lawyer: the court said also that they have to take a new decision within six weeks and **that is** next Tuesday.

42 المترجم: والمحكمة .. (غير واضح) خلال ست أسابيع بدّون يتّخذو قرار جديد (.) وهَدول بيخلصو (.) يوم التلاتاء (.) الجاي.
Interpreter: and the court .. [*unintelligible*] within six weeks they need to have taken a new decision (.) and those will end (.) coming (.) Tuesday.

43 اللاجئ: الجاي .. (غير واضح)
Immigrant: the coming .. [*rest unintelligible*]

44 Lawyer: .hh dus ik ben heel benieuwd (.) of het gaat gebeuren.
Lawyer: .hh thus I am very curious (.) whether it is going to happen.

45 المترجم: فهو متشوق متشوق كتي::ر (.) شو بدو يصير.
Interpreter: so he is longing really longing (.) [to know] what is going to happen.

46 اللاجئ: والله شكرا شكرا يعني هو عمل اللي عليه.
Immigrant: well thanks, thanks, he did what he had to do.

only three examples, not every notion was probed during the post-IME interview (as this was not the aim of this study and there were anyway time constraints). Further, the lawyer generally used informal language rather than challenging legal terms. The lawyer indicated during a 'corridor conversation' with me that he kept 'things' simple to facilitate the applicant's understanding. Furthermore, the interpreter also indicated during his post-IME interview that in this case, as in a number of other cases, he resorted to a lower register (using informal language) when he thought that his client (the applicant) might face difficulty in understanding closer renditions.

Despite this, during the post-IME interview with the applicant, he mentioned on several occasions that he generally encountered difficulties understanding the talk around the asylum procedure itself. This pre-encounter knowledge – in this case the legal knowledge he must have been exposed to during his residence in the Netherlands since 2009 (until the date of the meeting in 2013) – seems not to have always helped him to sufficiently understand the originals. For example, when asked in interview whether he knew what the High Court was, mentioned in turn 40, he said that he did not. He said he knew only 'the court'.

Yet, arguably, if the lawyer and the interpreter had not attempted to assist the applicant during the meaning-making process by utilising a lower register, the latter would have encountered even more difficulties in understanding. The 'material' which was afforded by the lawyer, through the interpreter, in a lower register, arguably empowered the applicant in his meaning-making.

5.3.2 Procedural confusion

Closely related to the topic of legal technical language is the challenging nature of the technicalities of the asylum procedure per se. This in itself might obstruct the applicant's understanding of the originals. In six originals (out of 18 in which the asylum procedure was being discussed) the meaning was miscommunicated, while in two others it was partly miscommunicated.

In Excerpt 4, extracted from the very start of the IME, the lawyer opens the meeting with the applicant and engages in the first interactional goal. He starts by reminding the applicant that they have been busy with the asylum procedure for a long time (turn 1). Then, he reminds him that they had attended a court session a few weeks earlier. After that, he presents some facts related to the procedure.

In turn 7, the lawyer indicates that the legal tool he used when he went to court some time ago (i.e. before the IME under investigation) was not an ordinary one: he went to court for the applicant at a time when the latter already had a residence permit (see Section 3.2.1 for information concerning the legal position of the applicant). The lawyer knows that the

From Excerpt 4

1 Lawyer: goed (….) .hhhh (.) ja we zijn al la:ng bezig met jouw:: asielprocedure.
Lawyer: good (….) .hhhh (.) yeah we have been busy with you::r asylum procedure for a lo:ng time.

2 المترجم: إحنا صارنّا فترة (.) عَم نشتغل مشغولين ب: (.) إجراءات لجو:ئك.
Interpreter: we have been working on been busy with: (.) your asylum proce:dure (.) for some time.

3 Lawyer: .hh we zijn e:: een aantal weken geleden bij de rechtbank geweest (.) in Den Helder.
Lawyer: .hh we went e:: to court a number of weeks ago (.) in Den Helder.

4 المترجم: قبل إي: عدة أسابي:ع (.) كنا: في محكمة في دن هيلدر.
Interpreter: several wee:ks ago e: (.) we had a court session in Den Helder.

5 اللاجئ: °صح صح°.
Immigrant: °correct correct°

6 Interpreter: klopt
Interpreter: correct

7 Lawyer: he:m dat was (.) e: een beetje bijzondere procedu:re (.) want ik ben in beroep gegaan tegen een beslissing van de IND (.) ter**wij**l je een verblijfsvergunning had.
Lawyer: he:m it was (.) e: a unusual procedu:re a little bit (.) for I lodged an appeal against a decision of the INS (.) at a **time** when you [already] had a residence permit.

8 المترجم: هذه الإجراءات كانت إيه استثنائية بعض الشيء لأنو هوىّ (.) عمل (.) إستئناف (.) ضد (.) قرا:ر (.) دائرة الهجرة والتجنيس في حين إنّو القرار كان إقامة،
Interpreter: this procedure was e somewhat exceptional for he (.) made [*sic*] (.) an appeal (.) against (.) the deci:sion of (.) the Immigration and Naturalisation Bureau when the decision [already taken by the INS] was a residence permit,

9 اللاجئ: صح (.) شكرا.
Immigrant: correct (.) thanks

10 Lawyer: en e: (.) de IND (.) heeft (.) daar op zitting ook gezegd dat ze vonden dat we eigenlijk=dat je helemaal geen recht had om in (.) beroep te gaan (.) omdat je geen belang had=want je hebt nu verblijfsvergunning .h dus dan kun je niet in beroep e e tegen een asielbesluit.
Lawyer: and e: (.) the INS (.) said (.) there during the [court] session indeed that they were of the opinion that we actually=that you had no right whatsoever to (.) lodge an appeal (.) because you had no interest=for you have now a residence permit .h so you cannot lodge an appeal e e against an asylum decision.

11 المترجم: وأثـ (.) وأثناء الجلسى (.) دائرة الهجرة والتجني:س قا:لت أنّو هنّى (.) إي بيشو إي يعني من رَأيُن إي أنوّ إنت إي ما من حقك أنو تتقدم ب: (..) طَلب إي إي ب: إستئناف ضد القرارْ لأنو ما من مصلحتك لأنّو انتى حصّلت (.) على الإقامة.
Interpreter: and du (.) and during the [court] session (.) the Immigration and Naturalisation Servi:ce sai:d that they (.) e: think e: yaʕni they are of the opinion e: that you e: have no right to lodge (..) e: e: an appeal against °the decision° because it is **not** in your interest because you [already] have (.) received the [residence] permit.

12 Lawyer: e: en ik heb toen uitgelegd (.) **bij** de rechtbank (.) dat ik vind dat er wel **de**gelijk belang is omdat jij .hh e een verblijfsvergunning heb gekregen vanwege de de algeme slechte siuatie in Syria (.) op dit momen.
Lawyer: e: and I explained then (.) **in** court (.) that I believe that there is **cer**tainly interest because you .hh e received a residence permit due to the the general bad situation in Syria (.) at this moment.

13 المترجم: وهو إي وضّح (.) مَعُن عند المحكمة (.) إنّهو (.) أنتى فعلا (.) في إلَك مصلحة (.) في الإستئناف (.) لأنّو إنتى حصلت على الإقامة (.) على ضوء (.) الوضع (.) إي: السيئ (.) حاليا (.) في (.) سوريا؟
Interpreter: And he e explained (.) with [*sic*] them at [*sic*] the court (.) that (.) you do indeed (.) have an interest (.) in [lodging] an appeal (.) because you have received the residence [permit] (.) in view of the (.) bad (.) e: situation (.) at present (.) in (.) Syria?

INS argues that if an applicant has been granted a subsidiary residence permit, they do not have any 'interest' in going to court (turn 10). This is why the lawyer mentions in turn 7 that the legal tool he utilised was 'unusual'. The interpreter translates the Dutch word 'bijzonder' ('unusual/ special') as إستثنائية ('istiṯna'iyya'; 'exceptional') (turn 8). The applicant says 'correct', followed by 'thank you' (turn 9). Because the lexical item إستثنائية ('istiṯna'iyya') is Modern Standard Arabic (MSA), rather than Syrian Arabic, the material discussed could be challenging and confusing due to its complex nature. Moreover, the applicant has been shown to have an uncritical attitude towards the renditions generally in the transcribed meeting with the lawyer. Accordingly, I decided to talk to the applicant about this.

At the very start of post-IME interview, my concerns were corroborated when the applicant mentioned that he had enjoyed only a few years of education. When I raised the issue with turn 8, the applicant indicated he had not understood the lawyer: the original was miscommunicated. He thought that the lawyer meant that the applicant had fled his homeland because he 'personally' had problems with the authorities, unlike some other asylum-seekers, who, as the applicant says the INS sometimes argues, leave their homeland because of the 'general' bad situation there, not necessarily because they themselves had encountered problems with the authorities. The applicant understood the word إستثنائية (istisna'iyya) in this last sense; that is, that the lawyer meant that the applicant personally had problems with the authorities and as such had exceptional circumstances warranting international protection. During the post-IME interview, when I explained to the applicant what the lawyer had actually said, he indicated that this was not the way he had understood the original during the IME. It is interesting to see that the next original (turn 10) contains the phrase 'indeed', connecting the reasoning of the previous original with the current one, while the corresponding rendition does not. This could have functioned as a 'clue' for the applicant to suspect that he might have misunderstood the first rendition under investigation (turn 8). The applicant does not give any response, which could mean that he was unable to follow the sequence of talk at that point.

In turn 11, a substitution was produced by the interpreter. The phrase 'because you had no interest' was substituted with 'it is **not** in your interest'. The post-IME interview revealed that this substitution made the applicant miscommunicate the entire original. The applicant thought that the lawyer meant that the INS said that lodging an appeal could turn out to be bad for him (this rendition was also discussed with the interpreter – see Section 4.3). In turn 13, it was unclear whether the applicant had understood the original where the lawyer was explaining some issues related to the procedure, and where the interpreter corrected the substitution he made in turn 11. The answer given by the applicant to me during the post-IME interview indicated that he did not understand the originals because the technicalities of the asylum procedure were challenging. The correction of the interpreter (the substitution in turn 11 to a close rendition) did not help the applicant to understand the original of the lawyer (turn 7), which was rendered in turn 8 by the interpreter.

Overall, on several occasions during post-IME interview, the applicant indicated that he found this kind of material challenging. He attributed this to not having enjoyed enough education, as he put it. In all the cases mentioned, the original turned to out to be miscommunicated due to the complexity of the asylum procedure. Thus, both *linguistic factors*, related to the choice of lexical items or expressions used by the interpreters, and *global factors*, related to understanding the bigger picture with relation to the legal procedure, can cause miscommunication.

Again, although the procedure had arguably been explained to the applicant or talked about on several occasions prior to the IME, pre-encounter knowledge does not seem to have helped the applicant sufficiently to understand this original and others, unlike those examined in Sections 5.2. The point can be reiterated that these insights would not have been possible if I had not interviewed the applicant.

5.3.3 Ambiguous responses

In Chapter 3, I raised some questions about certain originals, the corresponding renditions and the manner in which the applicant responded. I argued that there were reasons to think that the response 'correct' on the part of the applicant did not convince me entirely that he had understood the originals.

As we can see, the response 'correct' is made by the applicant to a series of the lawyer's originals in Excerpt 1. While at face value this would imply comprehension and agreement with the originals in questions, or at least the renditions, my ethnographic investigation into the sense-making experience here yielded some interesting answers. The applicant was found in some cases to understand the information related to the asylum procedure in a partial way (i.e. only parts of the informational content were understood) or vaguely (i.e. he did not show clear understanding). In these turns, the original was understood, partly understood, partly miscommunicated and miscommunicated (see online Appendix II). Another example of an ambiguous response follows:

Here we see another form of ambiguous response, an unintelligible remark. Such utterances are far from uncommon in speech; however, as 44 shows, this response was not addressed by any of the other interlocutors. It is possible that in the context of the IME, non-verbal cues may have afforded the lawyer enough of an indication of comprehension for him to continue. However, textually (i.e. in the transcript) there is nothing that indicates comprehension.

The post-IME interview with the applicant revealed that in many of instances the legal information was challenging. Thus, here also

From Excerpt 1

37 Lawyer: .hhh nou die beslissing van de rechtbank was op 15 oktober (.) en de IND had vier weken de tijd om daar tegen in hoger beroep te gaan.
Lawyer: .hhh well that decision of the court was on October 15 (.) and the INS had four weeks to lodge a higher appeal against it.

38 المترجم: قرار المحكمى كان صادر في 15 عشرة (.) ودائرة الهجرة والتجنيس كان الا (.) اربع اسابيع من الوقت (.) مشان تتقدم بإستئناف في المحكمة العليا.
Interpreter: the decislon of the court was issued on October 15 (.) and the Immigration and Naturalisation Service had (.) four weeks of time (.) in order to lodge an appeal at the Higher Court.

39 Lawyer: nou die zijn voorbij, (.) en ik heb niks gehoord (.) dus ze zijn niet in hoger beroep (.) gegaan.
Lawyer: these have passed (.) and I have heard nothing (.) so they have not lodged an appeal (.)

40 المترجم: الأربعة أسابيع (.) مرّوا (.) وخلصوا (.) وهو ما سم. شي فمشان هيك (.) دائرة الهجرة والتجنيس ما قدمت إستئناف في المحكمة العليا.
Interpreter: The four weeks (.) have pass.. (.) and come to an end (.) and he has not (heard?) anything and this is why (.) the Immigration and Naturalisation Service has not lodged an appeal at the High Court.

41 Lawyer: de rechtbank heeft ook gezegd dat ze binnen zes weken nieuwe besluit moeten nemen en **dat is** komende disnsdag.
Lawyer: the court said also that they have to take a new decision within six weeks and **that is** next Tuesday.

42 المترجم: والمحكمة .. (غير واضح) خلال ست أسابيع بدّون يتّخذو قرار جديد (.) وهَدول بيخلصو (.) يوم التلاتاء (.) الجاي.
Interpreter: and the court .. [*unintelligible*] within six weeks they need to have taken a new decision (.) and those will end (.) coming (.) Tuesday.

43 اللاجئ: الجاي .. (غير واضح)
Immigrant: the coming .. [*rest unintelligible*]

44 Lawyer: .hh dus ik ben heel benieuwd (.) of het gaat gebeuren.
Lawyer: .hh thus I am very curious (.) whether it is going to happen.

45 المترجم: فهو متشوق متشوق كتي::ر (.) شو بدو يصير.
Interpreter: so he is longing really longing (.) [to know] what is going to happen.

46 اللاجئ: والله شكرا شكرا يعني هو عمل اللي عليه.
Immigrant: well thanks, thanks, he did what he had to do.

pre-encounter knowledge did not help the applicant sufficiently to understand the originals. Notably, it would not have been possible to have gained this information if the applicant had not been interviewed.

5.3.4 Incomplete awareness of institutional roles

In this section, I discuss another topic where pre-encounter knowledge does not guarantee understanding of the originals, even though the applicant must have been exposed to this information repeatedly during the procedure. Rommetveit (1974: 50–51) states that '[s]ituated understandings are partial and fragmentary, dialogically constituted and only partially shared'. Wittgenstein (1953: 158) links situated understanding to '[n]ow I know how to go on'. I argue that both seem also to apply to understandings across encounters like the ones under investigation, which take place at different times. It seems that this partial understanding stays partial sometimes, even though the topic that is related to it has been discussed in earlier encounters.

In four cases which were probed during post-IME interview with the applicant (turns 10, 37, 39 and 41), the applicant encounters difficulties in understanding which legal organisation is responsible for which task (see Section 2.2.1). For example, the applicant indicated that he did not understand the difference between the INS and the court. In three of the four cases probed, the originals were miscommunicated and in one partly miscommunicated. The applicant did not know or could not clearly say which organisation performed the legal task under discussion, a factor which arguably contributed to miscommunication of the originals.

In Excerpt 1, it becomes clear that the court had ruled in favour of the applicant (turn 37) and had given the INS two choices: to accept the court's decision, in which case the INS would be expected to make a new decision, which would annul the previous decision; or to reject the decision of the court, in which case the INS would lodge an appeal, in which case the INS would have four weeks to do so. If the INS did not lodge this appeal (as in fact was the case – see turn 39), then it would have two choices: either to grant the applicant the more permanent asylum residence permit he sought or to come up with a 'decision in principle' in which the INS would indicate that it is planning to refuse the request of the applicant for an asylum permit. In the latter case, the applicant would be given an opportunity to convince the INS that it should change its mind and grant him the asylum residence permit (Section 1.2.3). During the IME, the lawyer was preparing for this last scenario; he double-checked the information in his report in order to base his response to the INS on factually correct information.

According to the lawyer, the INS cannot have filed an appeal, as the four-week deadline had expired (see turn 39). The lawyer explains that the INS now had six weeks, and that deadline was 'next Tuesday' (turn 41).

Before the post-IME interview, when the audio and the transcription were analysed, in Excerpt 1, due to certain linguistic choices made by the interpreter, I considered the rendition not clear enough and expected that it could have been problematic for the applicant. The pronoun 'they' in turn 42 was not specific enough and I saw the possibility of miscommunication. The post-IME interview made clear that in fact this had been the case. The applicant had thought it was the lower court that had to take the new decision, not the INS. When told that it was the INS that now had to take a decision, the applicant argued that the interpreter did not say this in his rendition. He followed this by saying that he generally did confuse the INS and the court. He attributed this to having gone to school for only a few years. Situational issues during the post-IME interview with me and during the IME with the lawyer could have contributed to this confusion over the tasks of different organisations, but under other circumstances the applicant might have been more capable of differentiating between these organisations.

The applicant will have heard the information during previous meetings with the lawyer, and with other institutions that hold meetings with applicants about their procedure such the Dutch Refugee Council (DRC), as explained in Chapter 2. However, the fact that understanding is generally partial, as discussed in Chapter 4, and as 'there is normally a considerable amount of vagueness in normal language use' (Linell, 2009) (see Section 4.3.2.7), this kind of miscommunication should not be considered strange, especially given that this is not 'normal language' and that legal information was found generally challenging by the applicant. But does this argument account for understanding in situated interactions only? Is there not a need to look at the notions of partial understanding and 'understanding for current purposes' in settings that deal with information across encounters, as in this case? I believe there is. Understanding across encounters, like the one under investigation, also seems to be partial, and interlocutors in these settings, too, seem to engage in understanding for 'current (practical) purposes'. Just as understanding during the current legal consultation is not complete, understanding across the procedure also is partial. Asylum-seekers cannot be expected to come to know everything about the procedure. In all probability, their understanding is partial – enough only for 'current (practical) purposes'.

5.4 Exploring Interpreter Strategies: Insights from Reflective Interviews

In this section, I explore the interpreter's strategic decision-making, drawing on the post-IME reflective interview. These findings show that the interpreter, while probably unaware of dialogism as a theory (see Chapter 4), was to a considerable extent aware of how sense-making takes place in IMEs. His answers during the reflective interview suggest that, unlike some other interpreters who may think that their job is to translate what is said rather than accommodate understanding actively, the interpreter in this case study believed his role was to help realise shared understanding between the lawyer and the applicant, and he repeatedly mentioned this. The interpreter's responses also indicated on several occasions that he thought he had to bridge the differences in knowledge between the applicant and the lawyer, and where necessary make use of various interventions, including reductions, expansions and substitutions.

The interpreter's responses in the interview indicate that he was aware that the nature of communication in IMEs requires interpreters to take on a different role from that of a translator. He noted that this brought with it challenges. The interpreter also indicated that it is important to consider the context in which a communicative event takes place when renditions are produced, and noted that the previous knowledge of the primary interlocutors has an influence on how communication progresses.

These reflections on the communicative process, and by extension sense-making within it, correspond to several central concepts in dialogism: (1) the notion of intersubjectivity; (2) the notion of alterity; (3) the fact that the interrelationship between notions like implicitness and vagueness and context (all resulting from the dialogical nature of situated interactions) leads to understanding becoming fragmentary, partial and partially shared; (4) the notion of contextualism; and (5) the notion of pre-encounter knowledge. These views must have had an influence on the manner in which the interpreter produced his renditions. That is, his translation decisions can be understood by utilising these central dialogical concepts (see Section 4.1.4).

In the sections below, I will discuss the translation decisions of the interpreter and link them to the corresponding dialogical concepts. For each concept, an excerpt provide context.

5.4.1 Fostering mutual understanding: The role of intersubjectivity in IMEs

As noted in Chapter 4, in dialogism intersubjectivity is a term that is generally used to refer to the interrelationship of communicating individuals with respect to cooperating communicatively during a social event with the aim of making sense of the world. Dialogism gives the 'other' an important role with regard to the 'acquisition of knowledge' (Lourenço *et al.*, 2013: 423) during the sense-making process. In the collected data, the interpreter shows a tendency to want to help the applicant understand the originals of the lawyer and vice versa. The 'others', in this case both the applicant and the lawyer, were constantly referred to by the interpreter when asked about his decisions. An example of this can be seen in Excerpt 10 (turn 361), where the interpreter expanded the original by adding على

Excerpt 10

360 Lawyer: waar ben je het meeste bang voor, voor de authoriteiten,je vader of voor de familie (.) Hussein,
Lawyer: what are you afraid of the most, of the authorities, your father or of the Hussein (.) family,

361 المترجم: مين أكتر (.) ناس او جهة بتخاف عل حياتك منا؟ (.) بَيَّك؟ النظام، ولا عائلة الحسين؟
Interpreter: which (.) people or party are you afraid the most of for your life? (.) your father? the regime, or the Hussein family?

362 اللاجئ: (بنبرة فاترة حزينة) والله الكلّ.
Immigrant: [*In a flat, sad tone*] Actually all of them.

363 …

364 Lawyer: waarom ben je bang voor de authoriteiten,
Lawyer: why are you afraid of the authorities,

365 المترجم: لشو انتى خايف من السلطات، او النظام،
Interpreter: why are you afraid of the authorities, or the regime,

حياتك ('for your life'). When asked about this during the reflective interview, the interpreter explained that these expansions are necessary for 'tāwḍīīḥ' ('making clear'). At the end of Excerpt 10, in turn 365, the expansion is similarly attributed to a need for 'tāwḍīīḥ'. The interpreter mentioned he expanded 'authoriteiten' ('authorities') to السلطات أو النظام ('sulutaat aw nidham'; 'authorities', or 'the regime') to ensure that the applicant understood what was meant by the lawyer. Generally, he said, Syrians do not use the word السلطات ('authorities'); rather, they use النظام ('the regime'). By expanding the original, he wanted to ensure that the meaning his rendition conveyed stayed close to the original, thus ensuring that the applicant understood the original, demonstrating his practical (although perhaps not theoretical or conceptual) understanding of the principle of intersubjectivity in communicative events (in addition to the use of his own pre-encounter knowledge).

Taking the 'other' into account (even when not aware of this dialogical concept) while making his translation decisions for the applicant, the interpreter was found also to take the other 'other' (that is the lawyer) into account in his pursuit to help both interlocutors to achieve shared understanding. The interpreter made clear during the reflective interview that he took the differences in the knowledge of the two others (the applicant and the lawyer) into account when he produced his renditions for the applicant. Taking the differences in knowledge into account relates also to the concept of alterity in dialogism.

5.4.2 Navigating alterity: The interpreter's adaptation to client knowledge and language use

Within dialogism alterity highlights the importance of recognising and valuing the unique perspectives each participant brings to a dialogue, serving as a counterbalance to intersubjectivity which focuses on shared understanding. Alterity enriches communication by embracing these differences, allowing for a more inclusive and comprehensive dialogue.

In his post-IME interview, the interpreter repeatedly stated that he often chooses to lower the register during encounters where he acts as interpreter, by using colloquial (informal) Arabic in his renditions. He said that this is necessary as otherwise, 'our people', here referring to the applicant in this study as an example, would not understand certain renditions. He mentioned that he tries at the beginning of an encounter to get an impression of the literacy/educational level of the client, without explicitly asking questions about it, and that he achieves this by listening to the way the applicant talks and examining the vocabulary he utilises. He then adapts the register he uses accordingly.

According to the interpreter, unlike at the INS, the court and other official bodies which hold that the interpreter has to translate 'word for word' (Mizori, 2017), it is permissible when interpreting with lawyers to raise or lower the register. The atmosphere in legal consultations is flexible and more informal, according to the interpreter, who stated that one can intervene, talk, add and correct if needed, 'even though this is not the work of the interpreter' (Mizori, 2017). Notably, the interpreter also added that he thinks that it is the primary responsibility of the lawyer to ensure that the register is adapted to the level of the applicant, but that the majority of the lawyers do not take this responsibility: 'The lawyer talks and ما إله علاقة هو ['ma ila ilaaqa howa'; 'it is not his concern'] whether the applicant understood or not'; he proceeded to state, 'I try, بقدر الإمكان ['bi qadar al imkaan'; 'as far as possible'], to make him understand if I see that the level is too low'.

This is illustrated by Excerpt 5, when the interpreter was asked why 'op een geven moment' ('at a given moment') was reduced (turns 55–56):

From Excerpt 5

55 Lawyer: e:m ik heb begrepen dat e: tus ik heb het verhaal zo begrepen= jouw vriendin (.) of nee jouw jouw neef had een vriendin e: een meisje leren kennen .hh waarmee e: ja die wat aanrommelde [*Laughs nasally*] om het zo maar te zeggen .hh (.) en (.) en op een gegeven moment heeft **jou** neef aan jou gevraagd om mee te gaan= zodat het meisje **ook** een vriendin mee zou nemen (.) en dan zou het allemaal wat minder (..) opvallen.

Lawyer: e:m I have understood that e: tog. I have understood the story in such a way=your **girl**friend (.) or no your your cousin had a girlfriend e: had met a girl .hh with whom e: yeah he used to mess around a little bit (*chuckles*) to put it this way .hh (.) and (.) and at a given moment **your** cousin asked you to accompany [them]=so that the girl **too** would take along a [girl] friend (.) and then things would be less (..) noticeable.

56 المترجم: يعني: (.) حسب ما هوى (.) فهم انّو ابن عمك (.) كان عندو رفيقة: (.) وعمل معا شغلا:ت، (.) وقال لك قال لك انّو تجي معو مشان هي كمان تجيب رفيقتها معا= مشان تغطو على هالموضوع.

Interpreter: yaʕni: (.) according to how he (.) has understood your cousin had a girl:friend (.) and he did things to her (.) and he said he said to you to come with him so that she too brings her [girl] friend with her=so you cover up this thing.

The interpreter said that the 'literacy/educational level' of the applicant would not have allowed him to understand it if rendered as في لحظة معينة ('lahtha mo ayana'; 'at a given moment'), as it would have been too formal. This expression was considered to be Modern Standard Arabic by the interpreter, and as the applicant would have found it difficult to understand, he chose not to translate it.

I believe that what the interpreter meant by 'lowering the register', in addition to choosing the informal mode of Arabic, was that he used less complex syntax (compared with the syntax used by lawyers) and less challenging vocabulary, resulting in a communicative style which is accessible to lay people. Of course, it is not unthinkable that he mentioned that he lowered the register during the reflective interview partly to save professional face. If this was the case, changing register, rather, reflected a means of easing the interpretation process. Despite the possibility of this more banal explanation, however, the interpreter's explanation for his change in register in and of itself (regardless of his actual motivation) demonstrated an awareness of the differences in interlocuters' understandings and its potential to influence sense-making, demonstrating a practical understanding of alterity's role in IMEs.

There are no 'textual' or 'activity' (as understood by Wadensjö) clues that the interpreter was using this strategy, and it would not have been possible to have reached that conclusion had I not spoken to him personally. The utility of post-IME interviews is clear here. Although these particular interventions did not have significant effects on the core meaning of the originals, such interventions may do so, particularly when dealing with complex backstories, legal technicalities, the intricacies of the asylum process, or the argumentation of institutions such as the INS. As explored in Chapter 2, miscommunication on any of these fronts can have severe implications for an applicant, given the importance of consistency in credibility assessments.

In summary, the interpreter adapted his translation decisions/strategies to suit the educational level of the applicant. He took into account the differences in the knowledge of the lawyer and the applicant and chose a translation strategy accordingly, demonstrating his awareness of alterity, even if he would not call it that. Adaptation of register and this kind of translation strategy are meant to serve the interests of the applicant with regard to understanding the originals of the lawyer. In the data, the interpreter is found to place more emphasis on alterity than on intersubjectivity when he discusses his strategies. He mentions that his renditions need to bridge the differences between the lawyer and the applicant, otherwise the applicant would not understand. He placed more importance on making the rendition understandable than on producing close renditions. The interpreter said in this regard that, nevertheless, he works within the degree of freedom granted to him by the lawyer. The largest group of renditions are in fact close renditions, constituting 35% of the interpreter's renditions.

5.4.3 Navigating implicitness and vagueness: The dialogic nature of interpreter-mediated communication

Talk is characterised by implicitness and vagueness, making understanding a challenging task. During talk, not everything is said or can be said and, as such, understanding can become fragmentary, partial and only partly shared. Context plays an important role in sense-making and meaning-making when interlocutors talk (see Section 4.3.2.4). It is context that helps the interlocutors make sense of what is said, as it helps them to determine which meanings are meant by the other interlocutor(s) among the (sometimes many) potential meanings words and expressions can hold. This is the third dialogical principle and my analysis shows that the interpreter was very well aware of this when formulating his renditions.

The interpreter expressed views to this effect on four occasions, noting: 'interpreting is not written translation'; and 'It is not translating word for word. It is important that you tāwḍīīḥ [make clear]) the idea as much as possible. Because languages and dialects are different' (Mizori, 2017). He contrasted the translation of written texts, where nothing is added or omitted, with interpreting, where it was sometimes necessary to help the applicant understand by providing extra contextual information.

In the examples that follow, I show that the interpreter was indeed aware of the challenges arising from the (generally) dialogic nature of interpreting, as well as of the fragmentary nature of meaning-making in communicative encounters. Words do not 'contain' meaning but represent potential meanings, and the interpreter seemed to know this.

In Excerpt 8 (pp. 89/152), the lawyer recounts how the backstory goes according to the information he has in his files, which is his second interactional goal during the IME. The lawyer expects the applicant either to confirm this information or to correct and/or complement it. Here, the interpreter produces an expansion. When requested to explain his expansion of the rendition with the adverbial بعد هالموضوع ('ba ad hal mawdo'; 'after this incident'), the interpreter indicated that he did so 'in order to make things clear for the applicant, in order to avoid questions like "when?" being asked'. The interpreter therefore seems to have provided context in order to empower the applicant to understand the rendition.

A range of contexts might have been assumed by the applicant in relation to the original 'you too did not seek to contact her for a number of weeks'. The original is in fact unproblematic, and so the lawyer did not provide the extra context. Interlocutors do not make every aspect of meaning explicit – some of it is left implicit (see Section 4.3.2.7). Implicitness forms an essential part of talk. The fact that the interpreter makes it explicit here could be viewed as an attempt to empower the applicant, to help the applicant in sense-making. Of course, it is also possible that the interpreter, not wanting to appear a 'bad' professional, provided this rationale as a cover for his divergence for the original, but this seems unlikely given the interpreter's understanding of alterity and intersubjectivity examined in the preceding sections.

5.4.4 Contextual influences on interpreter strategies: Settings and situations

In this section, I consider further how the interpreter incorporated context in his decision-making. He was found to take into consideration two types of context during the evaluation of the afforded material and the re-evaluation of his own thinking in the process of sense-making (i.e. in his internal dialogue): (1) that relating to the setting where the IME took place; and (2) that relating to the influence of the content of the conversation.

With regard to the former, the interpreter indicated that the setting where he worked influenced how he chose his translation decisions. As noted above (Section 5.5.2), the interpreter contrasted interpreting for formal institutions like the INS or the police, where the translation had to be 'word for word', with interpreting in a lawyers' offices, where he could adapt his strategy because of its 'shwayya' ('somewhat') informal nature.

In turn 57 of Excerpt 5, the applicant had corrected a piece of information for the lawyer: the girl he went out with was the sister of the girlfriend of his cousin, not her friend. In Excerpt 7, in turn 119, while reading the backstory of the applicant, the lawyer notices in his notes that the information corrected in turn 57 had already been corrected by the applicant in a previous IME between him and the applicant, and declares this to the applicant. In turn 120, the interpreter reduced 'goed' ('good') and 'trouwens' ('by the way').

When asked if he could explain this decision, the interpreter responded that the setting where he was working, that is, for the lawyer, must have influenced him, but he was not sure anymore. He said that at that point he must have thought these words unimportant and could be 'neglected' (Mizori, 2017) – they did not add to the meaning, nor did their absence affect it, as he said – or that in the context of the lawyer's office he took the free choice of just not translating them. He would have chosen to translate 'word for word' if this encounter had taken place in a police station or in an INS setting, for example, or in another official setting. I think this is a critical point – if as this case study suggests even individual interpreters alter their translation practices across settings (even within a single application process), the deficit of monological approaches in terms of identifying the influence of contextual factors on interpretation is a significant flaw in prevailing procedure design. Indeed, it is clear that that the interpreter in this case study adheres strictly to the how the INS theorises sense-making and meaning-making when involved in IMEs with them, as mentioned by the interpreter himself. Given that the INS generally adheres to monologism as theoretical framework (see Chapter 2), and the design of the procedure unsurprisingly is impacted by this theorisation, we have even more reason to critically engage with how sense-making and meaning-making are done during hearings. It must be noted of course that this finding, that the interpreter alters his translation strategies depending on the setting of a given IME, is bound to a single case study. Other interpreters may not do so, and rather elect to pursue a word-for-word translation (such that this is possible) across all settings. Nevertheless, the point stands that without a dialogical perspective of interpreting, in which the interpreter is an active agent in sense-making rather than a conduit of fixed linguistic meaning, this agency cannot be accounted for. On this basis, as will be explored further in Chapter 6, I further argue that an awareness of this agency is significantly augmented by the use of tools such as post-IME interviews in its capacity to identify if and where renditions have been subject to the influence of translation strategies.

The context and position of the applicant in the legal procedure also seems to have an influence on the interpreter's decision-making process. The interpreter mentioned that during this meeting, the backstory of the applicant was being revisited and the material was thus not new to the applicant. Accordingly, there was no need to produce close renditions. The applicant must have understood the original, he said. Again, looking at the findings of post-IME interview with the applicant, it appears that the applicant had indeed understood the rendition. In turn 120, the interpreter uses 'he corrected this matter' to remind the applicant that this subject had already been mentioned.

5.4.5 The influence of pre-encounter knowledge on interpreting strategies

The relevance of contextual influences discussed in the previous section is closely tied to the of concept of pre-encounter knowledge. The interpreter is well aware of the influence of pre-encounter knowledge on sense-making and that he takes it into account when he makes decisions with regard to translation strategies.

The interpreter was found to integrate pre-encounter knowledge in his internal dialogue when he makes translation decisions, whether this knowledge was information he himself had gained from his previous work, or information he thought had been gained by the applicant. The former is shown in how the interpreter altered his translation strategies when working with the INS, the police, and other formal institutions. An example of the applicant's pre-encounter knowledge type is the information dealt with during his previous meetings with the lawyer. The focus of this section is of this type of pre-encounter knowledge. The interpreter attributed some divergent renditions to his assumption that the applicant would understand these renditions, even though they were not close, because he had discussed those materials with his lawyer during previous meetings.

In Excerpt 6 (turn 95), the lawyer revisits the applicant's backstory. The interpreter produced a substituted rendition. The applicant agrees with the rendition: 'klap krijgen' ('to get hit/a slap') was substituted with ضربك

Excerpt 6

94 Lawyer: en jij krijgt toen een klap (.) van een van de agenten.
Lawyer: and then you received a blow (.) from one of the policemen.

95 المترجم: واحد منّون (.) من هدول الشرطة ضربك؟
Interpreter: one of them (.) of these policemen hit you?

96 اللاجئ: صح
Immigrant: correct

('darabak'; 'beat you'). During the post-IME interview with the interpreter, I argued that ضربك was not as specific as 'klap krijgen'. The interpreter responded that a close translation would be وجهلك ضربة ('wajjah lak darba'; 'to deal you a blow') but this is not used in Syrian colloquial Arabic, where one would say ضربك ('beat you'). I then reminded him that ضربك can refer to various types of physical contact, such as punching, slapping or other forms of hitting, without specifying the method or intensity – it is a general word for beating. He responded: '[the translation] gives the intended meaning; it suffices'. When asked if there were any other possible reasons, he responded 'e::, because both [the applicant and the lawyer] are talking about something they already know, they understand it and I thought the word ضربك is sufficient and the meaning is clear to both parties already'.

While one cannot guarantee that the interpreter accurately remembered the specific details of the encounter, the type of explanation he offers has been given repeatedly (see previous sections), suggesting that it reflects how he believes he should be translating. The rendition in this excerpt may thus be shaped by pre-encounter knowledge he had accumulated, including from earlier interpreting experiences. His awareness of colloquialisms in Syrian Arabic and their contextual appropriateness further illustrates the role of such pre-encounter knowledge. Moreover, his explanation underscores its importance in the process of sense-making during interpreter-mediated encounters.

Thus, across the 'interpreter strategies' grouping of renditions, multiple dialogical concepts can be seen to be at play. Here, too, the interpreter's claim 'it suffices' alludes to the notion of knowledge that is good enough for current practical purposes, the subject of the following section.

5.4.6 Interpreting for 'current (practical) purposes': Pragmatic understandings in IMEs

The interpreter was often found to be working towards producing understanding that was 'sufficient' for the applicant. In Section 4.3.2.6 it was noted that Linell (2009: 226) stresses that understanding is needed only for 'current (practical) purposes'. In Excerpt 9, the lawyer revisits the backstory of the applicant (turn 244). The interpreter does not start translating immediately. He engages in a side-sequence with the lawyer. He first wants to asked about something mentioned by the lawyer. When he gets an answer, without back-channelling with the applicant, the interpreter produces a rendition where the last sentence of the original is reduced (turn 248). When asked why, he said that it يفي بالغرض ('yafi bil gharadh'; 'suffices for the purpose'). He mentioned similar instances repeatedly during the reflective interview (Mizori, 2017).

It is probable that the side-sequence caused the interpreter to forget the detailed structure of the lawyer's original. However, because 'the family', a major character in the backstory, was well known to the applicant, he

Excerpt 9

244 Lawyer: en mense mensen zeiden hoe (.) **h**aal het je in je hoofd om met **die** familie e problemen te maken. De familie van (.) jouw vriendin bedoelde ze.
Lawyer: and people people said how (.) **d**id you get it into your head to make e problems with **that** e family. They meant the family (.) of your girlfriend.

245 Interpreter: mensen zei u?
Interpreter: you said people, Sir?

246 Lawyer: ja de politieagenten
Lawyer: yes the police officers

247 Interpreter: o de politie.
Interpreter: oh the police.

248 المترجم: وقلّك (.) الشرطة قلّك شو: (.) كي:ف خطر ببالك انّو تعمل (.) مشكل مع هيك (.) عائلة (.) مع هدولى الناس.
Interpreter: and (.) the police said what the hell (.) how did you get it into your head to make (.) problems with such (.) a family (.) with those people.

249 اللاجئ: صح
Immigrant: correct

must have known what the interpreter meant by 'such a family', especially because this original was used in the context of discussing the consequences of the enmity of this family for him. The interpreter might have thought that his rendition was not a close one but that the applicant had probably already understood which family the lawyer was talking about. During the post-IME interview with the applicant, he did indeed seem to have understood the original.

5.5 The 'No Conscious Strategy' Group

In certain cases, the interpreter did not or could not provide in his post-IME interview an explanation for some of his translation decisions. I have grouped these into one overarching 'no conscious strategy' group. During the post-IME interview, I developed an understanding of the professional identity of the interpreter and his theorisation interpreting. Our interaction lasted several hours and was of sufficient depth for me to infer certain possibilities when he said that he had 'no conscious strategy' in relation to a particular translation decision.

When considered against the backdrop of sense-making in asylum procedures, this grouping highlights the contrast between the reality of sense-making in IMEs, on the one hand, and the illusion of certainty and precision of meaning created by monological approaches and entextualisation, on the other. The fundamental nature of interpreting fosters challenges to sense-making and meaning-making, predicated on immediacy of communication, the nature of discourse and the faculties and limitations of the human mind. Without a reflective tool, such as post-IME interviews, an asylum procedure is largely unable to account for such potential sources of miscommunication.

5.5.1 Immediate nature of the communicative event

Interpreting is practised in real-time. The interpreter did not refer to this fact explicitly when explaining his decisions, but indirectly, for example when he said that 'Interpreting is not written translation' (Mizori, 2017). While producing renditions, he might not have had (enough) time to reflect on or (re-)evaluate some of the afforded material or some of the decisions he had made. When the process of evaluation and re-evaluation in the interpreter's internal dialogue is strained by external factors such as immediacy, it may unfold differently than it would without such strain. For example, at turn 11 in Excerpt 4, the interpreter indicated that this rendition was what he was able to think of at that moment: 'this is what I what was able to think of back then'. This suggests that, at another moment, the interpreter could have thought of another rendition. This phenomenon is represented seven times in the data but I will focus on this example in Excerpt 4.

During the IME, the lawyer revisited the legal procedure of the applicant, which was the first of three interactional goals he pursued. To recap, he started the IME by outlining how the legal procedure had developed so far. At a certain point (turn 10), he started to introduce the view of the INS. The lawyer told the applicant that the INS had made

From Excerpt 4

10 Lawyer: en e: (.) de IND (.) heeft (.) daar op zitting ook gezegd dat ze vonden dat we eigenlijk=dat je helemaal geen recht had om in (.) beroep te gaan (.) omdat je geen belang had=want je hebt nu verblijfsvergunning .h dus dan kun je niet in beroep e e tegen een asielbesluit.

Lawyer: and e: (.) the INS (.) said (.) there during the [court] session indeed that they were of the opinion that we actually=that you had no right whatsoever to (.) lodge an appeal (.) because you had no interest=for you have now a residence permit .h so you cannot lodge an appeal e e against an asylum decision.

11 المترجم: وأث (.) وأثناء الجلسى (.) دائرة الهجرة والتجني:س قا:لت أنّو هنّى (.) إي بيشو إي يعني من رَأيُن إي أنوّ إنت إي ما من حقك أنو تتقدم ب: (..) طَلب إي إي ب: إستئناف ضد القرارْ لأنو ما من مصلحتك لأنّو أنتى حصّلت (.) على الإقامة.

Interpreter: and du (.) and during the [court] session (.) the Immigration and Naturalisation Servi:ce sai:d that they (.) e: think e: yaʕni they are of the opinion e: that you e: have no right to lodge (..) e: e: an appeal against °the decision° because it is **not** in your interest because you [already] have (.) received the [residence] permit.

12 Lawyer: e: en ik heb toen uitgelegd (.) **bij** de rechtbank (.) dat ik vind dat er wel **de**gelijk belang is omdat jij .hh e een verblijfsvergunning heb gekregen vanwege de de algeme slechte siuatie in Syria (.) op dit momen.

Lawyer: e: and I explained then (.) **in** court (.) that I believe that there is **cer**tainly interest because you .hh e received a residence permit due to the the general bad situation in Syria (.) at this moment.

13 المترجم: وهو إي وضّح (.) مَعُن عند المحكمة (.) إنّهو (.) أنتى فعلا (.) في إلَك مصلحة (.) في الإستئناف (.) لأنّو إنتى حصلت على الإقامة (.) على ضوء (.) الوضع (.) إي: السيئ (.) حاليا (.) في (.) سوريا؟

Interpreter: And he e explained (.) with [*sic*] them at [*sic*] the court (.) that (.) you do indeed (.) have an interest (.) in [lodging] an appeal (.) because you have received the residence [permit] (.) in view of the (.) bad (.) e: situation (.) at present (.) in (.) Syria?

it clear during the court session, in which the appeal of the applicant against an earlier decision of the INS was being heard, that in its view the applicant had no interest in submitting an appeal because he had already been granted a residence permit. This is where Excerpt 4 begins.

The interpreter produces a rendition at turn 11, where he makes a substitution. It concerns the clause 'omdat je geen belang had' ('because you had no interest'), which was translated as لأنو ما من مصلحتك ('Li anno ma min maslahtak'; '([because it is **not** in your interest'), which in Arabic could carry the pragmatic meaning that something could turn out to be bad for you. During the post-IME interview with the applicant, conducted a week earlier than the interview with the interpreter, it turned out that the applicant had not understood the rendition as meant by the lawyer/INS but, rather, as meaning 'because it is not in your interest' as rendered by the interpreter, carrying the negative connotation referred to above. The interpreter mentioned during his post-IME interview that this was what he was able to think of at that moment, admitting that this element should have been translated differently.

The same phrase 'omdat je geen belang had' ('because you had no interest') was used again by the lawyer in the following turn 12. It is noticeable that the interpreter produced a closer rendition this time. This might be an indication that on this occasion the interpreter had had enough time to think of a closer rendition and that the substitution produced the first time was probably due to immediacy. It seems that in the time interval between his last rendition (turn 13) and the first version of it (turn 11), the interpreter found enough time to re-evaluate the afforded material and his own thinking, and produce a better rendition.

5.5.2 Influence of the nature of discourse

In the previous section, I examined decisions the interpreter could not directly explain during the post-IME interview. Here, I explore the unfolding nature of talk and its impact on sense-making in such encounters, focusing on an instance where the interpreter offered no explanation for his translation.

During the IME, the lawyer discussed the legal procedure with the applicant, which was one of the three interactional goals of the IME. In Excerpt 11, the lawyer is discussing a weak point (from his perspective) in the applicant's backstory and tries to elicit information from the applicant that might be used to form counter-arguments to the INS. In the excerpt, the interpreter reduces (the underlined part in turn 373) an important part of the original in which the lawyer explains why the INS might have a strong point.

During the post-IME interview with the interpreter, I wanted to identify why the interpreter made this reduction, but the interpreter said that he had 'no idea why' (Mizori, 2017). However, the unfolding nature

Excerpt 11

373 Lawyer: .hh dat is al een belangrijk punt in je verhaal= waar de waar de IND ook op gaat **zitten** (.) van **waarom waarom** hebben die politieagenten dit gedaan, ik bedoel= ze kregen de opdrach om jou (.) **op** te pakken =want ze wisten waar je was (.) en ze laten je gewoon (.) lopen= zo zullen ze **zelf** ook in problemen komen.
Lawyer: .hh this is already an important point in your backstory= which which the INS will **scrutinise** (.) in the sense **why why** did those police agents did this, I mean=they were assigned to (.) arrest you=for they knew where you were (.) and they just let you (.) go=this way they will get into trouble **themselves** too.

374 المترجم: يعني هاي النقطة بَدها تركز عليها دائرة الهجرة والتجنيس إي الشرطة لشو عملو هوك هيك هنّي إي كانو عرفانين انت وين وجايين لعندك ومسكوك (صوت اللاجئ يُسمع قائلا «صحيح») ولو كان بدّون ايّاك كانوا أخذوك هيك ما كانوا خلّوك هيك تهرب!
Interpreter: yaʕni this point the Immigration and Naturalisation Service will concentrate on e: the police why did they do this they e knew where you were and they came to you and caught you [*Immigrant interjects: 'correct'*] and if they had wanted you they would've taken you just like that they wouldn't have let you escape so easily!

375 اللاجئ: والله .. (غير واضح) تنزل تحت تس تسمع ضرب رصاص .. (غير واضح) نقوس تهرب انت (.) ابوك عَدنا ترجع تسلم حالك.
Immigrant: well [*unintelligible*] you go down when you hear hear shots [*unintelligible*] we shoot you run away (.) we have your father later you give yourself up again.

376–377
Interpreter: Dat weet ik niet .. [*unintelligible: muddled talk.*] je gaat naar buit= je gaat naar beneden (.) en als je beschietingen hoort [*last four words are pronounced in a nonchalant manner unlike how the immigrant had talked*] dan moet je vluchten en daarna weer melden want (.) wij hebben jouw vader (.) toen ik waarom (.) naar rede vroeg e e zeiden ze e e dat ik m'n mond maar moest doen [*especially the last seven words pronounced in a flat and thinking manner*].
Interpreter: I don't know .. [*unintelligible: muddled talk.*] you go outsi= you go down (.) and if you hear shellings [*sic*] [*last four words are pronounced in a nonchalant manner unlike how the immigrant had talked*] then you must run away and then report again for (.) we have your father (.) when I why (.) informed about the reason e e they said e e that I had to shut up [*especially the last seven words pronounced in a flat and thinking manner*].

of discourse provides some insight into this. Repetition could have been the reason why the interpreter might have felt that it was not necessary to mention that piece of information, but the transcribed text does not support this. It seems more likely that the complex linguistic nature of the original made it in fact impossible for the interpreter to keep the reduced part. Using the second personal pronoun, the lawyer directs his utterance towards the applicant. He provides an evaluation of what he will say next: 'hh that is already an important point in your backstory'. Then, the lawyer changes footing, and talks from the perspective of the INS. He does this by predicting that the INS will come up with an argument, which he introduces from the perspective of the INS: 'which which the INS will **scrutinise**'. Note the stressed lexical item '**scrutinise**'; arguably, the accent placed on this, together with the accent placed on the lexical items '**why why**' (in the same turn 373: '**why why** those police agents did this'), shows that he is adopting the perspective of the INS itself. Then, the lawyer again changes footing again and introduces his own point of view by saying, 'I mean=...'.

In his rendition, the interpreter does seem to to match these changes of footing, but at some cost. Possibly, the change of footing required more attention from him, made even more challenging when the applicant produced the interjection 'correct' close to where the reduced part came, interrupting the interpreter's train of thought (turn 374). When the applicant takes his turn (turn 375), no trace is found of the missing (reduced) part, which could mean that the interpreter's reduction caused him to miss that part. It is interesting that when the interpreter translates this response of the applicant in turn 376, he produces an expanded rendition in which he appears to add information not said by the applicant but sought by the lawyer. This is the explanation the lawyer was searching for in his original (turn 373): '[...] **why why** those police agents did this'. It is not clear whether the interpreter made this expanded rendition because he found it difficult to produce a close rendition for linguistic reasons, or because he realised that the lawyer wanted an answer to the missing part, which he had by then realised he had reduced in the previous rendition. It is possible that the interpreter realised at this latter point (turns 376–377) that the lawyer's question had been left unanswered, and as such he might have felt during the interaction that he had to compensate. It is impossible to know if the interpreter was aware he had made a reduced rendition at the time of its utterance but nevertheless later became aware that the answer sought by the lawyer had not been given. It is also interesting that the interpreter made his expansion in a way that could be understood to be the answer to the lawyer's question. This part was produced in a vague way, possibly to prevent the applicant from knowing he was making a rendition which diverged from his original. It was possibly produced to satisfy the need of the lawyer for an answer. No clear-cut reference to the lawyer's question was made. The lawyer then proceeded to another point.

While the interpreter said during his post-IME interview that he had 'no idea why' he had made this reduction (possibly because he did not remember what had happened at that point), based on my professional experience as an interpreter, I tend to think that the interpreter was distracted by the interjection of the applicant and later realised that he had reduced this part of the original.

The point here is that the complex, unfolding nature of talk during such communicative activities (with responses) constituted a challenge for the interpreter. Time constraints, in combination with the complex nature of talk, could lead to translation decisions the interpreter might not have made if he had had more time. In Excerpt 11, the interpreter found the process of evaluating and re-evaluating his own thinking (i.e. his internal dialogue) challenging because of the complex nature of talk and its immediacy. The fact that the interpreter in Excerpt 11, and in Excerpt 4 in the previous section, appeared to have realised that he had to repair the mistake he had made in the previous rendition could be evidence of this point. It is notable also that during his post-IME interview, the applicant turned out to have understood the rendition.

5.5.3 Memory/recollection

The interpreter has to deal with discourse almost as fast as it is being produced: interpretation takes place in real-time (Lai & Mulayim, 2014). In turn, the interpreter's sense-making begins the moment the lawyer starts to produce his original and goes on until the rendition has been produced, because the applicant also contributes to this sense-making. The very presence of the applicant influences the meaning-making, even if he does not say anything (see Chapter 4). Unlike translators, interpreters often do not have (enough) time to reflect on their translations; and often do not have enough time to take (enough) notes because of the 'immediacy' of the event (Lai & Mulayim, 2014).

The interpreter might also simply forget to translate something. For example, in Excerpt 4 (turn 1), the lawyer has just started the meeting with the applicant. He tells the applicant that he and the applicant have long been busy with the asylum procedure. It is noticeable that the adverbial 'lo:ng' (with the elongation showing displeasure) has been reduced by the interpreter and replaced by 'some', without the elongation. During his post-IME interview, the interpreter said he must have forgotten to translate it (Mizori, 2017) and was unable to find another reason.

The original is not very long, the interpreter was still fresh, as meeting had just started and was not at the end of a long day. It is possible that while developing his thoughts during his internal dialogue, he was distracted by some afforded material provided by one of the primary interlocutors. It is also possible that this was visual material as nothing could be heard in the recorded audio. The turns that follow do not provide any interactional indications about this. It is possible that because this piece of information was not decisive for understanding the original and because the applicant already knew that he had been busy with his immigration procedure, no attention was given to it, or it went unnoticed. The interpreter relativised the impact of this reduction during his post-IME interview by saying that the applicant knew that he had been busy with the procedure for a long time.

The very nature of interpreting engenders the loss of some afforded material in an IME. A translator would be less likely to make a similar omission in a written text. During the post-IME interview with the applicant, it seemed that he had understood the original and so the reduction does not seem to have influenced his understanding. Some eight occurrences relating to memory/forgetting were in the data (see Table 1).

5.5.4 Interpreter's strategies: Summary

For the group of renditions for which the interpreter did not or could not provide explanations during his post-IME interview, it is necessary to refer instead to the nature of the profession, that of its discourse and the transcribed text. Nevertheless, the interpreter did give me rich material which I have drawn on in the discussion. I have divided the discussion above into three parts for organisational purposes, not to suggest that the phenomena happen separately: they can all occur in one rendition and across a number of renditions.

The 'no conscious strategy' grouping of renditions underscores the relevance of dialogical perspectives. While monologism and the process of entextualisation create a false impression of certainty in terms of sense-making and meaning-making, dialogism accounts for the human dimension of communication. The three phenomena examined are all influenced by the human nature of the interpreter. The immediacy of translation demands much of even the most skilled interpreter. Similarly, the unfolding nature of discourse means that the task of an interpreter operates, in a sense, both forwards and backwards across the communicative event, even in a single rendition. What has been said, is being said and will likely be said all have a bearing on the suitability of a rendition. A given piece of talk morphs as additional words are spoken, with the ensuing meaning-making similarly shifting as interlocutors assess and reassess afforded material and their own internal dialogues. Memory, or rather the limitations of it, adds another layer of complexity to the interpreting process.

Dialogism, unlike monologism, foregrounds these factors. While the post-IME interview with the interpreter did not produce the strategies behind the discussed renditions, they succeeded in identifying the absence of them. As Chapter 3 noted, these are cases where the text itself offers little in the way of insight into meaning-making. The post-IME interview, coupled with a dialogical awareness of the nature of talk, allows an observer potentially problematic renditions to be identified. This is significant in itself, for, as Chapter 2 highlighted, an asylum application largely succeeds or fails on the basis of credibility. In a post-IME interview, a problematic rendition or series of exchanges can be reassessed.

5.6 Synthesis of the Findings: The Crucial Role of Reflective Interviews in Legal Interpreter-Mediated Communication

This chapter has shown how the use of post-IME interviews can generate valuable insights into the sense-making process in IMEs. Unlike traditional reliance on transcribed data, which decision-makers and legal representatives in asylum procedures depend on, this study's approach includes post-encounter interviews with the interlocutors, which allows much of the information that is frequently overlooked without reflective interviews to be recognised and utilised. This can greatly enhance understanding among all parties involved and thereby promote fairness.

The chapter's core argument is that integrating interview data alongside entextualised data allows decision-makers to form a fuller picture of the interactions within IMEs, such as the detailing of applicant backgrounds and stories, and responses to questions from asylum authorities. By highlighting the applicants' perspectives and the interpreters' decision-making processes, it becomes possible to address potential misunderstandings and biases more effectively, promoting a fairer asylum process. The chapter therefore advocates for systemic changes in asylum procedures that integrate dialogist principles into interpreting practices.

This chapter also answers the second research question in this case study in showing that the applicant comprehended the majority of the renditions (see Section 5.2). This can be explained by his reliance not only on the renditions but also, significantly, on his pre-encounter knowledge. For instance, he often made assumptions about the interpreter's material, incorporating his previous knowledge into the sense-making process. This integration of pre-encounter knowledge with the current interaction explains why most renditions were understood; the applicant was already familiar with much of the information from previous IMEs with the lawyer.

Some originals were, though, still challenging for the applicant (see Section 5.2). Despite prior exposure, the complex nature of legal discourse proved difficult to grasp fully, as would be true for any non-professional.

Section 5.3 showed that the post-IME interview with the interpreter provided information which would be difficult, if not impossible, to infer. The interpreter, understandably, did not have explanations for every translation decision due to constraints related to the nature of the profession, its discourse, the situational context and memory.

Where reasons for translation decisions were provided, the interpreter had adopted a dialogic approach to communication, striving to help primary interlocutors understand each other and adapting his decisions to the applicant's abilities. This approach took into account the nature of oral communication, contextual influences and pre-encounter knowledge, highlighting the complexity of the sense-making process. Excluding the perspectives of interlocutors impoverishes the understanding of these processes. When participants enter IMEs, they bring with them their life experiences, which play a crucial role in their interactions and need to be carefully considered.

For researchers, integrating dialogist principles into interpreting practices offers a robust framework for investigating interpreter-mediated communication. Furthermore, by showcasing the importance of reflective interviews, the chapter enriches the analytical toolkit available to researchers and practitioners.

6 Asylum Interviews and Hearings: The Problem of Information Loss in Asylum Procedures and How to Address It

Deficiencies in the design of contemporary asylum procedures lead to the loss of key elements of contextual information, as shown by the case study. Much of this information could be effectively (re)captured through the use of interviews, during or after IMEs, especially when guided by the contemporary theoretical framework of dialogism. Utilising this often-overlooked and/or neglected contextual data could significantly enhance both the efficacy and the equity of asylum processes in the Global North. Such a shift would contribute to mitigating the influence of fear-driven populist politics that has increasingly shaped asylum discourse, thereby realigning these processes with the original principles and humanitarian ethos underpinning the Convention on Refugees. The chapter summarises the three key reasons why this valuable information remains unexploited:

(1) As Chapter 2 showed, the current procedure is generally founded on an outdated, monological view of communication. Chapter 2 also explained the influence of politics on the design of asylum procedures, and that that design needs reform because its lack of a contemporary grounding inhibits the identification of vital information, as explained in Chapter 3. Chapter 5 expanded on this point to show how dialogism (explored theoretically in Chapter 4) and tools such as reflective interviews can capture contextual information that would otherwise be lost.
(2) Key stakeholders, such as legal professionals and immigration officials, are largely unaware of the significance of this type of data and where this data can be found and/or is stored – in the minds of interlocutors in a communicative event. They are likely to be unaware of theories of language which emphasise the importance of this information that could support more informed decision-making.
(3) Even when stakeholders (including legal professionals and immigration offices) as well do recognise this information's value, they may hesitate to allocate additional time and resources for its extraction. Chapters 1

and 2 explained the influence of politics on the asylum procedure, particularly the pressures that limit not only time and resources but also the type and scope of collectable information, as a byproduct of the policies and procedures designed to discourage asylum applications by creating a 'hostile environment' (see Chapter 2).

The book strongly advocates the adoption of the contemporary version of dialogism as the primary theoretical framework in interpreting in asylum procedures and their associated legal consultations. This unified and cohesive theoretical approach would benefit not only interpreters but also scholars in the field, interpretation educators and users of interpretation services.

6.1 Restating My Research

This book revolves around the quality of communication during interpreter-mediated encounters (IMEs) during asylum procedures, especially the legal consultations between applicants and lawyers. The insights into the communicative dynamics at play in IMEs in the Dutch asylum procedure are highly likely to apply in asylum procedures across the Global North. While the focus has been on these legal consultations, the findings allow for careful inferences about the broader asylum procedure. As I have argued throughout this book, asylum procedures are unfair to asylum applicants, as a consequence of deficiencies in their design, and in particular their overreliance o on a monological understanding of language and the mind, as explained in Chapter 2. Chapters 3 and 5 have shown that much relevant information can stay hidden within the minds of interlocutors during a given procedure. These inadequacies are not only to the disadvantage of the asylum applicant and interpreter, but also the Dutch Immigration and Naturalisation Service (INS) and the state itself.

This information in the minds of the interlocutors is, though, recoverable. The textual reports of hearings and meetings are not the entire story. Capturing this information in a manner that allows its use both during and after an asylum procedure does not require a significant change to the process as much as it requires a new mindset. The addition of post-IME interviews (be they detailed or short), if and when deemed necessary by a party to the procedure, would allow for the recovery of this otherwise lost contextual information without disrupting the overall structure of asylum procedures. Such interviews need not be laborious. Their ultimate goal is to build some reflexive capacity into IMEs and by extension the asylum procedure. Even during IMEs, this reflexivity with regard to sense-making might be achieved by a legal representative or caseworker asking questions like, 'What did you understand here?', 'Can you tell me what you thought about ... ?', or 'What did you make of this translation?' and so forth. With specific reference to the interpreter, question such as, 'How did you translate this?', 'Can you explain why you chose this strategy/made this decision' can help to make the sense-making process more transparent. Such questions create the capacity to monitor sense-making as it occurs, providing an opportunity to revisit areas of communication that may produce miscommunications if left unresolved. In my experience as an interpreter, the vast majority of cases of linguistic miscommunication in IMEs can be averted by such minimally intrusive interventions. Some cases, certainly, may require a full post-IME interview of the sort presented in the case study, but this would still offer a significant economy of time and resources if an appeal process is thereby avoided.

The recovery of such information, through the methods recommended in this chapter, would be to the benefit of all parties involved. Applicants would have reduced chances of unfair verdicts by having more opportunity to tell their stories and clarify misunderstandings. Interpreters would be afforded a safeguard against the potential negative consequences of the pressures on them by the current design of procedures and the inherent nature of their profession (see Chapter 2, and Sections 5.4 and 5.5, respectively). Lawyers would be provided an additional stream of information, giving them a broader and more accurate basis for their legal arguments. The INS (and analogous institutions) would enjoy the prospect of fewer appeals on the basis of missed information or inaccurate characterisations of the applicant, as well as having its core task of assessing credibility greatly facilitated. Lastly, the state, regardless of the prevailing social and political attitudes towards asylum and migration, would find itself with a reformed process better suited to fulfilling whatever mandate it sets.

I call here for a re-engagement with the communication process throughout the procedure. The procedure should prioritise legal, scholarly and communicative aspects over political considerations. This entails states conducting procedures in line with legal obligations under the 1951 Refugee Convention, and in a manner informed by sound scholarly principles. The goal should be to move away from political manoeuvring aimed at reducing asylum applications or the number of recognised claims, and closer to the development of approaches that honour the spirit of international obligations. This approach will benefit all parties, including those who implement policy. When asylum-seekers and their legal representatives are satisfied with the communicative aspects of the hearings, they will have fewer reasons to appeal. Within this, I call for more engagement on the part of immigration services, legal representatives and the judiciary with sociolinguistic scholarship which looks into sense-making and meaning-making. I argue that there is currently both the need and the capacity for such an effort to facilitate the recovery of this type of information. Critically, such change entails abandoning monological approaches towards understanding communication. As I argue throughout this book, I believe this is best achieved by adopting dialogism, or aspects of it. Further, implementing these recommendations does not necessarily and automatically need to lead to increased costs or resources if carried out with strategic insight, as I will explain below.

The case study investigated the sense-making processes (constituting communication) in an asylum-related IME in a lawyer's office in the Netherlands. This IME was a meeting between a Dutch-speaking lawyer and a Syrian-Arabic-speaking asylum applicant who had been granted 'subsidiary protection', in the form of a temporary residence permit, but was who therefore still seeking international protection and full residence rights. The interpreter was Middle Eastern and Arabic-speaking. The case study investigated how this interpreter rendered the originals of the lawyer, and whether or not the applicant understood the translated originals. Both lines of enquiry sought to understand how the sense-making and meaning-making processes unfolded during the IME from the perspective of the applicant and the interpreter, and how this influenced the meaning-making processes on the part of both participants. More concretely, during fieldwork, I had three research questions in mind:

(1) How does the interpreter render the originals of the lawyer?
(2) Does the applicant understand these originals (via the renditions), and what can be learned from the applicant's answers in terms of the sense-making and meaning-making processes?
(3) How does the interpreter explain his translation decisions, and what can be learned from them in terms of the sense-making and meaning-making processes?

The remainder of this chapter in structured as follows. Section 6.2 provides a summary of the findings related to the renditions produced in the case study. From there, Section 6.3 draws together the analysis of interpreting made in this book, focusing on the need to integrate dialogism into professional practice, particularly in asylum contexts. Section 6.4 addresses the limitations of this study, while Section 6.5 suggests areas for further research. Section 6.6 articulates the book's core message – the need to reform asylum procedures to incorporate aspects of the advances made in the theory of dialogism. Section 6.7 concludes with some final thoughts and reflections on my position as a researcher, interpreter and former asylum applicant.

6.2 Summary of the Findings

This section is divided into two parts, organised largely along the lines of the second and third research questions. The data relating to the first research question was presented in Table 1 (Section 5.1). To briefly recap, just under 36% of the total 110 renditions recorded in this IME were categorised as close renditions. The interpreter employed a number of interventions, including substitutions, expansions and reductions, to facilitate the interpretation process. As Chapter 3 explained, many of these renditions when examined purely textually raise questions related to their influence on the sense-making process or as to the translation strategies employed in producing them. Chapter 5 revisited some of the more salient renditions, producing the findings summarised in the following sub-sections.

The interpreter in the case study already had a working understanding of several dialogist principles. This opens the question as to whether similar insights have been intuited by other interpreters, as well as caseworkers and decision-makers, and utilised due to sheer necessity. Briefing all stakeholders working with virtually any mandate concerning asylum that values accurate, informed and effective decision-making (i.e. regardless of a desire to reduce or increase the number of successful applications) on dialogism's core tenets can only improve asylum procedures. Consider the absurdity of the proposition 'everyone always means exactly what they say, exactly as it is heard'. This is the world that monologism implies to be the case when coupled with ridig entextualisation. That procedures are designed, staff trained and verdicts rendered with this implicit claim is a problem that has an easy, dialogical, solution.

6.2.1 Renditions understood (or not): The applicant's sense-making

Chapter 4 showed that the process of sense-making needs to be studied holistically. Sense-making is contributed to by all the participants during the interaction. Therefore, all the participants' perspectives need to be incorporated into its analysis. In the context of the second research question, Chapter 5 showed that the applicant depended not only on the renditions produced during the interaction but also on his internal dialogue and 'material' learned, among other things, during previous interactions with the lawyer and various asylum organisations (pre-meeting/pre-encounter knowledge). While pre-encounter knowledge is very important to the applicant's understanding (Section 5.2), it does not allow him to understand all the originals (Section 5.3). In this regard, nodding or giving a semiotic response suggesting understanding does not necessarily mean that the applicant had indeed understood. The post-IME interview method utilised in this study, inspired by dialogism, was able to elicit insights into this issue and raised questions regarding the interrelationship between pre- encounter knowledge and the different IMEs. The results lead me to argue that notions such as 'partial understanding' and 'understanding for current (practical) purposes' (see Section 4.3.2.6) are not confined to one IME but could also be seen in relation to communication across IMEs.

In the next section, I bring to the fore the outcomes related to the interpreter (and thus the third research question), which are related to those of the second research question.

6.2.2 Renditions justified: The interpreter's decisions

Chapter 5 showed that the process of meaning-making is complicated. While the interpreter may not have been able to fully reconstruct his internal dialogue during the post-IME interview, he did provide insightful information regarding the process of meaning-making. Although he was probably unaware of dialogism as a theory, he was aware of how sense-making takes place in IMEs (see Section 5.5 and online Appendix II):

(1) he thought it was his job as an interpreter to help realise something akin to 'shared understanding' (Wadensjö, 1998) between the lawyer and the applicant;
(2) he thought he had to bridge the differences in knowledge between the applicant and the lawyer;
(3) he was aware that the nature of communication in 'communicative event(s)' such as the one under investigation is different from that dealt with by translators working with written texts, and that this brings challenges for the interpreter;
(4) he thought that the context in which a communicative event takes place needs to be taken into consideration when renditions are produced;
(5) he thought that the previous knowledge of the primary interlocutors influences how communication progresses during such communicative events.

These points correspond to central concepts in dialogism regarding how sense is made during conversations. As noted in Chapter 4, the dialogical, cognitivist theorisation of communication posits that communication is a subjective, negotiated process in which meaning is co-constructed by discourse participants. The interpreter's conceptions of his role above thus refer correspondingly to: (1) the notion of intersubjectivity; (2) the notion of alterity; (3) the fact that the interrelationship between notions like implicitness and vagueness with context (which bring about the dialogic nature of situated interactions) leads to understanding becoming 'fragmentary', 'partial' and 'partially shared' (Rommetveit, 1974); (4) the notion of contextualism (Linell, 2009); and (5) the notion of pre-encounter knowledge (see Section 4.3.2.9). I argue that these views must have influenced how the interpreter produced his renditions during the IME and that his translation decisions can be understood by utilising the central dialogical concepts referred to here.

6.3 Theoretical Development: Merging Academic Advances and Professional Perspectives

The theorisation of interpreting studies, particularly in the realm of dialogue interpreting, is more recent than has been the case in translation studies, and even more so than in other academic disciplines. Interpreting studies currently lacks a dominant theory that underpins either academic research or practice. Cecilia Wadensjö's *Interpreting as Interaction* (1998) has been influential but cannot be considered to provide a definitive theoretical framework. This gap is critical in specialised settings such as asylum procedures, where the role of the interpreter is not only pivotal but also fraught with complexities that demand a well-grounded theoretical approach. Furthermore, the role and responsibilities of the other interlocutors in IMEs is not agreed upon, or at least in a manner that would have scholarly backing. The need for a robust theoretical framework is therefore pressing.

Nevertheless, interpreting studies has developed several influential frameworks, including sociolinguistic approaches, cognitive models and discourse analysis. These frameworks reflect the field's diversity. For instance, the cognitive load model explores how interpreters manage cognitive resources during interpretation, which is crucial in high-pressure environments like courtrooms and asylum hearings. Discourse analysis has been instrumental in understanding how interpreters navigate and shape conversations in real-time, particularly in settings where power dynamics are at play. This section brings together the analysis presented across this book to advocate for the increased use of dialogism in relation to the role of interpreters in asylum settings.

6.3.1 Historical context and the evolution of theoretical approaches to interpreting

Historically translators and interpreters have often been viewed with scepticism or relegated to the margins, by those outside the scholarly field, such as regulating bodies. This marginalisation likely stems from a combination of factors, including a limited understanding of the complex dynamics of language and communication within interpreting, compounded by reliance on earlier linguistic theories that do not fully capture these intricacies. These early linguistic models often treated language as a static conduit of meaning, leading to the belief that interpreters could and should remain neutral and invisible, simply transferring content unaltered. This perspective ignored the reality that interpreters inevitably influence the discourse in IMEs. The move away from monological perceptions of language is crucial for recognising the interpreter's active participation in communication and the complex, context-dependent nature of their responsibilities.

Moreover, the marginalisation of interpreters can be linked to broader social and political factors. For many years, interpreting was viewed as a skill rather than a profession requiring specialised training and theoretical knowledge. This perception has gradually changed as scholars and practitioners have worked to professionalise the field, advocating for certification processes, ethical guidelines and specialised training programmes. The shift towards recognising interpreting as a profession has been marked by the establishment of professional organisations and the development of codes of ethics that emphasise the interpreter's role as an active participant in communication.

With the shift towards a more nuanced understanding of the interpreter's role, recognising the complexity and context-dependent nature of their responsibilities within communicative interactions, the concept of interpreter visibility has become an important theme in interpreting studies. Traditionally, visibility was seen as unwanted, but in a dialogic framework it is seen as part of the communicative process. In this framework, all interlocutors, including interpreters, are active co-constructors of meaning.

However, it is still the case that some service users prefer (or even require) their interpreter to remain as inconspicuous as possible, although this does vary significantly across sectors. For example, in legal interpreting, visibility might be minimised to maintain the perception of impartiality, while in medical interpreting, interpreters are more often active participants in the conversation to ensure clarity and understanding.

6.3.2 From conduits to active participants: Reassessing the interpreter's role in academic and practical contexts

Misconceptions about interpreting, such as the metaphorical representation of interpreters as mere 'conveyor belts' or 'conduits', though largely discredited within scholarly circles, continue to affect how interpreting services are received and evaluated in practice settings. For instance, in legal settings, there is often an expectation that interpreters should only translate verbatim, with no recognition that such a simplistic approach can lead to misunderstandings and misrepresentations of the original message. Many service users are unconnected to the academic research that challenges these misconceptions. This gap between academic research and practical application underscores the need for ongoing professional development and education for interpreters, as well as for the users of interpreting services.

Even within academic discourse, however, there is no clear consensus on the precise role and responsibilities of interpreters, and different interpretations of how sense-making and meaning-making occur during IMEs. For example, scholars who align with dialogic theories emphasise the interpreter's role as a co-constructor of meaning, while those who adopt a more traditional, linguistic perspective focus on the interpreter's responsibility to remain as neutral as possible. This theoretical fragmentation means that interpreters lack consistent guidelines on practice and service users' misunderstandings persist.

There is, thus, an urgent need for well defined, nuanced guidelines grounded in contemporary communication and interpretation theories, namely dialogism, within asylum procedures in the Global North. Traditional directives such as 'just translate' or 'translate verbatim' fail to capture the complexity of interpreting in these high-stakes environments. The provision of more precise guidelines, based on dialogism, would promote more consistent and accurate practice within these contexts.

To move towards realising such guidelines, I propose a four-tiered approach that addresses theory, regulation and adjudication.

First, a contemporary theory should be designated as the foundational guideline across interpreting settings within asylum and immigration procedures, related immigration lawyers and other relevant bodies. To this end, I propose dialogism. In particular, a comprehensive grasp of the concepts of sense-making and meaning-making, as contextualised in dialogism, is paramount. Recognising the dynamics of interactions during IMEs can enlighten all stakeholders. This includes emphasising the importance of pre-encounter knowledge and the critical approach of not accepting IMEs at face value.

Second, an independent body should periodically review the regulations governing interpreting practices to ensure the effective application of the selected theory within these specific contexts. Regular review should maintain the theory's relevance and efficacy and could be done by the existing oversight bodies rather than new entities.

Third, a non-governmental organisation or professional association should mediate differing viewpoints on national asylum policies and regulations, related immigration lawyers and similar institutions in the Global North. This mediation will allow for balanced input, preventing undue influence from any single governing body or interest group, and ensuring that interpreting practices remain consistent across various institutions.

Finally, a regulatory body or ombudsman should be responsible for assessing whether national and international standards are met in specific cases, such as asylum applications, to ensure that interpreters' work within these contexts is not only theoretically sound but also legally accountable.

6.3.3 Enhancing the interpreter's role and status through dialogism

A better understanding of interpreters' work, which will follow should the reforms listed above, will lead to better outcomes in IMEs. This understanding should focus on the work of the interpreter, not solely on what the role of the interpreter is. Dialogism will help achieve this. Historically, the simplistic, monological understanding of an interpreter's work has contributed to a perception of the profession as requiring little skill or education. This dehumanising view, which idealises interpreters as machines or advanced pieces of software, dangerously obscures the complexities and risks inherent in converting meaning from one language to another. Although perceptions have started to shift, the low status of the profession has been persistent and demoralising. This is partly because interpreting scholars have not sufficiently communicated the intricacies of an interpreter's work and the complex decision-making it requires.

A contemporary version of dialogism, sufficiently detailed, could serve as a framework to enhance the interpreter's role and status. Too often, the evaluation of an interpreter's work has been framed in terms of perceived shortcomings rather than an understanding of why they acted in a certain way. Adopting a dialogic framework can illuminate the intricate skillset and decision-making involved in interpreting. This approach will shift the analytical focus to why the interpreter acted in a particular way and whether the IME participants agreed upon such a role distribution.

6.3.4 The need for scholarly consensus and institutional engagement

Broadly, I call for a greater scholarly consensus on the theory explaining the practice of interpreting and the role of interpreters, as such consensus would benefit regulators and users of interpreter services. More tangibly, and with specific reference to this books area of investigation, I call for greater institutional engagement from government agencies and other bodies that preside over asylum with the theoretical dimensions of interpreting as they pertain to sense-making and meaning-making. A scholarly consensus will lead to clearer expectations and guidelines, reflected in the training of interpreters. At present, interpreters are found to be 'very active participants in lawyer–client interviews, as manifested in their various forms of intervention and in their adoption of roles not stipulated in their professional ethics' (Xu, 2021: 617) and a broadly accepted framework would counter any tendency for the interpreter's practice to be not what was expected or not wanted.

Within national asylum procedures, there are simply too many variables influencing interpreting practice, particularly across the varied settings of courts, hearings, legal consultations, medical procedures and so on. A unified dialogical approach across the full remit of the relevant bodies' area of activities is essential.

Naturally, theorising about the nature of communication and interpreting is not the aim nor the purview of organisations like the INS. Rather, and in light of the roadmap to reform presented above, what is recommended here is akin to a process of review and reflection, guided by a dialogist methodology. Specifically, the methodology I am proposing involves examining the interpreters' perspective as to why they acted in a certain way, and seeking other interlocutors' perspectives on why they did not intervene, and what they understood. The contexts of the interaction need to be included in this dialogist methodology: understanding who did what, when and why. Only by doing so can contextual information be acquired that is lost when the utterances of an IME are only entextualised. Simply put, if the meaning-carrying layers of an IME are ignored the results are not as rich as they could be – a poorer understanding of an applicant's backstory, or less certainty if a briefing on procedure has been comprehended, for instance.

When organisations that use interpretation services achieve greater consensus on how to theorise interpreting and the associated role of the interpreter, it will simplify the interpreter's task and make the expectations of them clearer. Similarly, it will do much to facilitate the process of regulation, reflection and review described above. As a result, users of interpreter services, such as lawyers, will have a clearer understanding of what to anticipate when working with interpreters.

When scholars of interpreting studies – at a local, regional or global level – reach a consensus on the theoretical approach to interpreting, it will enable interpreters to understand their role better. This shared framework will provide interpreters with a foundation upon which they can make better-informed decisions about their professional approach. The theoretical approach and practical methodology presented in this book represent my effort to catalyse this movement. While the most far-reaching means of driving reform lies with the organisations that preside over asylum procedures, much can be achieved by interpreters and the users of interpreting services themselves. Academic research will have the an opportunity to gather more data, investigate more scenarios and enrich our understanding of the internal processes of IMEs in a range of settings, including those related to asylum.

6.4 Limitations of the Study

This section highlights the salient limitations of the case study presented in this book, largely for academic researchers. A more detailed and academically oriented discussion of these limitations may be found in Mizori (2017).

The very nature of case studies involves some compromise; resource and time constraints must be balanced with sufficient depth of the investigation for meaningful conclusions to be drawn. Multiple case studies are often desirable, but sufficient depth often can be achieved only in a single case. Moreover, the data accumulated from a series of single case studies can lead to theory development. This is particularly true given that the methodology behind the case study – namely, the use of post-IME interviews based on a transcript of the IME – is innovative, at least within the study of interpreting in asylum- and immigration-related contexts.

Another limitation pertains the nature of dialogism, which theorises sense-making as not necessarily only between human beings. Artefacts, including recording equipment, also are a source of information during the process of meaning-making on the part of the individual. This may suggest that the data collected was not as 'pure' as it might have been if these devices were not present. During the two post-IME interviews, I was also in the room in addition to the audio-recorder, which again would have coloured the data. This, in a technical sense, was a limitation of the study's validity in terms of the possibility of recording 'pure' information – if such a thing can be said to exist in an externally observed communicative event. It is, however, also an opportunity for further research. Other researchers, with their own pre-encounter knowledge and perspectives, investigating other cases in similar or different institutional settings, will produce new data, having played their own role in sense-making. This will be discussed further in Section 6.7.

Closely related to the question of data validity is the matter of participant authenticity, for want of a better term. Although I took all the available precautions before holding these interviews, it cannot be ruled out that the participants might not have always said what they believed to be true, for a number of reasons – on different occasions they may have wanted to please me, have not remembered things or have guessed. Reasons related to confidentiality (on the part of both participants) and saving professional face (on the part of the interpreter) could have also contributed to answers that might not have been sincere.

In my capacity as an observer of sense-making, I was in a position somewhat similar to that of a caseworker or decision-maker. This is to say, sense-making was occurring, I was observing it and thus played some part in a dialogical sense in its formation. Afterwards, I looked at my research questions and the entextualised data produced, and drew my conclusions, and though they differed from the considerations of a caseworker, by the end of the asylum procedure we both would have undergone a similar experience in terms of our engagement with an IME, with the caveat I had the benefit of the additional data stream presented by the post-IME interviews. Thus, although the participants may have attempted to 'say the right thing' knowingly or unknowingly in relation to my study, the design of the study itself can be seen as an 'audit' of sense-making. The matter of participant validity in an IME and the second perspective of it created by the study (the first being the procedure itself) is, then, as much a data point as it is question of methodological validity.

6.5 Avenues for Future Research: Reflections on Methodology and Contextual Considerations in Asylum Procedures

Research is about generating knowledge, which this study has done. In addition, it has revealed some useful avenues for future research, some inspired by the data collected and discussed, some by its limitations.

6.5.1. In the case of the applicant

In Section 5.2.1, I argued that the development of an IME seems to depend not only on the originals and the renditions and their interrelation with the situated context but also on the co-construction of meaning, itself influenced by pre-encounter knowledge. In the present study, the applicant was seen to make assumptions about what the interpreter meant with his renditions, even when these were not based on the materials provided in these renditions. The assumptions related to 'realities' subscribed to by the applicant, realities that belonged to pre-encounter knowledge on the part of the applicant.

Based on this argument, several interesting questions arise. For example, what if the originals did not correspond with the 'reality' that the applicant subscribed to, in the sense that the lawyer had made mistakes, for example while revisiting the backstory of the applicant? Would that have influenced the outcome of the IME? This is made more likely by the fact that the renditions here were not all close renditions. Another question concerns the quality of the text in the lawyer's report regarding the backstory. Is it solely dependent on the quality of the work of this interpreter and the attentiveness of this applicant and lawyer, or also on how, among other things, individual applicants deal with the pre-encounter knowledge? The extent to which the applicant, the lawyer and the interpreter take into account the quality of the work produced collectively in an IME of this type seems to depend in part on the previous encounters between the lawyer, the applicant and this and other interpreters. How does this influence their behaviour with regard to meaning-making? One of the conclusions of this study is that understanding is not a static phenomenon related to the current IME but is interrelated with the understandings of previous meetings. In this regard, do the lawyer and the interpreter take a more relaxed attitude in relation to 'facilitating understanding' because they assume that the applicant has heard the material under discussion before?

In Section 5.2.2, 'Understanding something the interpreter has not said', the applicant was found to incorporate in his internal dialogue things that had not been mentioned in the rendition. More research is needed to see whether or not this could also be the case in other types of IME. Similarly, Section 5.2.3, 'Understanding the original directly via Dutch', points out that some applicants may not be totally dependent on the renditions. This opens up opportunities for research on how end-users and interpreters deal with this, that is, whether or not, and to what extent, the linguistic knowledge acquired by the applicant is taken into account during the IMEs.

Section 5.2.4, 'Not being able to say "something" but recognising it when mentioned by the researcher', dealt with a delicate matter. Sometimes in the post-IME interview the applicant was unable to clearly say what he had understood and I was unsure whether this was because he did not understand the rendition under investigation or whether it was because he encountered difficulties in expressing his thoughts. I argued that caution is advised when investigating understanding in the case of renditions dealing with the asylum procedure: the challenging nature of the asylum procedure may cause applicants to fail when explaining how they understood the rendition even if they had understood it. Future research could examine whether or to what extent this can be seen in other cases and contexts.

6.5.2 In the case of the interpreter

As discussed in Section 5.3.2, the findings of the post-IME interview with the interpreter show that he, while probably unaware of dialogism as a theory, was to a considerable extent aware of how sense-making takes place in IMEs. His answers corresponded to central concepts in dialogism regarding how sense is made during conversations. I believe that this opens up a rich starting point to do research into: whether or not, and if so to what extent, this can be observed in other lawyer–applicant IMEs; as well as whether or not, and if so to what extent, this can be seen in other types of IME.

Researchers can also share the results of this study and then use a quantitative research tool to investigate what other interpreters think. It is also possible to engage end-users (e.g. lawyers and applicants) with the results and investigate what they think of them.

6.5.3 In the case of the lawyer

As discussed in Chapters 5, the lawyer was found to take alterity into account while producing his originals: he said that he did not utilise a high register in order to avoid the applicant encountering difficulty in understanding the content of the IME. It is unknown how other lawyers handle sense-making in their offices. This opens up opportunities for researchers to study this type of interpreter-mediated discourse.

6.5.4 Inspired by the limitations of this study

Section 6.4 discussed the limitations of this study and pointed to the associated opportunities for further research, such as multiplying the number of cases. In more general terms, the fact that I had worked as a professional interpreter helped the lawyer and the interpreter to cooperate with me. I also believe that if the lawyer had not endorsed me, the applicant would have been less willing to participate. This image of myself (that is, the researcher) as a trustworthy professional is thought to have helped the participants to provide trustworthy information. Researchers should build on their image as trustworthy professionals. Once one is known as a trustworthy researcher, it is believed that professionals will want to cooperate and will be willing to divulge more information.

6.5.5 Within interpreting studies

One area for further research that arose over the course of this study pertains to the nature of the lost (but recoverable) information in IMEs. The approach taking to conceptualising such information in this study was broad; any information that seemed to affect sense-making but was not captured by the process of entextualisation was of interest. The question is then raised as to what sort of information is lost and in what relative proportions. Could such information be categorised as principally non-verbal, sub-textual information? Or perhaps (given the breath of inputs in a dialogical understanding of sense-making) a new concept is required. Further lines of enquiry may be considered in relation to this issue. Are some language combinations more prone to losing information of a certain type? Are certain interpretation strategies more prone to losing information of certain type? Such research could explore the efficacy of as well as the role of interpreters as active agents in sense-making.

6.6 Towards a Just and Humane Asylum Process: Enhancing Communication and Institutional Reform Through Dialogical Principles

This book has been written with the primary goal of making the asylum procedure equitable for applicants, particularly in terms of communication. The recommendations presented are designed to benefit not only the asylum-seekers and the organisations that assist them but also the asylum and immigration services and related professionals. I am confident that the insights and recommendations will not only enhance the fairness of the procedure but also improve the effectiveness of the work done by asylum lawyers and the INS. These improvements will lead to fewer mistakes, reduce the waste of time and resources, and a more efficient process, without necessarily requiring additional work or funding.

Before the recommendations of this study are presented, a simple point must be made: governments should invest more in implementing asylum procedures. The chronic underfunding of the asylum system, particularly in the Netherlands, has led to long waiting lists, poor accommodation and immense suffering for asylum applicants – many of whom are left to languish in camps for years. This policy is not only inhumane but also detrimental to the state's interests. Many asylum-seekers, particularly young men, are eager to work and contribute to the economy, yet they are prevented from doing so, which also hinders their integration into the community.

The inefficiencies and high number of appeals in the asylum process often stem from outdated approaches to sense-making and interpretation. Updating these procedures, grounded in a dialogical understanding of communication, is essential. As a member of the international community, the government of the Netherlands has a responsibility to process applications efficiently and fairly, and this responsibility is undermined by cost-saving measures.

It is essential that the INS grants interpreters more freedom to intervene when they perceive miscommunication, within frameworks inspired by dialogism. This includes alerting caseworkers to potential cultural and/or situational miscommunications. The INS should revisit its guidelines for working with interpreters, possibly building on existing frameworks but adapting them to incorporate dialogical theory as a foundational element. The findings in Chapter 5 offer valuable insights into what should be prioritised in these revisions.

For more profound changes in mindset, the INS and similar institutions in the Global North should reflect on the study's findings regarding sense-making and meaning-making. Revisiting the INS's adopted language ideology, as discussed in Chapters 3 and 5, could lead to significant improvements in how credibility assessments are conducted. Chapter 2 provides a detailed discussion of these criteria. I recommend that the INS consider making the entextualisation process within the procedure more open-ended. The current focus on standardisation should give way to a process that better captures and does justice to the applicant's story, all through the lens of dialogical theory. Moreover, there is a need for the INS to engage with asylum issues more from a legal perspective and less from a political one, as discussed in Chapters 1 and 2.

To implement these reforms effectively, a structured approach is necessary. This could be achieved through a three-tiered model that ensures consistency and accountability across all levels of the asylum process:

(1) *Theoretical framework.* Dialogism should be adopted as the foundational theoretical framework in asylum procedures. This would ensure that interpreters are seen as active participants in the communication process, aligning with the co-construction of meaning.
(2) *Regulatory oversight.* Independent bodies should be established to periodically review and update regulations within institutions like the INS. This oversight would ensure that the selected theoretical framework (dialogism) is effectively applied and remains relevant over time.
(3) *Professional mediation and judicial oversight.* A non-governmental organisation or professional association could mediate differing viewpoints on policies and regulations, while the judiciary or a regulatory body assesses whether national and international standards are being met. This approach would ensure that the work of interpreters is both theoretically sound and legally accountable.

Dialogical theorisation brings with it the possibility of conducting reflective interviews. These interviews are not always necessary, but they serve as a tool for deeper reflection and analysis, if required. Reflective interviews, whether conducted on the spot during an IME or afterwards, are a supplementary tool that, when applied appropriately, can enhance the fairness and thoroughness of the process, ensuring that the procedure aligns more closely with the intent of the system of international protection.

The INS should also reconsider its approach to handling a lawyer's response when declaring its intention to refuse an application. A dialogical approach demands that the INS re-engage with any new information provided by the applicant in response to such refusals. Dismissing this information as something that should have been mentioned earlier, a common practice when the INS is unconvinced by an applicant's declarations, is problematic. Instead, the new information should be recognised as a vital part of the ongoing dialogue, contributing to a fuller understanding of the asylum-seeker's narrative. However, this does not imply that the INS should accept everything at face value; rather, it should engage with the new information in a responsible manner, consistent with dialogical theory.

Lawyers and other legal representatives should engage with recent scholarship, especially the works of Jan Blommaert, Katrijn Maryns and Laura Smith-Khan, and update their practices accordingly. They should also refer to this scholarship when engaging with the INS and the judiciary. Lawyers and relevant elements of the judiciary who use interpreting services would benefit from a briefing or course on the fundamentals of interpreting services from a dialogical perspective. This form of outreach from the field of interpreting studies to service users could take many forms and need not be carried out by the INS or similar asylum institutions. Investing in such an understanding through courses, briefings and training can only reduce instances of miscommunication resulting from language barriers, thereby serving the interests of asylum organisations, particularly in reducing the likelihood of appeals.

Indeed, the benefits of such preparatory work run both ways. The challenges interpreters face in the asylum procedure and similar settings, such as courtrooms and hearings, highlight the need for adequate preparation on their part, in addition to recognition of their active role in shaping communication outcomes. As in court interpreting, where interpreters are often the least knowledgeable in a courtroom setting despite being responsible for ensuring that bilingual proceedings run smoothly, interpreters in hearings do not receive much information, if any, prior to the hearing session, despite the complex sense-making required by both the official and the applicant. It is likely that a lot of sense-making and meaning-making material is lost or not understood properly. This can even happen in legal consultations, even though some lawyers may be lenient and offer to give the interpreter some necessary context, as was the experience of the interpreter participating in the present case study.

In this regard, much can be gained from the exchange of information between participants in an asylum procedure. Working from the basis of a dialogical understanding of communication, interpreters stand to gain a better understanding of legal proceedings, and lawyers of the capabilities and limits of interpretation. While such goals may sound abstract, steps toward them need not be taxing. To provide a simple example, consider the benefits that may be gained from a lawyer's awareness of the different categories of translation strategies or from an interpreter knowing in advance the legal terminology pertinent to a case. Such exchanges of information would hardly upset the working environment of either party or require a significant outlay in time or funding.

Different recommendations can be addressed to the various stakeholders in the asylum procedure:

- Within the INS, immigration officials and staff must acknowledge the critical role they play in ensuring that interpreters are empowered to act when necessary, with a deeper understanding of the cultural and linguistic nuances that shape communication in asylum cases. The INS's adoption of a dialogical approach in its procedures will not only improve the accuracy and fairness of asylum decisions but also reduce the inefficiencies that currently plague the system.
- Lawyers are tasked with the responsibility not just of representing their clients but of actively shaping how their narratives are understood within the asylum process. By engaging deeply with the latest scholarship and understanding the dialogical nature of communication, lawyers can better advocate for their clients, ensuring that their stories are heard in their full complexity.
- Judges must move beyond the monological approach traditionally favoured in legal settings, recognising that the credibility of an asylum-seeker's narrative is co-constructed through interactions with various stakeholders. A more reflective and dialogical approach will enable judges to make more just and ethically responsible decisions, particularly where cultural and linguistic differences play a significant role.
- Assistance organisations have a pivotal role in empowering asylum-seekers, helping them articulate their narratives in a manner that resonates with the legal frameworks while remaining true to their lived experiences. These organisations must advocate for procedural reforms that address the communicative challenges inherent in the asylum process, ensuring that the voices of asylum-seekers are accurately and empathetically represented.
- Interpreters must embrace their role as active participants in the co-construction of meaning, recognising that their work extends far beyond mere translation. Continuous training and a deep understanding of the sociocultural and psychological factors influencing

communication are essential for interpreters to fulfil their responsibilities effectively.

- Interpreting and translation scholars should continue to explore the dynamics of communication in interpreter-mediated settings, particularly within the asylum process. Their research will be instrumental in developing more nuanced theories and practical applications that enhance the fairness and effectiveness of these procedures.
- Curriculum designers are responsible for ensuring that the next generation of interpreters is well equipped to handle the complexities of asylum cases. By integrating dialogical principles into interpreter training programmes, curriculum designers can prepare interpreters to navigate the ethical and communicative challenges they will face, ultimately contributing to a more just and equitable asylum process.

In summary, the asylum procedure in its current form requires significant reform, particularly in the context of communication. The recommendations provided in this book aim to address these issues by advocating for increased government funding, better training and preparation for interpreters, and a more dialogical approach across all levels of the asylum process. These changes would ensure that the asylum procedure becomes more efficient, just and humane for all parties involved.

6.7 Final Remarks: Immigration in the Modern Age

Migration has been present throughout human history. Politicians deal with the political dimensions of immigration, researcher with the academic dimensions. Powerful national organisations are tasked with dealing with asylum applicants. One of their main tools is communication, and within that communication the processes of sense-making and meaning-making are crucial for the applicant.

6.7.1 Articulating asylum stories: Meeting expectations and ensuring credibility

In the Dutch context, applicants must narrate their stories in a manner that aligns with the INS's expectations. That is, the narrative must also adhere to the criteria set out in the 1951 Geneva Convention and national asylum regulations, and resonate with the INS's interpretation of a credible account. If it fails to do so, the applicant may be returned to their homeland.

Any deficiency in the act of communication can critically diminish an applicant's chances of success, but the asylum procedure often overlooks a considerable amount of vital information, as a result of its design, leading to potential oversights and unfairness.

6.7.2 From asylum applicant to advocate: My journey through the labyrinth of communication

My journey in writing this book is deeply rooted in academia, my professional experience and my experiences as a former asylum applicant. Over the years, I have borne witness to countless narratives centred on interpreting challenges, as well as broader issues related to the asylum procedure, particularly in the realm of communication.

Enjoying the benefit of over a quarter century of experience as an interpreter in asylum cases, combined with my academic pursuits that led to a PhD in Interpreting Studies, I have immersed myself in the intricacies of asylum procedures. This extended tenure saw me collaborating closely with legal professionals and other stakeholders. This book was conceived from my first-hand observation of a poignant reality: many asylum applicants inadvertently lose their authentic voice during the procedure. The reason? The recording of their narratives often undergoes a transformation to fit the mould set by asylum institutions such as the INS. I endeavour to ensure that the heart-wrenching tales of asylum-seekers are relayed in a way that mirrors their true experiences and sentiments – if only they were provided with the time and resources to do so. Furthermore, it is my ardent hope to offer clarity to those working alongside interpreters and asylum-seekers, and to illuminate the nuances of communication during these pivotal encounters. The overarching aim is to foster a comprehensive understanding of the complexities of communication, which in turn can facilitate the achievement of a procedure that is imbued with fairness.

An epiphany struck me after years of service and scholarly pursuits: there is a wealth of knowledge to be unearthed about IMEs. Driven by an insatiable curiosity, I pondered if a case study could unravel strategies to recalibrate the focus of the procedure – shifting from an INS-centric approach to one prioritising equity. My academic endeavours found a nurturing environment at the University of Leeds, which provided the platform to explore these nuances further.

Dialogist interpretation, the approach I propose in this book, presents an opportunity to re-engage with IMEs in the asylum context, recovering lost information, context and, I hope, part of the applicants' authentic voice. My professional experience leaves me with no delusions as to the realities of the asylum process in much of the Global North. There will always be a bureaucratic element to proceedings, a pressure to 'get through' cases and process them to meet goals, address the needs of incoming applicants, and to coexist with the expectations and requirements of other branches of government. This pressure to mechanise and standardise procedures will inevitably play a role to some degree, but the asylum process need not be wholly captured by this potentially dehumanising force. The case study presented in this book recommends a new approach, *dialogist interpretation*, to provide solutions at numerous levels in this process.

In the most general sense, an awareness of dialogism among actors such as lawyers, caseworkers, interpreters and decision-makers will reframe the sense-making experience as one which is co-constructed. Through dialogism's many concepts, these parties can be made aware that the role they play is shaping sense-making and meaning-making, and in influencing narratives can be more open to exploring meaning where it is not immediately apparent, and can gain a deeper understanding of one another's roles and capabilities. Much benefit in this direction can be gained even from introductory courses and training, ideally offered by asylum organisations themselves as frequent users of interpreting services, or by professional bodies regulating interpretation.

More specifically, dialogist interpretation, as an approach and mindset for both interpreters and the users of their services, can do much to reduce instances of miscommunication and confusion in asylum applications, to the benefit of both applicants and organisations such as the INS. These benefits are achievable regardless of the political priorities assigned to asylum procedures. A reduction in unfair outcomes, resulting from lost information or erroneously introduced inconsistencies, will translate in a reduction in the number of appeals. The principal mechanism by which this may be achieved is the use of post-IME interviews. In cases that require this, be they cases where claims of miscommunication have been made, or the process needs to be extended to assess some element of a narrative, interviews investigating translation decisions and cross-checking the understandings of interlocutors can do much to clarify what brought about the co-constructed reality entextualised in a given report. Such interviews need not be applied in every case, but can serve as a tool which allows caseworkers, decision-makers and applicants to revisit the sense-making process on which an application may hinge.

Dialogist interpretation, as a theoretical approach, owes much to the wider developments in the field of interpreting studies and communication studies. It is still, though, in its infancy, and it is my hope this book will encourage its robust testing in theory and practice as a reinvigorating approach to interpretation. With the market pressures of non-human, AI-based 'solutions' to all areas of translation, a political climate eager for reform and reappraisal of asylum policies and practices and, most importantly, deteriorating conditions for many seeking protection in the Global North, this call for a new approach to interpretation is timely. The benefits of such an approach are not limited to IMEs in asylum processes, but in many respects the area of asylum provides ideal grounds to develop dialogist interpretation; the stakes are real, cases are frequent, language combinations are diverse and the prospect of doing meaningful good is tangible.

I am optimistic that every stakeholder within the asylum process – be they the INS, affiliated organisations, lawyers or interpreters – will find value in this book. My aspiration is that it catalyses further research, infusing newfound insights into daily interactions with interpreters and ultimately enhancing the fairness and efficacy of the asylum procedure.

References

Affolter, L. (2020) Keeping numbers low in the name of fairness. Ethos and ethics in a Swiss asylum administration. In J. Eckert (ed.) *The Bureaucratic Production of Difference* (pp. 27–57). Transcript.

Affolter, L. (2021a) Regular matters: Credibility determination and the institutional habitus in a Swiss asylum office. *Comparative Migration Studies* 9 (4), 1–16. https://doi.org/10.1186/s40878-020-00215-z (accessed 10 May 2024).

Affolter, L. (2021b) *Asylum Matters: On the Frontline of Administrative Decision-Making.* Palgrave Macmillan.

AIDA (2022) *Temporary Protection Netherlands.* https://asylumineurope.org/wp-content/uploads/2023/04/AIDA-NL_Temporary-Protection_2022.pdf (accessed 15 December 2023).

Akkerman, T. and Hagelund, A. (2007) 'Women and children first!' Anti-immigration parties and gender in Norway and the Netherlands. *Patterns of Prejudice* 41 (2), 197–214.

Aljazeera (2023) Dutch gov't falls over failure to agree on asylum seeker policy (accessed 20 September 2023).

Alonso, S. and da Fonseca, S.C. (2011) Immigration, left and right. *Party Politics* 18 (6), 865–884.

Al-Rubai'i, A.M.H.A. (2009) Instructing novice consecutive interpreters: Steps to improve the performance of memory. *Babel* 55 (4), 329–344.

Arksey, H. and Knight, P.T. (1999) *Interviewing for Social Scientists: An Introductory Resource with Examples.* Sage.

Australian Red Cross (2023) Refugee and asylum seeker facts. https://www.redcross.org.au/act/help-refugees/refugee-facts (accessed 14 September 2023).

Baade, B. and Gölz, L. (2023) An empirical analysis of credibility assessment in German asylum cases. *German Law Journal* 24 (2), 310–341.

Badshah, N. (2022) Rishi Sunak says as PM he would cap number of refugees UK accepts. https://www.theguardian.com/world/2022/jul/23/rishi-sunak-says-as-pm-he-would-cap-number-of-refugees-uk-accepts (accessed 15 September 2023).

Baillot, H., Cowan, S. and Munro, V.E. (2014) Reason to disbelieve: Evaluating the rape claims of women seeking asylum in the UK. *International Journal of Law in Context* 10 (1), 105–139.

Bakhtin, M.M. (1981) *The Dialogic Imagination: Four Essays by M.M. Bakhtin* (ed. M. Holquist; trans. C. Emerson and M. Holquist). University of Texas Press.

Bakhtin, M.M. (1986) *Speech Genres and Other Late Essays* (eds C. Emerson and M. Holquist; trans. V.W. McGee). University of Texas Press.

Barsky, R.F. (1993) The interpreter and the Canadian Convention refugee hearing: Crossing the potentially life-threatening boundaries between 'coccode-e-eh,' 'cluck-cluck,' and 'cot-cot-cot'. *TTR: traduction, terminologie, rédaction* 6 (2), 131–157.

Barsky, R.F. (1994) *Constructing a Productive Other: Discourse Theory and the Convention Refugee Hearing.* John Benjamins.

Barsky, R.F. (1995) The construction of the other and the destruction of the self: Efficacious discursive production in the Convention refugee hearing. In G. Brinker-Gabler (ed.)

Encountering the Other/s (pp. 79–100). SUNY.
Barsky, R.F. (1996) The interpreter as intercultural agent in Convention refugee hearings. *Translator* 2 (1), 45–63.
Bartlett, F.C. (1932) *Remembering: A Study in Experimental and Social Psychology*. Cambridge University Press.
Bateson, G. (1972) *Steps to an Ecology of Mind: Collected Essays in Anthropology, Psychiatry, Evolution, and Epistemology*. Intertext.
BBC (2017) UK overestimates non-EU students staying illegally, data suggests. https://www.bbc.com/news/uk-politics-41030304 (accessed 12 November 2023).
BBC (2022) Rwanda: We're committed to asylum plan, says Priti Patel. https://www.bbc.com/news/uk-61808120 (accessed 8 November 2023).
Bendel, P. (2019) Contemporary politics of international protection in Europe: From protection to prevention. In A. Weinar, S. Bonjour and L. Zhyznomirska (eds) *The Routledge Handbook of the Politics of Migration in Europe* (pp. 293–302). Routledge.
Berk-Seligson, S. (1989) The role of register in the bilingual courtroom: Evaluative reactions to interpreted testimony. *International Journal of the Sociology of Language* 79, 79–91.
Bernstein, B. (1972) A sociolinguistic approach to socialisation: With some reference to educability. In J.J. Gumperz and D. Hymes (eds) *Directions in Sociolinguistics: The Ethnography of Communication* (pp. 465–497). Basil Blackwell.
Betts, A. (2010) The refugee regime complex. *Refugee Survey Quarterly* 29 (1), 12–37. https://doi.org/10.1093/rsq/hdq009.
Bhabha, J. (2004) Seeking asylum alone: Treatment of separated and trafficked children in need of refugee protection. *International Migration* 42 (1), 141–148.
Bhabha, J. and Young, W. (1999) Not adults in miniature: Unaccompanied child asylum seekers and the new U.S. guidelines. *International Journal of Refugee Law* 11 (1), 84–125.
Binder, A. (2001) Gender and the 'Membership in a Particular Social Group' category of the 1951 Refugee Convention. *Columbia Journal of Gender and Law* 10 (2).
Birner, B.J. (2013) *Introduction to Pragmatics*. Wiley-Blackwell.
Bleiker, R., Campbell, D., Hutchison, E. and Nicholson, X. (2013) The visual dehumanisation of refugees. *Australian Journal of Political Science* 48 (4), 398–416.
Blommaert, J. (2001a) Context is/as critique. *Critique of Anthropology* 21 (1), 13–32.
Blommaert, J. (2001b) Investigating narrative inequality: African asylum seekers' stories in Belgium. *Discourse and Society* 12 (4), 413–449.
Bögner, D., Brewin, C. and Herlihy, J. (2010) Refugees' experiences of Home Office interviews: A qualitative study on the disclosure of sensitive personal information. *Journal of Ethnic and Migration Studies* 36 (3), 519–535.
Bohmer, C. and Shuman, A. (2007) Producing epistemologies of ignorance in the political asylum application process. *Identities: Global Studies in Culture and Power* 14 (5), 603–629.
Bohmer, C. and Shuman, A. (2010) Contradictory discourses of protection and control in transnational asylum law. *Journal of Legal Anthropology* 1 (2), 212–229.
Bohmer, C. and Shuman, A. (2018) *Political Asylum Deceptions: The Culture of Suspicion*. Springer.
Bonikowski, B. and Zhang, Y. (2023) Populism as dog-whistle politics: Anti-elite discourse and sentiments toward minority groups. *Social Forces* 102 (1), 180–201. https://doi.org/10.1093/sf/soad080.
Bontempo, K. and Napier, J. (2011) Evaluating emotional stability as a predictor of interpreter competence and aptitude for interpreting. *Interpreting* 13 (1), 85–105.
Boomgaarden, H.G. and Vliegenthart, R. (2009) How news content influences anti-immigration attitudes: Germany, 1993–2005. *European Journal of Political Research* 48 (4), 516–542.
Bot, H. and Verrept, H. (2013) Role issues in the Low Countries: Interpreting in mental healthcare in the Netherlands and Belgium. In C. Schäffner, K. Kredens and Y. Fowler

(eds) *Interpreting in a Changing Landscape: Selected Papers from Critical Link* (pp. 117–131). John Benjamins.

Bruner, J.S. (1990) *Acts of Meaning*. Harvard University Press.

Bullen, P. (2022) Why the UK government should rethink its plan to send asylum seekers from the UK to Rwanda. International Rescue Committee. https://www.rescue.org/uk/article/why-uk-government-should-rethink-its-plan-send-asylum-seekers-uk-rwanda (accessed 20 October 2023).

Butchard, P., Gower, M. and McKinny, CJ. (2024) The UK–Rwanda Migration and Economic Development Partnership. https://researchbriefings.files.parliament.uk/documents/CBP-9568/CBP-9568.pdf (accessed 20 July 2024).

Cameron, H.E. (2008) Risk theory and 'subjective fear': The role of risk perception, assessment, and management in refugee status determinations. *International Journal of Refugee Law* 20 (4), 567–585.

Campbell, J.R. (2020) The role of lawyers, judges, country experts, and officials in British asylum and immigration law. *International Journal of Law in Context* 16, 1–16.

Castles, S. (2000) International migration at the beginning of the twenty-first century: Global trends and issues. *International Social Science Journal* 52 (165), 269–281.

Castles, S. and Loughna, S. (2003) Trends in asylum migration to industrialized countries: 1990–2001. UNU/WIDER Discussion Paper No. 2003/31, Refugee Studies Centre, University of Oxford.

Castles, S. and Loughna, S. (2005) Trends in asylum migration to industrialized countries, 1990–2001. In G.J. Borjas and J. Crisp (eds) *Poverty, International Migration and Asylum: Studies in Development Economics and Policy* (pp. 39–69). Palgrave Macmillan.

Cea D'Ancona, M.Á. (2016) Immigration as a threat: Explaining the changing pattern of xenophobia in Spain. *International Migration and Integration* 17, 569–591.

Cheung, A.K.F. (2018) Non-renditions and the court interpreter's perceived impartiality: A role-play study. *Interpreting* 20 (2), 232–258.

Chin, A. and Cortes, K.E. (2015) The refugee/asylum seeker. In B. Chiswick and P.W. Miller (eds) *Handbook of the Economics of International Migration* (Vol. 1, pp. 585–658). Elsevier.

Clark, H.H. (1996) *Using Language*. Cambridge University Press.

Clifford, N.J. (2016) *Key Methods in Geography*. Sage.

Coffey, G. (2003) The credibility of credibility evidence at the refugee review tribunal. *International Journal of Refugee Law* 15 (3), 377–417.

Conway, C.M. (2014) *The Oxford Handbook of Qualitative Research in American Music Education*. Oxford Handbooks Online.

Creswell, J.W. (1994) *Research Design: Qualitative and Quantitative Approaches*. Sage.

Cucu, F. and Panon, L. (2023) Asylum policies and international tensions. *European Economic Review* 151, 104322.

Danso, R. and McDonald, D.A. (2001) Writing xenophobia: Immigration and the print media in post-apartheid South Africa. *Africa Today* 48 (3), 115–137.

Davidson, B. (2002) A model for the construction of conversational common ground in interpreted discourse. *Journal of Pragmatics* 34 (9), 1273–1300.

Davitti, E. (2012) Dialogue interpreting as intercultural mediation: Integrating talk and gaze in the analysis of mediated parent–teacher meetings. Doctor of Philosophy thesis, University of Manchester.

De Boe, E. (2015) The influence of governmental policy on public service: Interpreting in the Netherlands. *Translation and Interpreting* 7 (3), 166–185.

De Raad van State (2020) The Council of State. https://www.raadvanstate.nl/talen/artikel (accessed 17 July 2020).

Dempster, H. and Hargrave, K. (2017) *Understanding Public Attitudes Towards Refugees and Migrants*. Overseas Development Institute and Chatham House.

Dennison, J. and Dražanová, L. (2018) *Public Attitudes on Migration: Rethinking How People Perceive Migration: An Analysis of Existing Opinion Polls in the Euro-Mediterranean Region*. European University Institute.

Dimitrova, B.E. (1997) Degree of interpreter responsibility in the interaction process in community interpreting. In S.E. Carr, R.P. Roberts, A. Dufour and D. Steyn (eds) *The Critical Link: Interpreters in the Community: Papers from the First International Conference on Interpreting in Legal, Health, and Social Service Settings (Geneva Park, Canada, June 1–4, 1995)* (pp. 7–28). John Benjamins.

Doherty, B. (2015) This is Abyan's story, and it is Australia's story. *Guardian*, 28 October. https://www.theguardian.com/australia-news/2015/oct/28/this-is-abyans-story-and-it-is-australias-story (accessed 15 September 2023).

Doornbos, N. (2006) Op verhaal komen: Institutionele communicatie in de asielprocedure. Doctor of Philosophy thesis. University of Nijmegen.

Drew, P. and Heritage, J. (eds) (1992) *Talk at Work: Interaction in Institutional Settings*. Cambridge University Press.

Drugan, J. (2020) Complex collaborations: Interpreting and translating for the UK police. *Target* 32 (2), 307–326.

Duff, P. (2012) How to conduct case study research. In S. Gass and A. Mackey (eds) *Research Methodologies in Second Language Acquisition* (pp. 95–116). Wiley-Blackwell.

Dufva, H. (2004) Language, thinking and embodiment: Bakhtin, Whorf and Merleau-Ponty. In F. Bostad, C. Brandist, L.S. Evensen and H.C. Faber (eds) *Bakhtinian Perspectives on Language and Culture: Meaning in Language, Art, and New Media* (pp. 133–146). Palgrave Macmillan.

Eades, D. (2005) Applied linguistics and language analysis in asylum seeker cases. *Applied Linguistics* 26 (4), 503–526.

Eades, D. (2009) Testing the claims of asylum seekers: The role of language analysis. *Language Assessment Quarterly* 6 (1), 30–40.

Elliott, D., Mayadas, N.S. and Segal, U.A. (2010) Immigration worldwide: Trends and analysis. In U.A. Segal, D. Elliott and N.S. Mayadas (eds) *Immigration Worldwide: Policies, Practices, and Trends* (pp. 17–26). Oxford University Press.

EU Commission (2023) Common European Asylum System. https://home-affairs.ec.europa.eu/policies/migration-and-asylum/common-european-asylum-system_en (accessed 10 October 2023).

European Council (2024) Infographic – Asylum applications in the EU. https://www.consilium.europa.eu/en/infographics/asylum-applications-eu (accessed 8 November 2023).

Eurostat (2024) Population and population change statistics. https://ec.europa.eu/eurostat/statistics-explained/index.php?title=Population_and_population_change_statistics&oldid=608692#Population_change_at_national_level (accessed 18 September 2023).

Every, D. and Augoustinos, M. (2008) 'Taking advantage' or fleeing persecution? Opposing accounts of asylum seeking. *Journal of Sociolinguistics* 12 (5), 648–667.

Fairclough, N. (1989) *Language and Power*. Longman.

Fairclough, N. (2014) *Language and Power* (3rd edn). Longman.

Felberg, T.R. and Skaaden, H. (2012) The (de)construction of culture in interpreter-mediated medical discourse. *Linguistica Antverpiensia, New Series – Themes in Translation Studies* 11, 95–112,

Fernández, B. (2023) It's psychological warfare season on the US border. Aljazeera. https://www.aljazeera.com/opinions/2023/5/9/its-psychological-warfare-season-on-the-us-border (accessed 10 November 2023).

Fiske, L. and Kenny, M.A. (2004) 'Marriage of convenience' or a 'match made in heaven': Lawyers and social workers working with asylum seekers. *Australian Journal of Human Rights* 10 (1), 137–157.

Flick, U. (2006) *An Introduction to Qualitative Research* (3rd edn). Sage.

Fontanari, E. (2022) Germany, year 2020: The tension between asylum right, border control, and economy, through the imperative of deservingness. *Migration Studies* 10 (4), 766–788.

Forced Migration Review (2024) Non-signatory states and the international refugee regime. https://www.fmreview.org/issue67/janmyr/?utm_source=chatgpt.com (accessed 7 April 2025).

Forrest, A. (2023) Tories consider sending migrants 4,000 miles to Ascension Island if Rwanda plan fails. *Independent*. https://www.independent.co.uk/news/uk/politics/government-illegal-migrants-ascension-island-rwanda-b2388582.html (accessed 8 November 2023).

Fullerton, M. (2011) A tale of two decades: War refugees and asylum policy in the European Union. *Washington University Global Studies Law Review* 10 (1), 87.

Gallai, F. (2017) Pragmatic competence and interpreter-mediated police investigative interviews. *The Translator* 23 (2), 177–196.

Galletta, A. (2013) *Mastering the Semi-Structured Interview and Beyond: From Research Design to Analysis and Publication*. New York University Press.

Gallez, E. and Maryns, K. (2014) Orality and authenticity in an interpreter-mediated defendant's examination: A case study from the Belgian Assize Court. *Interpreting* 16 (1), 49–80.

Gentile, A., Ozolins, U. and Vasilakakos, M. (1996) *Liaison Interpreting: A Handbook*. Melbourne University Press.

Ghezelbash, D. and Feith Tan, N. (2020) The end of the right to seek asylum? COVID-19 and the future of refugee protection. *International Journal of Refugee Law* 32 (4), 668–679.

Gibb, R. and Good, A. (2014) Interpretation, translation and intercultural communication in refugee status determination procedures in the UK and France. *Language and Intercultural Communication* 14 (3), 385–399.

Gillespie, A. (2010) The dialogical turn. Turning the corner? [Review of Per Linell, *Rethinking Language, Mind, and World Dialogically: Interactional and Contextual Theories of Human Sense-Making*]. *Theory and Psychology* 20 (3), 461–463.

Gillham, B. (2000) *Case Study Research Methods*. Continuum.

Glynn, I. (2021) Becoming a continent of immigration: Charting Europe's migration history, 1919–2019. *International Review of Social History* 66 (2), 1–21.

Goffman, E. (1961) *Encounters: Two Studies in the Sociology of Interaction*. Bobbs-Merrill.

Goffman, E. (1981) *Forms of Talk*. University of Pennsylvania Press.

Gońda, M., Lesińska, M. and Pachocka, M. (2020) *Relations between Immigration and Integration Policies in Europe*. Routledge.

Goodwin-Gill, G.S. (2021) International refugee law in the early years. In C. Costello, M. Foster and J. McAdam (eds) *Oxford Handbook of International Refugee Law*. Oxford University Press.

Granhag, P.A., Strömwall, L.A. and Hartwig, M. (2005) Granting asylum or not? Migration board personnel's beliefs about deception. *Journal of Ethnic and Migration Studies* 31 (1), 29–50.

Graumann, C.F. (1990) Perspectival structure and dynamics in dialogues. In I. Marková and K. Foppa (eds) *The Dynamics of Dialogue* (pp. 105–126). Harvester Wheatsheaf.

Gray, D.E. (2009) *Doing Research in the Real World* (2nd edn). Sage.

Green-Pedersen, C. and Krogstrup, J. (2008) Immigration as a political issue in Denmark and Sweden. *European Journal of Political Research* 47, 610–634.

Gumperz, J.J. (1982) *Discourse Strategies*. Cambridge University Press.

Hahamovitch, C. (2003) Creating perfect immigrants: Guestworkers of the world in historical perspective 1. *Labor History* 44 (1), 69–94.

Hale, S. (2007) *Community Interpreting*. Palgrave Macmillan.

Hambly, J. (2019) Interactions and identities in UK asylum appeals: Lawyers and law in a quasi-legal setting. In N. Gill and A. Good (eds) *Asylum Determination in Europe: Ethnographic Perspectives* (pp. 195–216). Palgrave Macmillan.

Hammersley, M. and Traianou, A. (2012) *Ethics in Qualitative Research: Controversies and Contexts*. Sage.

Hartland, A. (2023) Salience, preference, and asylum outcomes in Germany and the UK, 2002–2019. *Journal of Public Policy* 43 (2), 284–306.

Harvey, C. (2015) Time for reform? Refugees, asylum-seekers, and protection under international human rights law. *Refugee Survey Quarterly* 34, 43–60.

Hatton, T.J. (2004) Seeking asylum in Europe. *Economic Policy* 19 (38), 6–62.

Hatton, T.J. (2016) Immigration, public opinion and the recession in Europe. *Economic Policy* 31 (86), 205–246.

Herlihy, J., Gleeson, K. and Turner, S. (2010) What assumptions about human behaviour underlie asylum judgments? *International Journal of Refugee Law* 22 (3), 351–366.

Hodkinson, P. (2016) Grounded theory and inductive research. In N. Gilbert and P. Stoneman (eds) *Researching Social Life* (4th edn) (pp. 80–100). Sage.

Hox, J.J. and Boeije, H.R. (2005) Data collection, primary versus secondary. In K. Kempf-Leonard (ed.) *Encyclopedia of Social Measurement* (pp. 593–599). Elsevier.

Huysmans, J. (2006) *The Politics of Insecurity: Fear, Migration and Asylum in the EU*. Routledge.

Huysmans, J. and Buonfino, A. (2008) Politics of exception and unease: Immigration, asylum and terrorism in parliamentary debates in the UK. *Political Studies* 56 (4), 766–788.

Immigratie- en Naturalisatiedienst (2014) Over de IND. https://ind.nl/EN/individuals/Pages/default.aspx (accessed 6 September 2014).

Immigratie- en Naturalisatiedienst (2015) De Asielprocedure. http://ind.nl/Documents/Nederlands%20-%20RVT_2015.pdf (accessed 6 July 2016).

Immigratie- en Naturalisatiedienst (2023a) Asylum: latest developments. https://ind.nl/en/asylum-latest-developments (accessed 25 November 2023).

Immigratie- en Naturalisatiedienst (2023b) De toelatingsorganisatie van Nederland. https://ind.nl/nl/formulieren/6070.pdf (accessed 29 November 2023).

Jacobs, L., Meeusen, C. and d'Haenens, L. (2016) News coverage and attitudes on immigration: Public and commercial television news compared. *European Journal of Communication* 31 (6), 642–660.

Jacobs, M. and Maryns, K. (2021) Managing narratives, managing identities: Language and credibility in legal consultations with asylum seekers. *Language in Society* 51 (3), 1–28.

Jacobs, M. and Maryns, K. (2023) Mediated disclosure in asylum encounters. *Multilingua* 42 (2), 165–189.

Jacobsen, B. (2009) The community interpreter: A question of role. *Hermes – Journal of Language and Communication in Business* 22 (42), 155–166.

Jacquemet, M. (2009) Transcribing refugees: The entextualization of asylum seekers' hearings in a transidiomatic environment. *Text and Talk* 29 (5), 525–546.

Jacquemet, M. (2011) Crosstalk 2.0: Asylum and communicative breakdowns. *Text and Talk* 31 (4), 475–497.

Jacquemet, M. (2013) Transidioma and asylum: Gumperz's legacy in intercultural institutional talk. *Journal of Linguistic Anthropology* 23 (3), 199–212.

Janmyr, M. (2024) FMR 67: Non-signatory states and the international refugee regime. https://www.fmreview.org/issue67/janmyr/ (accessed 24 July 2024).

Jick, T.D. (1979) Mixing qualitative and quantitative methods: Triangulation in action. *Administrative Science Quarterly* 24 (4), 602–611.

Josephs, I. (1998) 'Do you know Ragnar Rommetveit?' On dialogue and silence, poetry and pedantry, and cleverness and wisdom in psychology [interview with Ragnar Rommetveit]. *Culture and Psychology* 4 (2), 189–212.

Kälin, W. (1986) Troubled communication: Cross-cultural misunderstandings in the asylum-hearing. *International Migration Review* 20 (2), 230–241.

Kang, Y.D. (2021) Refugee crisis in Europe: Determinants of asylum seeking in European countries from 2008–2014. *Journal of European Integration* 43 (1), 33–48.

Karatani, R. (2005) How history separated refugee and migrant regimes: In search of their institutional origins. *International Journal of Refugee Law* 17 (3), 517–541.

Kaufmann, D. (2021) Debating responsibility-sharing: An analysis of the European Parliament's debates on the Common European Asylum System. *European Policy Analysis* 7 (1), 207–225.

Kelly, N. and Townsend, M. (2020) Revealed: Supermarket staff recruited to make 'life and death' asylum decisions. *Observer*, 5 November. https://www.theguardian.com/world/2022/nov/05/revealed-novice-staff-making-life-and-death-asylum-decisions (accessed 20 September 2023).

Keselman, O., Cederborg, A.-C. and Linell, P. (2010) 'That is not necessary for you to know!' Negotiation of participation status of unaccompanied children in interpreter-mediated asylum hearings. *Interpreting* 12 (1), 83–104.

King, D.E. (2005) Asylum seekers/patron seekers: Interpreting Iraqi Kurdish migration. *Human Organization* 64 (4), 316–327.

Kirkup, J. and Winnett, R. (2012) Theresa May interview: 'We're going to give illegal migrants a really hostile reception'. *The Telegraph*, 25 May. https://www.telegraph.co.uk/news/0/theresa-may-interview-going-give-illegal-migrants-really-hostile (accessed 18 July 2024).

Kjelsvik, B. (2014) 'Winning a battle, but losing the war': Contested identities, narratives, and interaction in asylum interviews. *Text and Talk* 34 (1), 89–115.

Kneebone, S. (ed.) (2009) *Refugees, Asylum Seekers and the Rule of Law: Comparative Perspectives*. Cambridge University Press.

Kox, M., van Liempt, I. and Smits, A. (2023) Shaping a climate of arrival: National and local media representations of refugees' arrival infrastructures in the Netherlands. *Journal of Refugee Studies* 36 (1), 46–64.

Kynsilehto, A. and Puumala, E. (2015) Persecution as experience and knowledge: The ontological dynamics of asylum interviews. *International Studies Perspectives* 16 (4), 446–464.

Lai, M. and Mulayim, S. (2014) Interpreter linguistic intervention in the strategies employed by police in investigative interviews. *Police Practice and Research* 15 (4), 307–321.

Lancaster, C.M. (2022) Immigration and the sociocultural divide in Central and Eastern Europe: Stasis or evolution? *European Journal of Political Research* 61 (2), 544–565.

Lesch, H.M. and Saulse, B. (2014) Revisiting the interpreting service in the healthcare sector: A descriptive overview. *Perspectives* 22 (3), 332–348.

Levinson, S.C. (1992) Activity types and language. In P. Drew and J. Heritage (eds) *Talk at Work: Interaction in Institutional Settings* (pp. 66–100). Cambridge University Press.

Li, S. (2011) Understanding interactions in interpreted triadic medical consultations in primary care. Doctoral thesis, University of Leeds.

Li, S. (2013) Co-construction of interpreted conversation in medical consultations. *Applied Linguistics Review* 4 (1), 127–149.

Li, X. (2015) Putting interpreting strategies in their place justifications for teaching strategies in interpreter training. *Babel-Revue Internationale De La Traduction / International Journal of Translation* 61 (2), 170–192.

Lian Ching, S.B.Z. (2017) Medical terminology rendition techniques employed by paraprofessional Chin-Hakha English interpreters. *Translation and Interpreting* 9 (2), 38–51.

Linell, P. (1982) *The Written Language Bias in Linguistics*. Department of Communication Studies, University of Linköping.

Linell, P. (2003) What is dialogism? Aspects and elements of a dialogical approach to language, communication and cognition. Lecture first presented at Växjö University, October 2000. https://cspeech.ucd.ie/Fred/docs/Linell.pdf (accessed 3 March 2025).

Linell, P. (2009) *Rethinking Language, Mind, and World Dialogically: Interactional and Contextual Theories of Human Sense-Making*. Information Age.

Long, K. (2013) When refugees stopped being migrants: Movement, labour and humanitarian protection. *Migration Studies* 1 (1), 4–26.

Lourenço, P., Basto, I., Cunha, C. and Bento, T. (2013) Dialogism in detail: Per Linell's *Rethinking Language, Mind, and World Dialogically* and its potentials. *Culture and Psychology* 19 (3), 421–430.

Lucassen, L. (2019) The rise of the European migration regime and its paradoxes (1945–2020). *International Review of Social History* 64 (3), 515–531.

Luedtke, A. (2019) Migration governance in Europe: A historical perspective. In A. Weinar, S. Bonjour and L. Zhyznomirska (eds) *The Routledge Handbook of the Politics of Migration in Europe* (pp. 15–25). Routledge.

Luhmann, N. (1995) *Social Systems.* Stanford University Press.

Lyons, K. and Huegler, N. (2010) European Union immigration and the European Union. In U.A. Segal, D. Elliott and N.S. Mayadas (eds) *Immigration Worldwide: Policies, Practices, and Trends* (pp. 437–448). Oxford University Press.

Macaron, J. (2018) Syrian refugees in Jordan and Lebanon: The politics of their return. Arab Center, Washington DC. https://arabcenterdc.org/resource/syrian-refugees-in-jordan-and-lebanon-the-politics-of-their-return/ (accessed 3 March 2025).

Macken-Horarik, M. (2003) Working the borders in racist discourse: The challenge of the 'Children Overboard Affair' in news media texts. *Social Semiotics* 13 (3), 283–303. https://doi.org/10.1080/1035033032000167024.

Marková, I. (1990) Introduction. In I. Marková and K. Foppa (eds) *The Dynamics of Dialogue* (pp. 1–22). Harvester Wheatsheaf.

Marková, I. (2000) Amédée or how to get rid of it: Social representations from a dialogical perspective. *Culture and Psychology* 6 (4), 419–460.

Marková, I. (2003) *Dialogicality and Social Representations: The Dynamics of Mind.* Cambridge University Press.

Marková, I., Linell, P., Grossen, M. and Salazar Orvig, A. (2007) *Dialogue in Focus Groups: Exploring Socially Shared Knowledge.* Equinox.

Marr, D. and Wilkinson, M. (2003) *Dark Victory*. Allen and Unwin.

Marshall, C. and Rossman, G.B. (2014) *Designing Qualitative Research* (6th edn). Sage.

Maryns, K. (2005) Monolingual language ideologies and code choice in the Belgian asylum procedure. *Language and Communication* 25, 299–314.

Maryns, K. (2006) *The Asylum Speaker: Language in the Belgian Asylum Procedure* (1st edn). Routledge.

Maryns, K. (2013a) Procedures without borders: The language-ideological anchorage of legal-administrative procedures in translocal institutional settings. *Language in Society* 42, 71–92.

Maryns, K. (2013b) Disclosure and (re)performance of gender-based evidence in an interpreter-mediated asylum interview. *Journal of Sociolinguistics* 17 (5), 661–686.

Maryns, K. (2015) Asylum settings. In F. Pöchhacker (ed.) *Routledge Encyclopedia of Interpreting Studies* (pp. 22–26). Routledge.

Maryns, K. (2017) The use of English as ad hoc institutional standard in the Belgian asylum interview. *Applied Linguistics* 38 (5), 737–758.

Maryns, K. (2020) Asylum. In M. Baker and G. Saldanha (eds) *Routledge Encyclopedia of Translation Studies* (3rd edn). Routledge.

Maryns, K. and Blommaert, J. (2001) Stylistic and thematic shifting as a narrative resource: Assessing asylum seekers' repertoires. *Multilingua – Journal of Cross-Cultural and Interlanguage Communication* 20 (1), 61–84.

Maryns, K. and Blommaert, J. (2002) Pretextuality and pretextual gaps: On de/refining linguistic inequality. *Pragmatics* 12 (1), 11–30.

Mason, I. (ed.) (2001) *Triadic Exchanges: Studies in Dialogue Interpreting.* St Jerome.

Mason, I. and Stewart, M. (2001) Interactional pragmatics, face and the dialogue interpreter. In I. Mason (ed.) *Triadic Exchanges: Studies in Dialogue Interpreting* (pp. 51–70). St Jerome.

Matera, M., Tubakovic, T. and Murray, P. (2023) Is Australia a model for the UK? A critical assessment of parallels of cruelty in refugee externalization policies. *Journal of Refugee Studies* 36 (2), 271–287.

Matthews, B. and Ross, L. (2010) *Research Methods: A Practical Guide for the Social Sciences*. Pearson Education.

Maxwell, J.A. (2005) *Qualitative Research Design: An Interactive Approach* (2nd edn). Sage.

Maxwell, J.A. (2013) *Qualitative Research Design: An Interactive Approach* (3rd edn). Sage.

McAdam, J. and Wood, T. (2021) The concept of 'international protection' in the global compacts on refugees and migration. *Interventions* 23 (2), 191–206.

McKinnon, S. (2009) Citizenship and the performance of credibility: Audiencing gender-based asylum seekers in U.S. Immigration Courts. *Text and Performance Quarterly* 29, 205–221.

Melloy, K. (2007) Telling truths: How the REAL ID Act's credibility provisions affect women asylum seekers. *Iowa Law Review* 92 (637), 637–676.

Merriam, S.B. and Tisdell, E.J. (2015) *Qualitative Research: A Guide to Design and Implementation*. Jossey-Bass.

Meyer, B. (1998) What transcriptions of authentic discourse can reveal about interpreting. *Interpreting* 3 (1), 65–83.

Ministry of Justice (2023) Appeal against a visa or immigration decision. https://www.gov.uk/immigration-asylum-tribunal (accessed 20 October 2023).

Mizori, H. (2017) Sense-making in an interpreter-mediated lawyer–immigrant encounter: Incorporating the perspectives of the participants utilizing dialogism. PhD thesis, University of Leeds.

Müller, T. (2018) Constructing cultural borders: Depictions of Muslim refugees in British and German media. *Zeitschrift für Vergleichende Politikwissenschaft* 12, 263–277.

Neumayer, E. (2005) Bogus refugees? The determinants of asylum migration to Western Europe. *International Studies Quarterly* 49, 389–409.

Nielsen, T.R. and Møller, N.H. (2022) Data as a lens for understanding what constitutes credibility in asylum decision-making. *Proceedings of the ACM on Human-Computer Interaction* 6, 1–23.

Nielsen, T.R., Menendez-Blanco, M. and Møller, N.H. (2023) Who cares about data? Ambivalence, translation, and attentiveness in asylum casework. *Computer Supported Cooperative Work* 32, 861–910.

Nikolaidou, Z., Rehnberg, H.S. and Wadensjö, C. (2023) 'Do I have to say exactly word by word?' (Re)producing and negotiating asymmetrical relations in asylum interviews. *Journal of International Migration and Integration* 24 (Suppl. 4), S745–S768.

Norman, S. (2007) Assessing the credibility of refugee applicants: A judicial perspective. *International Journal of Refugee Law* 19 (2), 273–292. https://doi.org/10.1093/ijrl/eem015.

Norström, E., Fioretos, I. and Gustafsson, K. (2012) Working conditions of community interpreters in Sweden: Opportunities and shortcomings. *Interpreting* 14 (2), 242–260.

NOS (2022) Artsen zonder Grenzen naar Ter Apel, waar opnieuw 700 mensen buiten sliepen. https://nos.nl/collectie/13898/artikel/2441954-artsen-zonder-grenzen-naar-ter-apel-waar-opnieuw-700-mensen-buiten-sliepen (accessed 18 October 2023).

NOS (2023) CBS: 35.500 eerste asielaanvragen in 2022, grootste aantal sinds 2015. https://nos.nl/artikel/2461786-cbs-35-500-eerste-asielaanvragen-in-2022-grootste-aantal-sinds-2015 (accessed 4 August 2023).

Nunan, D. (1992) *Research Methods in Language Learning*. Cambridge University Press.

O'Connell, D., Kowal, S. and Kaltenbacher, E. (1990) Turn-taking: A critical analysis of the research tradition. *Journal of Psycholinguistic Research* 19, 345–373.

Okólski, M. (2012) *European Immigrations: Trends, Structures and Policy Implications*. Amsterdam University Press.

Orchard, P. (2017) The dawn of international refugee protection: States, tacit cooperation and non-extradition. *Journal of Refugee Studies* 30 (2), 282–300.

Orchard, P. (2019) The historical development of refugee protection in Europe. In A. Weinar, S. Bonjour and L. Zhyznomirska (eds) *The Routledge Handbook of the Politics of Migration in Europe* (pp. 283–292). Routledge.

Pantti, M. and Ojala, M. (2019) Caught between sympathy and suspicion: Journalistic perceptions and practices of telling asylum seekers' personal stories. *Media, Culture and Society* 41 (8), 1031–1047.

Park, J.S.-Y. and Bucholtz, M. (2009) Introduction. Public transcripts: Entextualization and linguistic representation in institutional contexts. *Text and Talk* 29 (5), 485–502.

Patton, M.Q. (1990) *Qualitative Evaluation and Research Methods*. Sage.

Patton, M.Q. (1999) Enhancing the quality and credibility of qualitative analysis. *Health Services Research* 34 (5), 1189–1208.

Pöchhacker, F. (2004) *Introducing Interpreting Studies*. Routledge.

Pöllabauer, S. (2006) 'During the interview, the interpreter will provide a faithful translation'. The potentials and pitfalls of researching interpreting in immigration, asylum, and police settings: Methodology and research paradigms. *Linguistica Antverpiensia, New Series – Themes in Translation Studies* 5 (5), 229–244.

Potter, J. (1998) Cognition as context (whose cognition?). *Research on Language and Social Interaction* 31 (1), 29–44.

Potter, J. and Te Molder, H. (2005) Talking cognition: Mapping and making the terrain. In H. Te Molder and J. Potter (eds) *Conversation and Cognition* (pp. 1–54). Cambridge University Press.

Puggioni, R. (2017) *Rethinking International Protection: The Sovereign, the State, the Refugee*. Springer.

Raído, V.E. (2014) *Translation and Web Searching*. Routledge.

Reddy, M.J. (1979) The conduit metaphor: A case of frame conflict in our language about language. In A. Ortony (ed.) *Metaphor and Thought* (pp. 284–297). Cambridge University Press.

Reynolds, J.T. (2020a) Stability and hybridity in refugee legal advice meetings: Discursive structure as a resource for lawyer-client intercultural communication. *Journal of Applied Linguistics and Professional Practice* 15 (1), 91–115.

Reynolds, J.T. (2020b) Investigating the language–culture nexus in refugee legal advice meetings. *Multilingua* 39 (4), 395–429.

Ricatti, F. (2016) A country once great? Asylum seekers, historical imagination, and the moral privilege of whiteness. *Journal of Australian Studies* 40(4), 478–493. https://doi.org/10.1080/14443058.2016.1225783

Rillof, P. and Buysse, L. (2015) Getting organized to beat Babel in multilingual service encounters: The European Network for Public Service Interpreting and Translation (ENPSIT). *Translation and Interpreting* 7 (3), 186–197.

Rock, F. (2017) Shifting ground: Exploring the backdrop to translating and interpreting. *The Translator* 23 (2), 217–236.

Rommetveit, R. (1974) *On Message Structure: A Framework for the Study of Language and Communication*. Wiley-Interscience.

Roy, C.B. (2000) *Interpreting as a Discourse Process*. Oxford University Press.

Roy, C. and Metzger, M. (2014) Researching signed language interpreting research through a sociolinguistic lens. *Translation and Interpreting* 6 (1), 158–176.

Rudvin, M. (2007) Professionalism and ethics in community interpreting: The impact of individualist versus collective group identity. *Interpreting* 9 (1), 47–69.

Santana, A., Zagórski, P. and Rama, J. (2020) At odds with Europe: Explaining populist radical right voting in Central and Eastern Europe. *East European Politics* 36 (4), 1–22.

Schaart, E. (2023) Dutch government falls as ministers clash over migration. *Politico*, 7 July. https://www.politico.eu/article/dutch-government-pm-mark-rutte-in-crisis-over-asylum-measures/ (accessed 20 August 2024).

Schlueter, E. and Davidov, E. (2013) Contextual sources of perceived group threat: Negative immigration-related news reports, immigrant group size and their interaction, Spain 1996–2007. *European Sociological Review* 29 (2), 179–191.

Schittenhelm, K. (2019) Implementing and rethinking the European Union's asylum legislation: The Asylum Procedures Directive. *International Migration* 57 (1), 229–244.

Schmitt-Beck, R. and Wolsing, A. (2010) European TV environments and citizens' social trust: Evidence from multilevel analyses. *Communications* 35 (4), 461–483.

Schneider, S. (2019) Becoming a decision-maker, or: 'Don't turn your heart into a den of thieves and murderers'. In N. Gill and A. Good (eds) *Asylum Determination in Europe: Ethnographic Perspectives* (p. 285). Palgrave Macmillan.

Schuster, L. (2000) A comparative analysis of the asylum policy of seven European governments. *Journal of Refugee Studies* 13 (1), 118–132.

Searle, J.R. (1969) *Speech Acts: An Essay in the Philosophy of Language*. Cambridge University Press.

Segal, U.A., Elliott, D. and Mayadas, N.S. (eds) (2010) *Immigration Worldwide: Policies, Practices, and Trends*. Oxford University Press.

Seidman, I. (2006) *Interviewing as Qualitative Research: A Guide for Researchers in Education and the Social Sciences* (3rd edn). Teachers College Press.

Silverman, D. (2006) *Interpreting Qualitative Data: Methods for Analyzing Talk, Text and Interaction* (3rd edn). Sage.

Simeon, J.C. (2010) A comparative analysis of the response of the UNHCR and industrialized states to rapidly fluctuating refugee status and asylum applications: Lessons and best practices for RSD systems design and administration. *International Journal of Refugee Law* 22 (1), 72–103.

Smith-Khan, L. (2017a) Negotiating narratives, accessing asylum: Evaluating language policy as multi-level practice, beliefs and management. *Multilingua* 36 (1), 31–57.

Smith-Khan, L. (2017b) Telling stories: Credibility and the representation of social actors in Australian asylum appeals. *Discourse and Society* 28 (5), 512–534.

Smith-Khan, L. (2017c) Different in the same way? Language, diversity, and refugee credibility. *International Journal of Refugee Law* 29 (3), 389–416.

Smith-Khan, L. (2019a) Communicative resources and credibility in public discourse on refugees. *Language in Society* 48, 403–427.

Smith-Khan, L. (2019b) Why refugee visa credibility assessments lack credibility: A critical discourse analysis. *Griffith Law Review* 28 (4), 406–430.

Smith-Khan, L. (2020) Migration practitioners' roles in communicating credible refugee claims. *Alternative Law Journal* 45 (2), 119–124.

Smith-Khan, L. (2021) 'I try not to be dominant, but I'm a lawyer!' Advisor resources, context, and refugee credibility. *Journal of Refugee Studies* 34 (4), 3710–3733.

Snape, D. and Spencer, L. (2003) The foundations of qualitative research. In J. Ritchie and J. Lewis (eds) *Qualitative Research Practice: A Guide for Social Science Students and Researchers* (pp. 1–23.) Sage.

Sorgoni, B. (2019) The location of truth: Bodies and voices in the Italian asylum procedure. *PoLAR: Political and Legal Anthropology Review* 42 (1), 161–176.

Spijkerboer, T. (2010) *De Nieuwe Asielprocedure*. Universiteit Amsterdam.

Stake, R.E. (2000) The case study method in social inquiry. In R. Gomm, M. Hammersley and P. Foster (eds) *Case Study Method: Key Issues, Key Texts*. Sage.

Statista (2023) Estimated net migration figures in Europe in 2023, by country. https://www.statista.com/statistics/686124/net-migration-selected-european-countries/#statisticContainer (accessed 17 October 2023).

Stobb, M. (2019) Power of the pen or the gavel? Determining asylum standards on the courts of appeals. *Justice System Journal* 40 (3), 196–220.

Stoel, H. (2023) Dutch Prime Minister Mark Rutte is gone, but the turn to the right continues. *Jacobin*, 7 July. https://jacobin.com/2023/07/netherlands-pm-mark-rutte-vvd-elections-immigration (accessed 20 August 2024).

Sturge, G. (2023) *Asylum Statistics*, House of Commons Library, 12 September, Number SN01403. House of Commons Library.

Suchman, L.A. (1987) *Plans and Situated Actions: The Problem of Human–Machine Communication*. Cambridge University Press.

Susam-Sarajeva, Ş. (2009) The case study research method in translation studies. *Interpreter and Translator Trainer* 3 (1), 37–56.

Swanborn, P. (2010) *Case Study Research: What, Why and How?* Sage.

Syal, R. (2022) 'Invasion' of the UK? Experts dubious of Suella Braverman's claim. *Guardian*, 1 November. https://www.theguardian.com/uk-news/2022/nov/01/bravermans-invasion-claim-not-backed-by-facts-say-experts (accessed 12 November 2023).

Syal, R. and Stacey, K. (2023) Rishi Sunak 'extinguishing the right to seek refugee protection in UK'. *Guardian*, 7 March. https://www.theguardian.com/uk-news/2023/mar/07/suella-braverman-asylum-migration-bill-law-change-small-boats (accessed 6 November 2023).

Taylor, S.J. and Bogdan, R. (1984) *Introduction to Qualitative Research Methods: The Search for Meanings* (2nd edn). Wiley.

Taylor, S.J. and Bogdan, R. (1998) *Introduction to Qualitative Research Methods: A Guidebook and Resource* (3rd edn). Wiley.

Thomas, R. (2006) Assessing the credibility of asylum claims: EU and UK approaches examined. *European Journal of Migration and Law* 8, 79–96.

Tipton, R. (2008) Reflexivity and the social construction of identity in interpreter-mediated asylum interviews. *The Translator* 14 (1), 1–19.

Topping, A. (2023) Albanian PM hits out at Braverman over 'disgraceful' comments on migrants, *Guardian*, 23 March. https://www.theguardian.com/world/2023/mar/23/albanian-prime-minister-edi-rama-hits-out-at-braverman-over-disgraceful-comments-on-migrants (accessed 6 November 2023).

Tracy, S.J. (2013) *Qualitative Research Methods: Collecting Evidence, Crafting Analysis, Communicating Impact*. Wiley.

Trauner, F. (2016) Asylum policy: The EU's 'crises' and the looming policy regime failure. *Journal of European Integration* 38 (3), 311–325.

UNHCR (2001) *UNHCR Statistical Yearbook 2001*. UNHCR. https://www.unhcr.org/statistics/unhcrstats/4a02e3406/unhcr-statistical-yearbook-2001.html (accessed 16 July 2015).

UNHCR (2011) *The 1951 Convention Relating to the Status of Refugees and Its 1967 Protocol*. UNHCR.

UNHCR (2018) *Report of the Special Rapporteur on the Human Rights to Safe Drinking Water and Sanitation – Note by the Secretariat* (A/HRC/39/55). UNHCR.

UNHCR (2019) *Handbook on Procedures and Criteria for Determining Refugee Status and Guidelines on International Protection Under the 1951 Convention and the 1967 Protocol Relating to the Status of Refugees*. UNHCR.

UNHCR (2020) Situation Syria regional refugee response. UNHCR. https://data2.unhcr.org/en/situations/syria (accessed 31 August 2020).

UNHCR (2021) *Global Trends Report 2020*. UNHCR.

UNHCR (2022) *Global Trends Report 2022*. UNHCR.

UNHCR (2023a) Global Refugee Forum. https://www.unhcr.org/global-refugee-forum-2023 (accessed 5 October 2023).

UNHCR (2023b) Refugee Data Finder. https://www.unhcr.org/refugee-statistics (accessed 24 October 2023).

UNHCR (2023c) About statelessness. https://www.unhcr.org/ibelong/about-statelessness (accessed 24 October 2023).

UNHCR (2023d) *Global Trends Report 2022*. UNHCR.

Valero-Garcés, C. (2015) The impact of emotional and psychological factors on public service interpreters: Preliminary studies. *Translation and Interpreting* 7 (3), 90–102.

Valsiner, J. and van der Veer, R. (2000) *The Social Mind: Construction of the Idea*. Cambridge University Press.

Van Dale (2015) 'Asielzoeker', in Van Dale Groot woordenboek van de Nederlandse taal. https://www.vandale.nl (accessed:11 July 2023).

Van der Kist, J., Dijstelbloem, H. and De Goede, M. (2019) In the shadow of asylum decision-making: The knowledge politics of country-of-origin information. *International Political Sociology* 13 (1), 68–81.

van der Kleij, S. (2015) Interaction in Dutch asylum interviews: A corpus study of interpreter-mediated institutional discourse. PhD thesis, Radboud Universiteit.

van Selm, J. (2019) Does European refugee policy exist? Regional dimensions of the refugee protection approach in Europe. In A. Weinar, S. Bonjour and L. Zhyznomirska (eds) *The Routledge Handbook of the Politics of Migration in Europe* (pp. 303–314). Routledge.

Van Veldhuizen, T.S. (2022) Fact-finding in asylum cases. In S. Landström, P.A. Granhag and P.J. van Koppen (eds) *The Future of Forensic Psychology* (1st edn) (pp. 160–170). Routledge.

Van Veldhuizen, T.S., Maas, R.P.A.E., Horselenberg, R. and Van Koppen, P.J. (2018) Establishing origin: Analysing the questions asked in asylum interviews. *Psychiatry, Psychology and Law* 25 (2), 283–302.

Vanto, J., Peltonen, J. and Honkasalo, M.L. (2021) Collectivized discretion: Seeking explanations for decreased asylum recognition rates in Finland after Europe's 2015 'refugee crisis'. *International Migration Review* 56 (3), 754–779. https://doi.org/10.1177/01979183211044096 (accessed 3 March 2025).

Vigouroux, C.B. (2021) Tribute: Jan Blommaert, a citizen sociolinguist. *Journal of Sociolinguistics* 25, 504–510.

Vlasenko, S.V. (2019) Introduction: Interpreting in Russian contexts. *Translation and Interpreting Studies* 14 (3), 437–441.

VluchtelingenWerk Nederland (no date) Wat wij doen voor vluchtelingen. https://www.vluchtelingenwerk.nl/wat-wij-doen (accessed 24 May 2018).

VluchtelingenWerk Nederland (2023) *Country Report: Overview of the Main Changes since the Previous Report Update*. https://asylumineurope.org/reports/country/netherlands/overview-main-changes-previous-report-update/ (accessed 16 December 2023).

Wadensjö, C. (1995) Dialogue interpreting and the distribution of responsibility. *Hermes - Journal of Language and Communication in Business* 8 (14), 111–129.

Wadensjö, C. (1998) *Interpreting as Interaction*. Longman.

Walliman, N.S.R. (2006) *Social Research Methods*. Sage.

Weinar, A., Bonjour, S. and Zhyznomirska, L. (eds) (2019) *The Routledge Handbook of the Politics of Migration in Europe*. Routledge.

Wengraf, T. (2001) *Qualitative Research Interviewing: Biographic Narrative Methods and Semi-Structured Methods*. Sage.

Wetzel, A. (2019) Section commentary: Asylum and international protection. In A. Weinar, S. Bonjour and L. Zhyznomirska (eds) *The Routledge Handbook of the Politics of Migration in Europe*. Routledge.

White, E. (2017) The legal status of Russian refugees, 1921–1936. *Comparativ: Zeitschrift fur Globalgeschichte und Vergleichende Gesellshaftsforschung* 27 (1), 18–38.

Williams, L. (2005) Interpreting services for refugees: Hearing voices? *International Journal of Migration, Health and Social Care* 1 (1), 37–49.

Wilson-Shaw, L., Pistrang, N. and Herlihy, J. (2012) Non-clinicians' judgments about asylum seekers' mental health: How do legal representatives of asylum seekers decide when to request medico-legal reports? *European Journal of Psychotraumatology* 3.

Winn, M. (2020) The far-right and asylum outcomes: Assessing the impact of far-right politics on asylum decisions in Europe. *European Union Politics* 22 (1), 70–93.

Wittgenstein, L. (1953) *Philosophical Investigations*. Macmillan.

Xu, H. (2020) Interprofessional relations in interpreted lawyer–client interviews: An Australian case study. *Perspectives* 29 (4), 608–624.

Xu, H. (2021) Roles, ethics and lawyers' reactions: An ethnographic study of interpreters' role performance in interpreted lawyer–client interviews. *Multilingua* 40 (5), 617–646.

Yin, R.K. (2003) *Case Study Research: Design and Methods* (3rd edn). Sage.

Zaun, N., Leroch, M. and Thielemann, E. (2024) Why courts are the life buoys of migrant rights: Anti-immigrant pressure, variation in judicial independence, and asylum recognition rates. *Journal of European Public Policy* 31 (5), 1206–1230.

Zhan, C. and Zeng, L. (2017) Chinese medical interpreters' visibility through text ownership: An empirical study on interpreted dialogues at a hospital in Guangzhou. *Interpreting* 19 (1), 97–117.

Index

For Product Safety Concerns and Information please contact our EU Authorised Representative:

Easy Access System Europe

Mustamäe tee 50

10621 Tallinn

Estonia

gpsr.requests@easproject.com

www.ingramcontent.com/pod-product-compliance
Lightning Source LLC
Jackson TN
JSHW061642160925
91121JS00003B/9
9781836681311